Advanced Cases
in MIS

Advanced Cases in MIS

JOSEPH A. BRADY

ELLEN F. MONK

THE UNIVERSITY OF DELAWARE

COURSE
TECHNOLOGY

Thomson Learning™

ONE MAIN STREET, CAMBRIDGE, MA 02142

Australia • Canada • Denmark • Japan • Mexico • New Zealand • Philippines
Puerto Rico • Singapore • South Africa • Spain • United Kingdom • United States

Advanced Cases in MIS is published by Course Technology.

Associate Publisher	Kristen Duerr
Senior Editor	Jennifer Normandin
Developmental Editor	DeVona Dors
Production Editor	Megan Cap-Renzi
Quality Assurance	John Bosco
Editorial Assistant	Amanda Young
Marketing Manager	Susan E. Ogar
Text Designer	GEX Publishing Services
Cover Designer	Efrat Reis

Use of the Microsoft Approved Study Guide Logo on this product signifies that it has been independently reviewed and approved in complying with the following standards:

- acceptable coverage of all content related to Microsoft exam number 70-176, entitled Designing and Implementing Desktop Applications with Microsoft Visual Basic 6.0.
- sufficient performance-based exercises that relate closely to all required content; and
- technically accurate content, based on sampling of text.

Disclaimer

Course Technology reserves the right to revise this publication and make changes from time to time in its content without notice.

The Web addresses in this book are subject to change from time to time as necessary without notice.

For more information, contact Course Technology, One Main Street, Cambridge, MA 02142; or find us on the World Wide Web at *www.course.com*.

For permission to use material from this text or product, contact us by

- Web: www.thomsonrights.com
- Phone: 1-800-730-2214
- Fax: 1-800-730-2215

ISBN 0-619-00061-9

Printed in America
3 4 5 CODE 02

memory of my parents, Joseph D. and Helen M. Brady

For Peter, Caroline, and Catherine

Preface

For the last 10 years, we have taught MIS courses at the University of Delaware. From the start, we wanted to include good computer-based case studies in the database and decision-support parts of our courses.

Unfortunately, we could not find any textbooks that offered cases meeting our needs. This omission surprised us because our requirements, we thought, were not unreasonable. First, we wanted cases that asked the student to think about real-world business situations. Second, we wanted cases that provided students with hands-on experience, using the kind of software that students had encountered in their computer literacy course—and that they would later use in business. Third, we wanted cases that would strengthen students' ability to analyze a problem, examine alternative solutions, and implement the solution in software. Undeterred, we took to writing our own cases.

For years, our colleagues and book representatives have urged us to publish our cases. Clearly, we were not alone—others also wanted to teach MIS using computer-based case studies. So, we gathered up some of our best cases and related tutorials. We're happy to have Course Technology publish them in this book, so that you too can use our cases in your MIS teaching.

Each tutorial and case in this book has been completed at the University of Delaware by business students. The tutorials prepare the student to tackle the cases. The cases are challenging but not impossible. In addition, the cases are organized in a way that helps the student to think about the logic of the case and the appropriate software to solve it. We think the cases will fit in smoothly in an undergraduate MIS course or in an MBA Information Systems course.

❧ BOOK ORGANIZATION

This book is organized into three main sections: one section for databases and two sections for decision support systems. All three parts contain tutorials and case studies. The tutorials provide the kind of support for databases and spreadsheets that is generally lacking in the average book on Microsoft Access and Excel. The tutorials are designed to help the student use some of the software's more-advanced features.

Part I: Database Cases Using Microsoft Access

This section begins with two tutorials and then presents 10 case studies.

Tutorial A: Database Design

Tutorial A helps the student understand how to set up different tables for a database, without requiring the student to learn data normalization.

Tutorial B: Database Queries and Reports

Tutorial B teaches the student about more-advanced features of Access queries and reports—features the student must understand to solve the cases. This tutorial also includes a "pitfalls to avoid" section so students can trouble-shoot their own problems.

Cases 1 to 10: Database Cases

Ten database cases follow the two tutorials. The student's job is to implement each case's database in Access so its query and report outputs can help management understand the business situation.

The first two cases are designated as Preliminary (or "warm-up") Cases. You may want your students to begin with these somewhat easier cases. The eight cases that follow require a more-demanding database design and implementation effort.

Part II: Decision Support Cases Using Excel

This section begins with a tutorial and then presents five case studies.

Tutorial C: Building a Decision Support System (DSS) in Excel

Tutorial C covers the use of Excel for designing decision support spreadsheets. Fundamental spreadsheet design concepts are taught. Instruction on the Scenario Manager, which the student can use to organize the inputs and outputs of many "what-if" scenarios, is included as well. The tutorial concludes with a review of Excel basics—a self-help for students.

Cases 11 to 15: Excel DSS Cases

These five cases can be done either with or without the Scenario Manager. Case 11, a Preliminary Case, is somewhat easier than the other cases in this section. In each case, the student must use Excel to model two or more alternative solutions to a problem. The student then uses the outputs of the model to identify and document the preferred solution.

Part III: Decision Support Cases Using the Excel Solver

This section begins with a tutorial and then presents five case studies.

Tutorial D: Building a Decision Support System (DSS) Using Excel's Solver

Tutorial D covers the use of the Solver, which is a decision support tool employed to solve optimization problems. It concludes with a "trouble-shooter" section.

Cases 16 to 20: Excel Solver Cases

Five Solver cases follow, the first of which is a Preliminary Case. Once again, in these cases the student uses the spreadsheet to analyze alternatives and identify the preferred solution.

Individual Case Design

All 20 cases follow a similar template:

- Each case begins with a *Preview* that explains the purpose of the case and gives an overview of the student's task.

- The next section, *Preparation*, provides the student with the information necessary to complete the case successfully. (Of course, the tutorials are an excellent preparation for the cases.)

- The third section, *Background*, provides the business context that frames the case. These sections resemble the kinds of problems students could face in the working world.

- Next comes the *Assignment* section, which is organized in a way that helps the student develop the analysis.
- The last section, ***Deliverables***, clearly lists what the student must hand in: printouts, memoranda, and files on disk. These items are similar to the kinds of deliverables that a manager might demand at the end of a job assignment.

➤ USING THE CASES

As noted earlier, we have successfully used these cases in our undergraduate MIS courses. You may already have devised ways of incorporating cases into your courses. We usually start the semester's database instruction by assigning database tutorials and then assigning a case to each student. We allocate cases randomly, from a pool of three or four cases, to each student. That way, all students do not work on the same case. Then, for Excel DSS instruction, we do much the same thing: assign the tutorial and then a case to each student, drawn from the three or four cases selected for that semester.

An alternative approach would be to assign the tutorial, then a preliminary case, followed by one of the more difficult cases. This strategy would give the student more exposure to the topics.

A third approach might be to assign cases whose subject matter is taught in a student's major courses. For example, Finance majors might enjoy Case 18, which covers structuring a portfolio.

➤ COURSE TECHNOLOGY TEACHING TOOLS

An *Instructor's Manual* and *Solutions Files* accompany this book. The *Instructor's Manual* contains sample syllabi, teaching tips for each case, solutions for all case assignments, and hints on grading cases. Both the *Instructor's Manual* and the *Solutions Files* can be downloaded from Course Technology's World Wide Web site, located at www.course.com.

➤ ACKNOWLEDGMENTS

We would like to give many thanks to the team at Course Technology, especially to our senior editor, Jennifer Normandin, and editorial assistant, Amanda Young. We also thank DeVona Dors, our development editor, whose efforts made the cases more understandable. In addition, we would like to acknowledge the contributions of our students, who have tested the cases in this book.

Contents

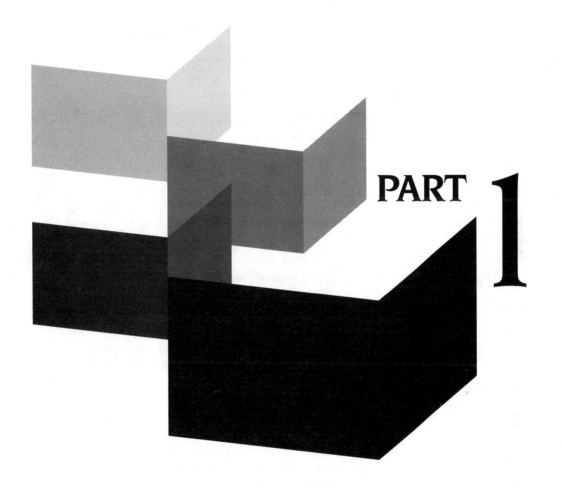

PART 1

Database Cases Using Access

A
TUTORIAL

Database Design

This database design tutorial has two sections. The first section briefly reviews basic database terminology. The second section teaches database design.

❧ REVIEW OF TERMINOLOGY

In Access, a **database** is a group of related objects that are saved into one file. An **object** can be a table, a form, a query, or a report. An Access database file has the suffix .mdb.

A **table** consists of data that is arrayed in rows and columns. A row of data is called a **record.** A record's columns are its **fields**. Thus, one way to think about a record is as a set of related fields. The fields in a table should be related to one another in some way. For example, a company might have employee data in a table called Employee. That table would have data fields about the people who work there. It would not have data about the company's customers—customer data would go into a Customer table. Each table should have a **key field**, which is a field whose value is guaranteed to be unique from one record to another. For example, in an Employee table, SSN (Social Security number) would be a good key because each record's SSN value is different from every other record's SSN value.

Data can be entered into a table directly, or by entering the data into a **form**, which is based on the table. The form then inserts the data into the table. A field's values have a **data type**. This is merely the way the values that are entered should be interpreted by the database package. Common data types are *text* for entries that should be treated as English words, *integer* for entries that are to be treated as numbers without decimal values, and *currency* for numbers that are to be treated as dollars and cents.

A **query** is a question that is asked about the data in a table (or tables). For example, a manager might want to know the names of employees who have worked for the company more than five years. A query can be designed to interrogate the Employee table in that way. The query would be "run," and the output would answer the question. A query can interrogate more than one table at a time. In that case, multiple tables must be *joined* by linking them on the values of fields that they have in common. To run the query, the query generator treats the joined table as one large temporary table.

Access also has a **report** generator that can be used to format a table's data or a query's output.

☙ DATABASE DESIGN

"Designing" a database entails structuring business data so it can be managed and retrieved. To do this, you must decide which tables need to be in the database and which fields need to be in each table.

Computer scientists have devised semimathematical ways to design databases. These ways can be time-consuming and difficult to learn. By contrast, this tutorial teaches database design in the context of practical examples, emphasizing business knowledge and common sense. This approach gives students a good grounding in the fundamentals and lets them design serviceable, if not technically perfect, databases.

Each database models the logic of some business situation, so your first task is to understand that situation. You do that by talking to managers and workers or by observation or by looking at business documents, such as sales records. Your purpose is to identify the business' objects (sometimes called its **entities**), which are the things or events that the database needs to keep track of. An object eventually becomes a table in the database. Consider a database for a video store. Two video store objects that should come quickly to mind are Video and Customer.

Example: The Talent Agency

Suppose you've been asked to build a database for a talent agency. The agency books bands into nightclubs. The agent needs a database to keep track of the agency's transactions and to answer the queries that arise in running the business. The most frequent query comes from club managers who call and want to know which bands are available on a certain date and at a particular time. Another query might be what fees were earned by the agent, grouped by band, in a month. Sometimes the agent just wants to see a list of all the people who play for all the bands and their instruments. Sometimes the agent wants to see a list of all guitar players in all the bands, and so on.

You have talked to the agent and found out many things about the business. Assume that your database must reflect these facts:

1. A "booking" is a certain band playing in a certain club on a certain date, starting at a certain time, and ending at a certain time, for a certain fee. A band can play more than once a day. The Heartbreakers, for example, could play at the East End Cafe in the afternoon and then at the West End Cafe that night. The club pays the agent, who keeps a five-percent fee and then gives the remainder to the band.

2. Each band that the agent handles has at least two members; there is no maximum number of members. The agent notes the phone number of just one band member, which is used when the agency needs to contact the band. No two bands have the same name.

3. No two band members in any of the bands have the same name. For example, if there is a "Sally Smith" in one band, there are no other Sally Smiths in any other bands.

4. The agency keeps track of the instrument that each band member plays. Each band member plays just one instrument. "Vocals" is an instrument for this recordkeeping purpose—a band's singer only sings.

5. Each band has a desired fee. For example, the Lightmetal band might want $700 a night and would expect the agent to try to get at least that amount for the band.

6. Each club has a name, an address, and a contact person. That person has a phone number that the agent uses to contact the club. No two clubs have the same name. Each club has a desired fee that they want to pay a band. The contact person tries to get the agent to accept that amount for a band's appearance.

7. Some clubs will feed the band members for free, and others will not.

✦ RULES GOVERNING DATABASE DESIGN

Rule 0: You do not need a table for the business itself. The database *represents* the entire business. Thus, Agent and Agency are not objects of the business because they are the business.

Rule 1: Look for *nouns* denoting the major "objects" in the business. Objects become tables in the database. All organizations have something they are selling (a service or an inventory item), and all have customers or clients. So, look for a noun denoting the customer, and look for the noun denoting what is being sold.

Here the thing that is offered is Bands. The customer is Clubs. Thus, the database needs a Band object and a Club object.

Rule 2: Look for attributes of each object. An **attribute** is like an *adjective* used to describe a noun, because an attribute describes some aspect of the object. Attributes become the table's fields. Denote one attribute as the key field.

The attributes of Band (based on what you are told, not what you think should be true) are the following: Band Name, Band Phone Number, and Desired Fee. No two names can be the same, so the key field is Band Name. The following definition would work for Band (in Access):

Table Name: Band

Field Name	Data Type
Band Name (key)	Text
Band Phone Number	Text
Desired Fee	Currency

Fig. A-1

These are two likely Band records:

Band Name (key)	Band Phone Number	Desired Fee
Heartbreakers	831 1765	$800
Lightmetal	831 2000	$700

Fig. A-2

Here is a question that a beginning database designer might ask: Why wouldn't Band Member be an attribute of Band? The answer: You don't know yet how many members will be in each band; therefore, you don't know how many fields to allocate in the Band table for members. We will cover this problem in more depth.

The attributes of Club are the following: Club Name, Address, Contact Name, Phone, Preferred Fee, and Feed Band? The following definition would work for Club (in Access):

Table Name: Club

Field Name	Data Type
Club Name (key)	Text
Address	Text
Contact Name	Text
Club Phone Number	Text
Preferred Fee	Currency
Feed Band?	Yes/No

Fig. A-3

Two likely Club records follow:

Club Name (key)	Address	Contact Name	Club Phone Number	Preferred Fee	Feed Band?
East End	1 Duce St.	Al Pots	444 8877	$600	Yes
West End	99 Duce St.	Val Dots	555 0011	$650	No

Fig. A-4

Why wouldn't Bands Booked Into Club be an attribute of Club? Again, you do not know yet how many bookings a Club will have. Furthermore, Bookings is the agency's business *transaction*. You need a table to record the business transaction. We get to that rule now.

Rule 3: Make an object representing the organization's business "transaction." That is, the selling event, which is a noun also. Here, the event is a Booking. That is what the agent *does*. The agent books a certain band into a certain club on a certain date, for a certain fee, starting at a certain time, and ending at a certain time. From that statement, we can see that the attributes are the following: Band Name, Club, Date, Start Time, End Time, and Fee. The following definition would work for Booking (in Access):

Table Name: Booking

Field Name	Data Type
Band Name	Text
Club Name	Text
Date	Date/Time
Start Time	Date/Time
End Time	Date/Time
Fee	Currency

Fig. A-5

Some likely Bookings records follow:

Band Name	Club Name	Date	Start Time	End Time	Fee
Heartbreakers	East End	3/6/99	18:00	23:30	$800
Heartbreakers	East End	3/7/99	19:00	23:30	$750
Heartbreakers	West End	3/8/99	13:00	18:00	$500
Lightmetal	East End	3/6/99	13:00	17:00	$700
Lightmetal	West End	3/6/99	18:00	23:30	$750

Fig. A-6

The records in the table will list all bookings in a period. Each band will be booked many times, and each club will be used many times. Each date and time could appear more than once. No single field is guaranteed to have unique values. So, no *one* field can be the key.

You must make a **compound key** whose field values *together* will be unique. Here, this combination would work: Band Name, Date, and Start Time. This would also work, since a band can only be in one place at one time: Club Name, Date, and Start Time.

A way around the compound key problem is to make a field called Booking Number. Each record gets its own number. This number is like an invoice number.

In this table, Band Name and Club Name are **foreign keys**, that is, they are fields that are keys in some other "foreign" table.

Rule 4: Avoid data redundancy. Why wouldn't Club Phone Number be in the Bookings table as a field? After all, the agent might have to call about some last minute change and could quickly look up the number in the Bookings table. The answer is that a query could be set up linking Club and Bookings, joining on Club Name, and the Phone Number field value shown that way. Redundant data wastes disk space and leads to data entry errors because you must enter the value in more than one table.

Rule 5: Do not include a field if it can be calculated from other fields. A **calculated field** is made using the query generator. Thus, the agent's fee is not included in Bookings. It can be calculated by query (some known percentage times the booking fee).

Rule 6: Do not include a field if you do not know in advance how many of that attribute the object will have. Make a separate table for that attribute. This answers the question: Why isn't Band Member in the Band Table? If you knew in advance exactly how many members each band had, you could set up fields for the attributes of each member in Band. Suppose the number was always three. You could set up fields like this:

MemberName1

MemberName2

MemberName3

MemberInstrument1

MemberInstrument2

MemberInstrument3

Member1Phone

(Additional fields continue)

That would create a lot of fields, and it would create a pretty ugly table, but it would work without redundancy. However, here you cannot make that assumption. If a band had four members (continuing the example), there would not be enough fields. If the band had two members, some fields would go to waste (and some disk space be wasted by the empty fields).

The answer is to make a Band Member table. The attributes are the following: Member Name, Band Name, Instrument, and Phone. The table definition would be as follows:

Table Name: Band Member

Field Name	Data Type
Member Name (key)	Text
Band Name	Text
Instrument	Text
Phone	Text

Fig. A-7

Some likely Band Member records follow:

Member Name (key)	Band Name	Instrument	Phone
Pete Goff	Heartbreakers	Guitar	302 444 1111
Joe Goff	Heartbreakers	Vocals	302 444 1234
Sue Smith	Heartbreakers	Keyboard	302 555 1199
Joe Jackson	Lightmetal	Sax	302 888 1654
Sue Hoopes	Lightmetal	Piano	302 888 1765

Fig. A-8

Member Name can be the key field because of the (somewhat arbitrary) assumption that no two members in any band have the same name. Alternately, Phone could be the key, if it could be assumed that no two members share a phone. Instrument can be included, because there is just one per member. Note! Band Name must be included as a foreign key, so you can tell who plays for whom.

You should test your understanding of this rule by dealing with this question. What if a Band Member could play any number of instruments, i.e., not just one? What would you do?

It's the same problem as seen between Band and Band Member. You must make a Member Instrument table (and take Instrument out of Band Member). The table definition would be as follows:

Table Name: Member Instrument

Field Name	Data Type
Band Member Name (key)	Text
Instrument (key)	Text

Fig. A-9

You would see records like this:

Band Member Name (key)	Instrument (key)
Pete Goff	Guitar
Pete Goff	Sax
Joe Jackson	Guitar
Joe Jackson	Sax
Sue Hoopes	Piano

Fig. A-10

Note that neither field has unique values, so you need a compound key. There could only be one record with the *combined* value "Pete Goff" and "Guitar." Note that assigning an "instrument number," as an alternative to the compound key, seems unpromising. Such a number seems contrived—not analogous to an invoice number, certainly.

Database Queries and Reports

B
TUTORIAL

Microsoft Access is a relational database package that runs under Windows on microcomputers. This tutorial was prepared using Access Version 7.0.

Before using this tutorial, you should know the fundamentals of Microsoft Access and know how to use Windows. This tutorial teaches you the more advanced Access skills you'll need to do the following database case studies. The tutorial concludes with a discussion of common Access problems and how to solve them.

A preliminary caution: Always observe proper file saving and closing steps. Use these steps to exit from Access: (1) With your diskette in drive A:, use these commands: File—Close, then (2) File—Exit. This gets you back to Windows. Always end your work with these two steps. Never pull out your diskette and walk away with work remaining on the screen. You could lose your work if you do.

To begin this tutorial, open a database called Employee.

AT THE KEYBOARD

Open a new database (File—New) and call it Employee. If you are saving to a floppy diskette, first select the drive (A:), and then enter the file name (Employee.mdb).

The opening screen looks like this:

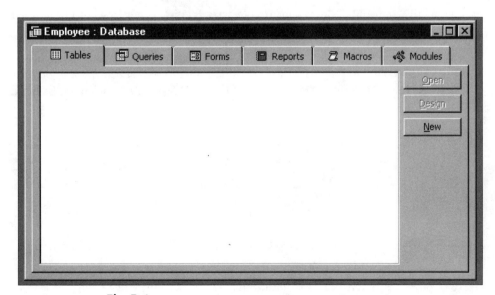

Fig. B-1

In this tutorial, this screen is called the "main objects menu." From this screen, you can create or change objects.

➤ CREATING TABLES

Your database will keep track of data about employees, their wage rates, and their hours worked.

Defining Tables

At the "main objects menu," make three new tables.

🖵 AT THE KEYBOARD

(1) **Define a table called Employee.** This table contains permanent data about employees: Click the New button in the main object menu, then Design View, and then define the table Employee. The table's fields are Last Name, First Name, SSN (Social Security number), Street Address, City, State, Zip, Date Hired, and US Citizen?. The SSN is the key field. Change the length of text fields from the default 50 spaces to more appropriate lengths; for example, Last Name might be 30 spaces, and Zip might be 15 spaces. Your completed definition should look like this:

	Field Name	Data Type	Description
	Last Name	Text	
	First Name	Text	
🔑	SSN	Text	
	Street Address	Text	
	City	Text	
	State	Text	
	Zip	Text	
	Date Hired	Date/Time	
	US Citizen?	Yes/No	

Fig. B-2

When you're finished, choose File—Save. Enter the name desired for the table (here, Employee). Important! Save the table *Within the Current Database*. If you save it as a separate external file, you will have much trouble later relating other tables to this one. Specify the name of the *table*, not of the database itself. (It is coincidence that "Employee" has the same name as its database file.)

(2) **Define a table called Wage Data.** This table contains permanent data about employees and their wage rates. The table's fields are SSN (Text), Wage Rate (Currency), Salaried (Y/N). SSN is the key field. The definition should look like this:

	Field Name	Data Type	Description
🔑	SSN	Text	
	Wage Rate	Currency	
	Salaried	Yes/No	

Fig. B-3

Use File—Save to save the table definition. Name the table Wage Data.

(3) **Define a table called Hours Worked.** The purpose of this table is to record the number of hours employees worked each week in the year. The table's fields are: SSN (Text), Week # (Number – Long Integer), Hours (Number – Double). The SSN and Week # constitute the "compound key."

In the following example, SSN 089-65-9000 worked 40 hours in week 1 of the year and 52 hours in week 2. These are the records for that person for the first two weeks of the year:

SSN	Week #	Hours
089-65-9000	1	40
089-65-9000	2	52

Notice that 089-65-9000 is an entry for each week. If the employee works each week of the year, at the end of the year there will be 52 records with that value. Thus, SSN values will not distinguish records. However, no other single field can distinguish these records either. Other employees will have worked during the same week number, and some employees will have worked the same number of hours (40 would be common). No single field by itself can be the key field.

However, a table must have a key field. The solution? Use a "compound" key; that is, use values from more than one field. The compound key to use here is SSN plus Week #. There is only *one* combination of SSN 114-11-2333 and Week# 1—those values *can occur in only one record*; therefore, the combination distinguishes that record from all others.

How do you set a compound key? The first step is to highlight the fields in the key. These must appear one after the other in the table definition screen. (Plan ahead for this.)

AT THE KEYBOARD

For the Hours Worked table, click in the first field's left prefix area, hold the button down, then drag down to highlight names of all fields in the compound key.

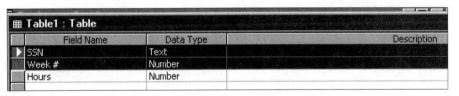

Fig. B-4

Now, click the key icon. Your screen should look like this:

Fig. B-5

That completes the key and the table definition. Use File—Save to save as Hours Worked.

Adding Records to the Table

At this point, all you have done is to set up the skeletons for three tables. The tables have no data records yet. If you were to print the tables out, all you would see would be column headings (the field names). The most direct way to enter data into tables is to select the table, open it, and type the data directly into the cells.

AT THE KEYBOARD

At the main objects menu, select Tables, then Employee. Then select Open. Your data entry screen should look like this:

Fig. B-6

The table has many fields, and some of them may be off the screen, to the right. Scroll to see obscured fields. (Scrolling happens automatically as data is entered.)

Type in your data, one field value at a time. Note that the first row is empty when you begin. Each time you finish a value, hit Enter, and the cursor will move to the next cell. After the last cell in a row, the cursor moves to the first cell of the next row, *and* Access automatically saves the record. (Thus, there is no File—Save step after entering data into a table.)

Dates (e.g., Date Hired) are entered as "6/15/99" (without the quotes). Access automatically expands the entry to the proper format in output.

Yes/No variables are clicked on (checked) for Yes; otherwise, (for No) the box is left blank. You can click the box from Yes to No, like using a toggle switch.

If you make errors in data entry, click in the cell, backspace out the error, and type the correction.

Enter this data in the Employee table:

Last Name	First Name	SSN	Street Address	City	State	ZIP	Date Hired	US Citizen?
Howard	Jane	114-11-2333	28 Sally Dr.	Glasgow	DE	19702	8/1/94	Yes
Smith	John	123-45-6789	30 Elm St.	Newark	DE	19711	6/1/96	Yes
Smith	Albert	148-90-1234	44 Duce St.	Odessa	DE	19722	7/15/87	Yes
Jones	Sue	222-82-1122	18 Spruce St.	Newark	DE	19716	7/15/92	No
Ruth	Billy	714-60-1927	1 Tater Dr.	Baltimore	MD	20111	8/15/95	No
<< Add your data here>>				Newark	MN	33776	Today	Yes

Fig. B-7

Note that the sixth record is *your* data record. Assume you live in Newark, *Minnesota*, were hired on today's date (enter the date) and you are a U.S. citizen. (Later in this tutorial, you will see Joe Brady's name and the SSN 099-11-3344 for this record.)

Open the Wage Data table and enter this data:

SSN	Wage Rate	Salaried?
114-11-2333	10.00	No
123-45-6789	0.00	Yes
148-90-1234	12.00	No
222-82-1122	0.00	Yes
714-60-1927	0.00	Yes
<<Your SSN!>>	8.00	No

Fig. B-8

Again, you must enter your SSN. Assume you earn $8 an hour and are not salaried. (Note that Salaried = No implies someone is paid by the hour. Those who are salaried do not get paid by the hour, so their hourly rate is shown as 0.00.)

Open the Hours Worked table and enter this data:

SSN	Week #	Hours
114-11-2333	1	40
114-11-2333	2	50
123-45-6789	1	40
123-45-6789	2	40
148-90-1234	1	38
148-90-1234	2	40
222-82-1122	1	40
222-82-1122	2	40
714-60-1927	1	40
714-60-1927	2	60
<<Your SSN>>	1	60
<<Your SSN>>	2	55

Fig. B-9

Notice that salaried employees are always given 40 hours. Nonsalaried employees (including you) might work any number of hours. For your record, enter your SSN, 60 hours worked for week 1, and 55 hours worked for week 2.

Since you can already create basic queries, this section teaches you the kinds of advanced queries you will do in the Case Studies. In many of the computer screens shown in the section, you'll see author Joe Brady's name and SSN 999-11-3344. Your name and SSN should replace his in your screens.

Using Calculated Fields in Queries

A calculated field is an output field that is made from *other* field values. The calculated field is **not** a field in a table; it is created in the query generator. The calculated field does not become part of the table—it is just part of query output. The best way to explain this process is by working through an example.

⊟ AT THE KEYBOARD

Suppose you want to see the SSNs and wage rates of hourly workers, and you want to see what the wage rates would be if all employees were given a 10% raise. To do this, show the SSN, the current wage rate, and the higher rate (which should be titled "New Rate" in the output). Here is how to set up the query:

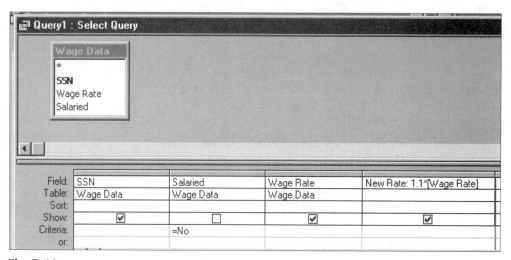

Fig. B-10

The Salaried field is needed, with the Criteria =No, to select hourly workers. The Show box for that field has been turned off, so the Salaried field values will not show in the query output.

Note the expression for the calculated field, which you see in the rightmost field cell:

New Rate:1.1*[Wage Rate]

"New Rate:" merely specifies the desired output heading (don't forget the colon). 1.1*[Wage Rate] multiplies the old rate by 110%, which results in the 10% raise.

In the expression, the field name Wage Rate must be enclosed in square brackets. The rule is this: *Anytime a field name is referred to in an Access expression, it must be enclosed in square brackets.*

If you run this query, the output will look something like this (if your SSN were 099-11-3344):

SSN	Wage Rate	New Rate
114-11-2333	$10.00	11
148-90-1234	$12.00	13.2
099-11-3344	$8.00	8.8
	$0.00	

Query1 : Select Query

Fig. B-11

Notice that the calculated field output is not shown in Currency format; it's shown as a Double—a number with digits after the decimal point. To convert the output to Currency format, click on the line above the calculated field expression, thus activating the column (it darkens):

Field:	SSN	Salaried	Wage Rate	New Rate: 1.1*[Wage Rate]	
Table:	Wage Data	Wage Data	Wage Data		
Sort:					
Show:	☑	☐	☑	☑	
Criteria:		=No			
or:					

Fig. B-12

Then select View—Properties. A window like this pops up:

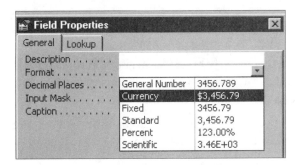

Field Properties

General | Lookup

Description . . . .
Format . . . .
Decimal Places . . . . .
Input Mask . . . .
Caption . . . .

General Number	3456.789
Currency	$3,456.79
Fixed	3456.79
Standard	3,456.79
Percent	123.00%
Scientific	3.46E+03

Fig. B-13

Select General Properties, then Format, then click on Currency. Then click the upper-right X to close the window. Now when you run the query, the output looks like this (if your SSN were 099-11-3344):

SSN	Wage Rate	New Rate
114-11-2333	$10.00	$11.00
148-90-1234	$12.00	$13.20
099-11-3344	$8.00	$8.80
	$0.00	

Fig. B-14

There is no need to print the query output or to save it. Go back to the design view and close the query. Here are some additional pointers on making calculated fields.

Avoiding Errors in Making Calculated Fields

- Don't put the expression in the *Criteria* cell, as if the field definition were a filter. You are making a *Field*; so put the expression in the Field cell.

- Spell, capitalize, and space a field's name *exactly* as you did in the table definition. If the table definition differs from what you type, Access thinks you're defining a new field by that name. Access then prompts you to enter values for the new field, which it calls a "Parameter Query" field. This is easy to debug because of the tag "Parameter Query." If Access asks you to enter values for a "Parameter," you almost certainly have misspelled a field name in an expression in a calculated field or in a criterion.

  Example: Here are some errors you might make for Wage Rate:

    Misspelling: (Wag Rate)
    Case change: (wage Rate / WAGE RATE)
    Spacing change: (WageRate / Wage Rate)

- Don't use parentheses or curly braces instead of the square brackets. Also, don't put parentheses inside square brackets. You *are* allowed to use parentheses outside of the square brackets, in the normal algebraic manner.

  Example: Suppose you want to multiply Hours times Wage Rate, to get a field called Wages Owed. This is the correct expression:

    Wages Owed:[Wage Rate]*[Hours]

  This would also be correct:

    Wages Owed:([Wage Rate]*[Hours])

  But it would **not** be correct to leave out the inside brackets, which is a common error:

    Wages Owed:[Wage Rate*Hours]

"Relating" Two (or More) Tables by the "Join" Operation

Often, the data you need for a query is in more than one table. To complete the query, you must join the tables. One rule of thumb is that joins are usually made on key fields that have common *values*. The names of the join fields are irrelevant—the names may be the same, but that is not a requirement for an effective join.

Make a join by first bringing in (Adding) the tables needed. Next, decide which fields you will join. Then click on one field name and hold down the button, dragging the cursor over to the other field's name in its window. Release the button. Access puts a line in, signifying the join. (Note: If there are two key fields in the tables with the same name, Access will put the line in automatically, so you do not have to do the click-and-drag operation.)

You can join more than two tables together. The common fields *need not* be the same in all tables; that is, you can "daisy chain" them together.

A common join error is to Add a table to the query and then fail to link it to another table. You have a table just "floating" in the top part of the QBE screen! When you run the query, your output will show the same records over and over. This error is unmistakable because there is *so much* redundant output. The rules are (1) add only the tables you need, and (2) link all tables.

Here is an example of a query needing a join.

AT THE KEYBOARD

Suppose you want to see the last name, SSN, wage rate, salary status, and citizenship for only U.S. Citizens and hourly workers. The data is spread across two tables, Employee and Wage Data, so both tables are added and five fields pulled down. Criteria are then added. Set it up this way:

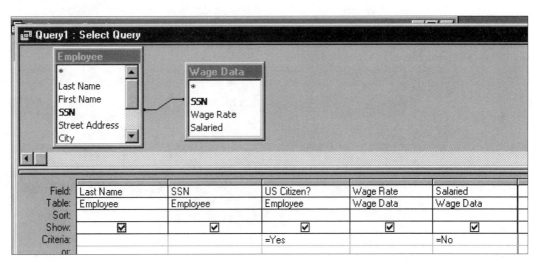

Fig. B-15

The join is on SSN. A field by that name is in both tables, so Access automatically puts in the join. If one field had been spelled SSN and the other Social Security Number, you would still join on these fields (because of the *common values*). You would click and drag to do this operation.

Run this query. The output should look like this (if your name were Brady with SSN 099-11-3344):

Last Name	SSN	US Citizen?	Wage Rate	Salaried
Howard	114-11-2333	☑	$10.00	☐
Smith	148-90-1234	☑	$12.00	☐
Brady	099-11-3344	☑	$8.00	☐

Query1 : Select Query

Fig. B-16

Here is a quick review of Criteria. In this example, if you want data for employees who are U.S. citizens *and* who are hourly workers, the Criteria expressions must go into the *same* Criteria row. If you want data for employees who are U.S. citizens *or* who are hourly workers, one of the expressions must go into the second Criteria row (the one that has the "Or:" notation in it).

There is no need to print the query output or to save it. Go back to the Design View and close the query. Here is another query that you should set up and try.

AT THE KEYBOARD

Suppose you want to see the wages owed to hourly employees for week 2. Show the last name, the SSN, the salaried status, the hours worked, and the wages owed. Wages will have to be a calculated field ([Wage Rate]*[Hours]). The criteria are =No for Salaried and =2 for the Week #. (Another "And" query, note!) When you add the tables, your screen may show the links differently. Click and drag the Employee, Hours Worked, and Wage Data table icons to look like this:

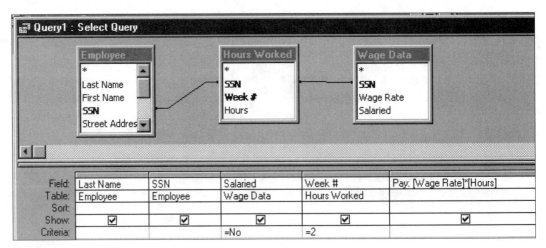

Fig. B-17

(Note: In the previous table, the calculated field column was widened so you can see the whole expression. Review: To widen a column, you click on the column boundary line, and drag to the right.) Run the query. If your name were Brady with SSN 099-11-3344, the output should be something like this:

Last Name	SSN	Salaried	Week #	Pay
Howard	114-11-2333	☐	2	$500.00
Smith	148-90-1234	☐	2	$480.00
Brady	099-11-3344	☐	2	$440.00

Query1 : Select Query

Fig. B-18

Notice that it was not necessary to pull down the Wage Rate and Hours fields to make this query work. Return to the Design View. There is no need to save. File—Close.

Summarizing Data From Multiple Records ("Sigma" Queries)

You may want data that summarizes values from a field for more than one record (or possibly all records) in a table. For example, you might want to know the average hours worked for all employees in a week, or perhaps the total (sum) of all the hours worked. Furthermore, you might want data grouped ("stratified") in some way. For example, you might want to know the average hours worked, grouped by all U.S. citizens vs. all non-U.S. citizens. Access calls this kind of query a "summary" query or a "sigma" query. Unfortunately, this terminology is not intuitive, but the statistical operations that are allowed will be familiar. These operations include the following:

Sum	The total of a field's values
Count	A count of the number of instances in a field, i.e., the number of records. Here, to get the number of employees, you'd count the number of SSN numbers.
Average	The average of a field's values
Min	The minimum of a field's values
Var	The variance of a field's values
StDev	The standard deviation of a field's values

AT THE KEYBOARD

Suppose you want to know how many employees are represented in a database. The first step is to bring the Employee table into the QBE screen. Do that now. The query will Count the number of SSNs, which is a sigma query operation. Thus, you must bring down the SSN field.

To tell Access you want a sigma query, click the little "Sigma" icon in the menu:

Fig. B-19

This opens up a new row in the lower part of the QBE screen, called the Total row. At this point the screen would look like this:

Fig. B-20

Note the Total cell says "Group By." Until you specify a statistical operation, Access just assumes that a field will be used for grouping (stratifying) data.

To Count the number of SSNs, click next to "Group By," revealing a little arrow. Click the arrow to reveal a drop-down menu.

Fig. B-21

Select the Count operator. (With this menu, you may need to scroll to see the operator you want.) Your screen should now look like this:

Fig. B-22

Run the query. Your output should look like this:

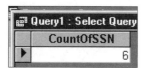

Fig. B-23

Notice that Access has made a pseudo-heading "CountOfSSN". To do this, it just spliced together the statistical operation ("Count"), the word "Of," and the name of the field ("SSN"). What if you wanted an English phrase as a heading, such as, "Count of Employees"? In the Design View, you'd change the query this way:

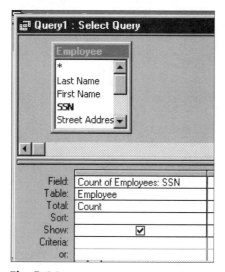

Fig. B-24

Now when you run the query, the output looks like this:

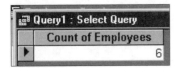

Fig. B-25

There is no need to save this query. Go back to the Design View and Close.

Here is another example. Suppose you want to know the Average wage rate of employees, grouped by whether they are salaried.

Here is the setup:

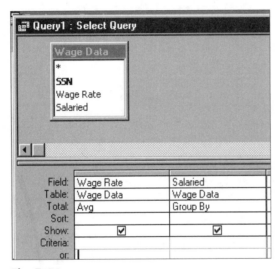

Fig. B-26

When you run the query this is what you get:

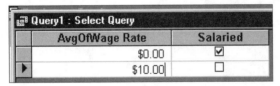

Fig. B-27

Recall the convention that salaried workers are assigned zero dollars an hour. Suppose you want to eliminate the output line for zero dollars an hour because only hourly-rate workers matter for this query. This is the setup:

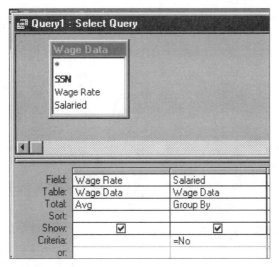

Fig. B-28

When you run the query, you'll get output for nonsalaried employees only:

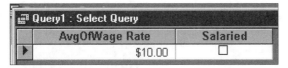

Fig. B-29

Thus, it's possible to use Criteria in a sigma query without any problem, just as you would with a "regular" query.

There is no need to save the query. Go back to the Design View and Close.

AT THE KEYBOARD

You can make a calculated field in a sigma query. Assume that you want to see two things for hourly workers: (1) the average wage rate—call it Average Rate in the output, and (2) 110% of this average rate—call it the "Increased Rate."

You already know how to do certain things for this query. The revised heading for the average rate would be Average Rate (Average Rate:Wage Rate, in the Field cell). You want the Average of that field. Grouping would be by the Salaried field (with Criteria: =No, for hourly workers).

The most difficult part of this query is to construct the expression for the calculated field. Conceptually it is:

Increased Rate:1.1*[The current average, however that is denoted]

The question is how to represent this:

[The current average, however that is denoted]

You cannot use Wage Rate for this because that heading denotes the wages before they are averaged. Surprisingly, it turns out that you can use the new heading ("Average Rate") to denote the averaged amount. Thus:

Increased Rate:1.1*[Average Rate]

Thus, unintuitively, *you can treat "Average Rate" as if it were an actual field name.* Use this setup:

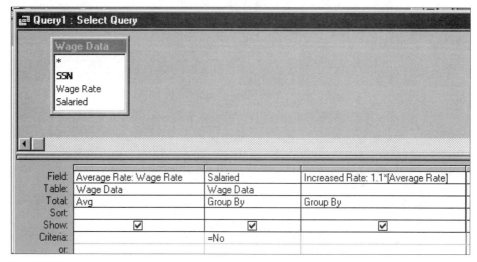

Fig. B-30

However, if you ran the query now, you'd get some sort of error message. You do not want Group By in the calculated field's Total cell.

There is not a *statistical* operator that applies to the calculated field. You must change the Group By operator to Expression. You may have to scroll to get to Expression in the list. Here is what that looks like:

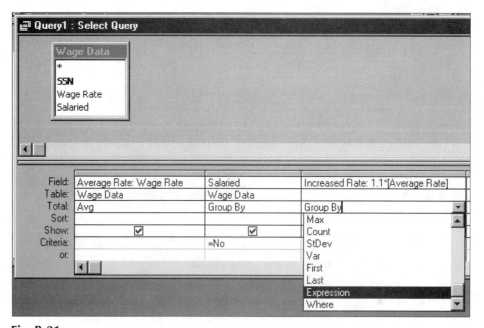

Fig. B-31

This is how the screen looks before running:

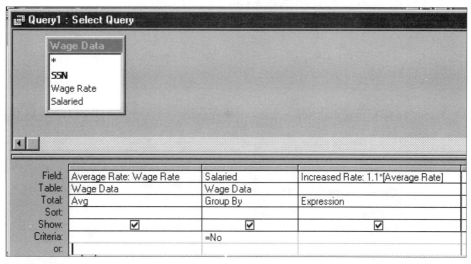

Fig. B-32

This is what the output of the query should look like:

Fig. B-33

There is no need to save the query definition. Go back to the Design View. File—Close.

Using the Date () Function in Queries

Access has two date function features that you should know about.

1. This *built-in function* gives you today's date:

    Date()

    You can use this function in a query criterion or in a calculated field. The function "returns" the day in which the query is run (i.e., puts that value into the place where the function is in an expression).

2. *Date arithmetic* lets you subtract one date from another to get the number of days' difference. Access would evaluate the expression

    10/9/98 - 10/4/98

    to the integer 5 (9 less 4 is 5).

Here is an example of how this would work in Access. Suppose you wanted to give each employee a bonus equaling a dollar for each day the employee had worked for you. You'd need to calculate the number of days between the employee's date of hire and the day that the query is run, then multiply that number by 1.

The number of elapsed days is:

Date() - [Date Hired]

Suppose you want to see the last name, the SSN, and the bonus. You'd set the query up this way:

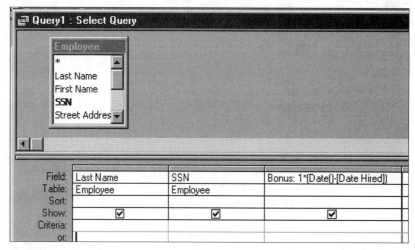

Fig. B-34

Assume you set the format of the Bonus field to Currency. The output will be something like this (if your name were Brady with SSN 099-11-3344):

Last Name	SSN	Bonus
Brady	099-11-3344	$0.00
Howard	114-11-2333	$1,703.00
Smith	123-45-6789	$1,033.00
Smith	148-90-1234	$4,277.00
Jones	222-82-1122	$2,450.00
Ruth	714-60-1927	$1,324.00

Fig. B-35

(Your Bonus data will be different because you are working on a date different than the date on which this tutorial was written.)

Using Time Arithmetic in Queries

Access will also let you subtract the values of time fields to get an elapsed time. Assume that our database had a JobAssignments table showing the times that nonsalaried employees were at work in the day. The definition is as follows:

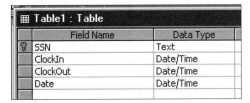

Fig. B-36

Assume the Date field is formatted for Long Date and that the ClockIn and ClockOut fields are formatted for Medium Time. Assume your SSN is 099-11-3344. Also assume, for a particular day, nonsalaried workers were scheduled as follows:

JobAssignments : Table

SSN	ClockIn	ClockOut	Date
099-11-3344	8:30 AM	4:30 PM	Wednesday, March 31, 1999
114-11-2333	9:00 AM	3:00 PM	Wednesday, March 31, 1999
148-90-1234	7:00 AM	5:00 PM	Wednesday, March 31, 1999

Fig. B-37

You want a query that will show the elapsed time on premises for the day. When you add the tables, your screen may show the links differently. Click and drag the Job Assignments, Employee, and Wage Data table icons to look like this:

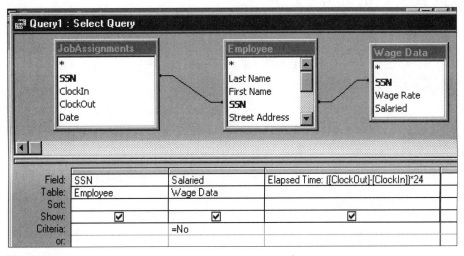

Fig. B-38

This is the output (If your SSN were 099-11-3344):

SSN	Salaried	Elapsed Time
114-11-2333		6
148-90-1234		10
099-11-3344		8

Fig. B-39

The output looks right. For example, employee 099-11-3344 was here from 8:30 a.m. to 4:40 p.m., which is 8 hours. But how does the odd expression

([ClockOut] - [ClockIn]) * 24

yield the correct answers? Why wouldn't this expression, alone, work?:

[ClockOut] - [ClockIn]

This is the answer: In Access, subtracting one time from the other *yields the decimal portion of a 24-hour day*. Employee 099-11-3344 worked 8 hours, which is a third of a day, so .3333 would result. That is why you must multiply by 24—to convert to an hours basis. Continuing with 099-11-3344, 1/3 x 24 = 8.

Note that parentheses are needed to force Access to do the *subtraction first*, before the multiplication. Without parentheses, multiplication takes precedence over subtraction. With this expression:

[ClockOut] - [ClockIn] * 24

ClockIn would be multiplied by 24 and then that value would be subtracted from ClockOut. The output would be a nonsense decimal number.

Five Practice Queries

This portion of the tutorial is designed to provide additional practice making queries. Before making these queries, you must create the specified tables and enter the records shown in the Creating Tables section of this tutorial.

At the Keyboard

In each query that follows, you are given a problem statement and a "scratch area." You are also shown what the query output should look like. Set up each query in Access. Run the query. When satisfied with the results, save the query, and continue. You will be working with the Employee, Hours Worked, and Wage Data tables.

1. Create a query that shows the SSN, last name, state, and date hired for those living in Delaware *and* who were hired after 12/31/92. Sort (ascending) by SSN. (Sorting review: Click in the Sort cell of the field. Choose Ascending or Descending.)

Field						
Table						
Sort						
Show						
Criteria						
Or:						

JobAssignments : Table

SSN	ClockIn	ClockOut	Date
099-11-3344	8:30 AM	4:30 PM	Wednesday, March 31,
114-11-2333	9:00 AM	3:00 PM	Wednesday, March 31,
148-90-1234	7:00 AM	5:00 PM	Wednesday, March 31

Fig. B-40

2. Create a query that shows the last name, first name, date hired, and state for those living in Delaware *or* who were hired after 12/31/92. The primary sort (ascending) is on last name, and secondary sort (ascending) is on first name. (Review: The primary sort field must be left of the secondary sort field in the query setup.)

Field						
Table						
Sort						
Show						
Criteria						
Or:						

If your name were Joseph Brady, your output would look like this:

Query1 : Select Query

Last Name	First Name	Date Hired	State
Brady	Joseph	Wednesday, March 31, 1999	MN
Howard	Jane	Monday, August 01, 1994	DE
Jones	Sue	Wednesday, July 15, 1992	DE
Ruth	Billy	Tuesday, August 15, 1995	MD
Smith	Albert	Wednesday, July 15, 1987	DE
Smith	John	Saturday, June 01, 1996	DE

Fig. B-41

3. Create a query that shows the sum of hours worked by U.S. citizens and by non-U.S. citizens; i.e., group on citizenship. The heading for total hours worked should be Total of Hours Worked.

Field						
Table						
Total						
Sort						
Show						
Criteria						
Or:						

US Citizen?	Total Hours Worked
☑	363
☐	180

Query1 : Select Query

Fig. B-42

4. Create a query that shows the wages owed to hourly workers for week 1. The heading for the wages owed should be Total Owed. The output headings should be: Last Name, SSN, Week #, and Total Owed.

Field						
Table						
Sort						
Show						
Criteria						
Or:						

If your last name were Brady, your output would look like this:

Query1 : Select Query

Last Name	SSN	Week #	Total Owed
Howard	114-11-2333	1	$400.00
Smith	148-90-1234	1	$456.00
Brady	099-11-3344	1	$480.00
*			

Fig. B-43

5. Create a query that shows the last name, SSN, hours worked, and overtime amount owed for employees paid hourly who earned overtime during week 2. Overtime is paid at 1.5 times the normal hourly rate for hours over 40. The amount shown should be just the overtime portion of the wages paid. This is not a sigma query—amounts should be shown for individual workers.

Field						
Table						
Sort						
Show						
Criteria						
Or:						

If your last name were Brady, your output would look like this:

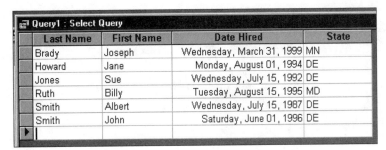

Query1 : Select Query

Last Name	First Name	Date Hired	State
Brady	Joseph	Wednesday, March 31, 1999	MN
Howard	Jane	Monday, August 01, 1994	DE
Jones	Sue	Wednesday, July 15, 1992	DE
Ruth	Billy	Tuesday, August 15, 1995	MD
Smith	Albert	Wednesday, July 15, 1987	DE
Smith	John	Saturday, June 01, 1996	DE

Fig. B-44

➤ CREATING REPORTS

Database packages let you make attractive management reports from a table's records or from a query's output. If you are making a report from a table, Access' report generator looks up the data in the table and puts it into report format. If you are making a report from a query's output, Access runs the query in the background and then puts the output in report format.

There are three ways to make a report. One is to handcraft the report in the so-called "Design View," from scratch. This is tedious and is not shown in this tutorial. The second way is to use the so-called "Report Wizard," during which Access leads you through a menu-driven construction. This method is shown in this tutorial. The third way is to start in the Wizard and then use the Design View to tailor what the Wizard produces. This method is shown in this tutorial.

Creating a Grouped Report

This tutorial assumes you can use the Wizard to make a basic ungrouped report. This section of the tutorial teaches you how to make a grouped report. (If you cannot make an ungrouped report, you might learn how to make one by following the first example below.)

🖫 **AT THE KEYBOARD**

Suppose you want to make a report out of the Hours Worked table. At the main objects menu, start a new report by choosing Report—New. Select the Report Wizard and select the Hours Worked table from the drop-down menu as the report basis. Select OK. In the next screen, select all the fields (use the >> button):

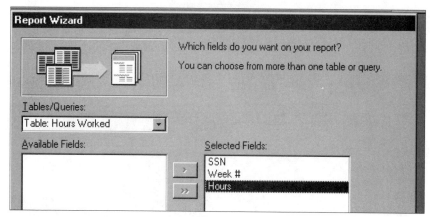

Fig. B-45

Click Next. Then tell Access that you want to group on Week # by double-clicking on that field name. You'll see this:

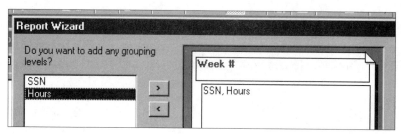

Fig. B-46

Click Next. You'll see this screen for Sorting and for Summary Options:

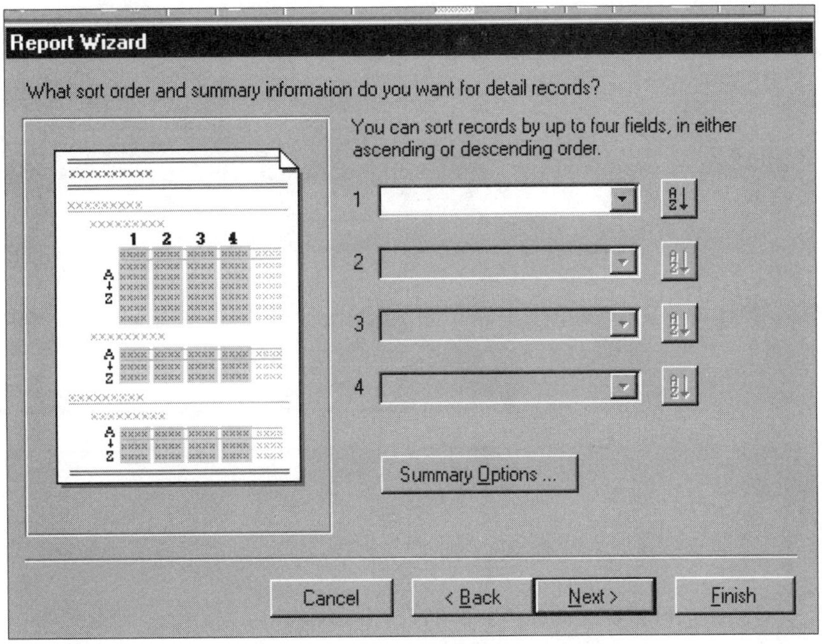

Fig. B-47

Because you chose a grouping field, Access will now let you decide whether you want to see group subtotals and/or report grand totals for numerical fields. In this example, group subtotals are for total hours in each week. Assume you *do* want the total of hours by week. Click Summary Options. You'll get a screen like this:

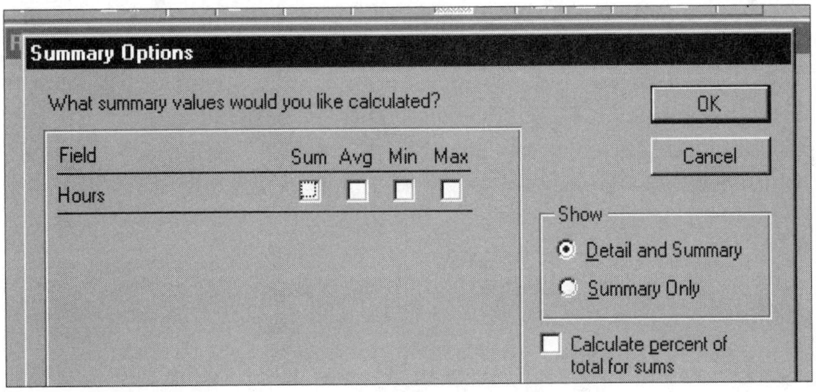

Fig. B-48

Click the Sum box for Hours (to sum the hours in the group), and choose Detail and Summary if that is not already chosen. (Detail equates with "group" and Summary with "grand total for the report.") Then click OK. This takes you back to the Sorting screen, where you can pick an ordering within the group, if desired. (In this case, none is.) Then click Next to continue.

In the Layout screen (not shown here) choose Stepped and Portrait. Click *off* the Adjust the Field Width option, then click Next. In the Style screen (not shown), accept Corporate, then click Next. Provide a title—Hours Worked by Week would be appropriate. The Preview button should be selected. Click Finish. If your SSN were 099-11-3344, the top portion of your report will look like this:

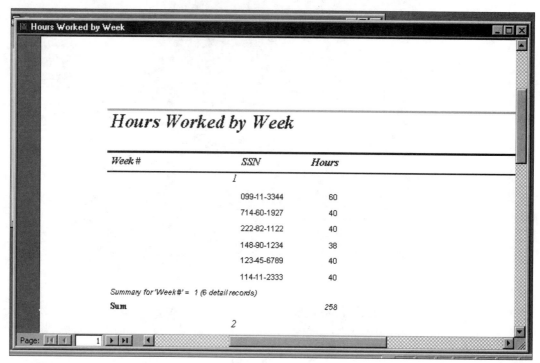

Fig. B-49

Notice that data is shown grouped by weeks, with week 1 on top, then a subtotal for that week. Week 2 data is next, then there is a grand total (which you can scroll down to see). The subtotal is labeled "Sum," which is not very descriptive. This can be changed later in the Design View. Also, there is the apparently useless italicized line that starts out *"Summary for 'Week ..."* This also can be deleted later in the Design View. At this point, you should save the file. Then File—Close to get back the main objects menu. Try it. You will see this:

Fig. B-50

To edit the report in the Design View, click on the report title, then on the Design button. You will see this complex (and intimidating) screen:

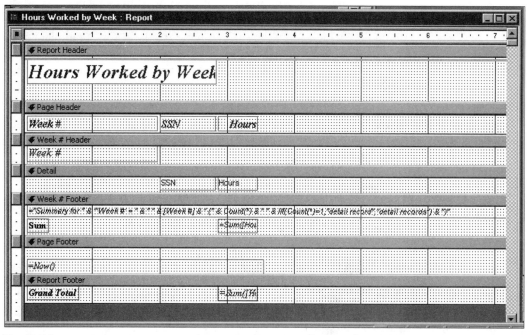

Fig. B-51

The organization of the screen is hierarchical. The top organization is the Report level. The next level down (within a report) is the Page level. The next level or levels down (within a page) are for any data groupings you have specified.

If you told Access to make group (summary) totals, your report will have a "header" and a grand report total. The report header is usually just the title you have specified, and often the date is put in by default.

A page also has a header, which is usually just the names of the fields you have told Access to put in the report (here, Week #, SSN, and Hours). Sometimes the page number is put in by default.

The header structure of reports with grouped data is complex. There is a header for the group—in this case, the *value* of the Week # will be the header. (For example, there is a group of data for the first week, then one for the second—the values shown will be 1 and 2.) Within each data grouping is the other "detail" that you've asked for. In this case, there will be data for each SSN and the related hours.

Each Week # gets a "footer," which is a labeled sum—recall that you asked for that to be shown (Detail and Summary were requested). The Week # footer is indicated by three things: (1) the italicized line that starts "=Summary for ..." and (2) the Sum label and (3) the adjacent expression "=Sum(Hours)."

The italicized line beneath the Week # footer will be printed unless you eliminate it. Similarly, the word "Sum" will be printed as the subtotal label unless you eliminate it. The "=Sum(Hours)" is an expression that tells Access to add up quantity *for the header in question* and put that number into the report as the subtotal. (In this example, that would be the sum of hours, by Week #.)

Each report also gets a footer—the grand total (in this case, of hours) for the report.

If you look closely, each of the detail items appears to be doubly inserted in the design. For example, you will see the notation for SSN twice, once in the Page Header and then again in the Detail band. Hours are treated similarly.

The data items will not actually be printed twice because each data element is an object in the report; each object is denoted by a label and by its value. There is a representation of the name, which is the boldfaced name itself (in this example, "SSN" in the page header), and there is a representation, in less-bold type for the value "SSN" in the detail band.

Sometimes the Wizard is arbitrary about where it puts labels and data. However, if you do not like where the Wizard puts data, it can be moved around in the Design View. You can click and drag within the band, or across bands. Often, a box will be too small to allow full numerical values to show. When that happens, select the box and then click one of the sides to stretch it. This will allow full values to show. At other times an object's box will be very long. When that happens, the box can be clicked, resized, then dragged right or left in its panel to reposition the output.

Suppose you do *not* want the italicized line to appear in the report. Also suppose that you would like different subtotal and grand total labels. The italicized line is an object that can be activated by clicking on it. Do that. "Handles" (little squares) appear around its edges:

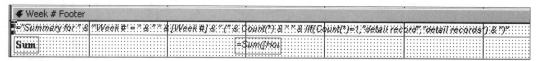

Fig. B-52

Press the Delete key to get rid of the highlighted object.

To change the subtotal heading, click on the Sum object:

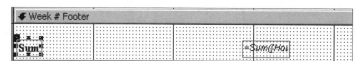

Fig. B-53

Click again. This gives you an insertion point from which you can type:

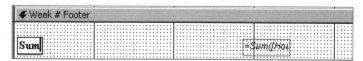

Fig. B-54

Change the label to something like Sum of Hours for Week, then hit Enter, or click somewhere else in the report to deactivate. Your screen should look like this:

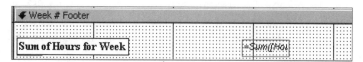

Fig. B-55

You can change the Grand Total in the same way.

File—Save. Then File—Print Preview. If your SSN were 099-11-3344, you should see a report like this (top part shown):

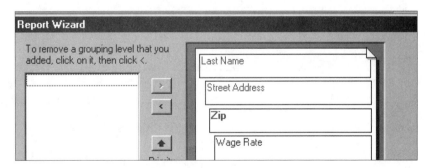

Hours Worked by Week

Week #	SSN	Hours
1		
	099-11-3344	60
	714-60-1927	40
	222-82-1122	40
	148-90-1234	38
	123-45-6789	40
	114-11-2333	40
Sum of Hours for Week		258

Fig. B-56

Notice that the data is grouped by week number (data for week 1 is shown) and subtotaled for that week. The report would also have a grand total at the bottom.

Moving Fields in the Design View

When you group on more than one field in the Report Wizard, the report has an odd "staircase" look. There is a way to overcome that effect in the Design View.

Suppose you make a query showing an employee's last name, street address, Zip Code and wage rate. Then you make a report from that query, grouping on last name, street address, and Zip Code. (Why you would want to organize a report in this way is not clear, but for the moment accept the organization for the purpose of the example.)

Report Wizard

To remove a grouping level that you added, click on it, then click <.

Last Name

Street Address

Zip

Wage Rate

Fig. B-57

Click Next. You do not Sum anything in Summary Options. Click off the "Adjust the Field Width" option. Select Landscape. Select Stepped. Select Corporate. Type in a title (Wage Rates for Employees).

When you run the report, it comes out with a staircase-grouped organization. In the report that follows, notice Zip is shown below street address, and street address is shown below name. (The detail field Wage Rate is shown subordinate to all others, as desired. Wage rates may not show on the screen without scrolling.) If your last name were Brady, your Wage Rate screen will look like this:

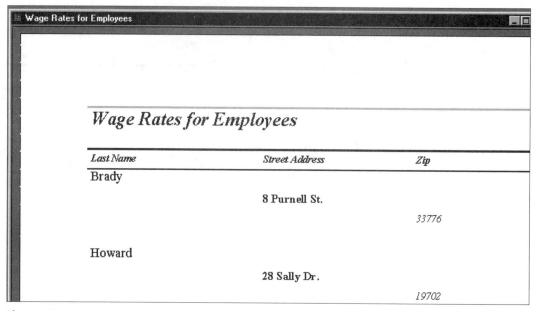

Fig. B-58

Suppose you want the last name, street address, and Zip all on the same line. The way to do that is to take the report into the Design View for editing. At the main objects menu, select the report and Design. At this point, the "headers" look like this:

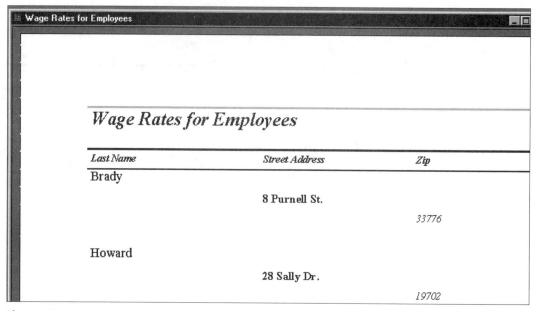

Fig. B-59

Your goal is to get the address and Zip fields into the last name header (*not* into the page header!), so they will then print on the same line.

The first step is to click the Street Address object:

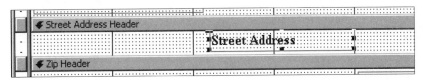

Fig. B-60

Hold the button down with the little "paw" icon, and drag the object up into the Last Name header:

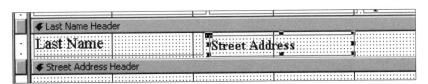

Fig. B-61

Do the same thing with the Zip object:

Fig. B-62

To get a more compactly printed report, tighten up the "dotted" area between each header. Put the cursor on the top of the header panel. The arrow changes to something that looks like a crossbar. Click and drag up to close the distance. After both headers are moved up, the screen looks like this:

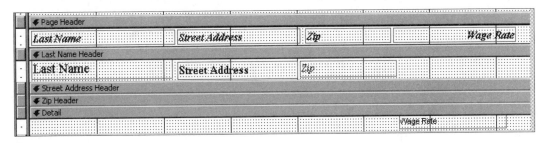

Fig. B-63

If your name were Brady, here is how your report should now look:

Wage Rates for Employees

Last Name	Street Address	Zip	Wage Rate
Brady	8 Purnell St.	33776	
			$8.00
Howard	28 Sally Dr.	19702	
			$10.00
Smith	44 Duce St.	19722	
			$12.00

Fig. B-64

❧ CREATING FORMS

Forms simplify adding new records to a table. The Form Wizard is easy to use and will not be reviewed; however, making a form out of more than one table needs to be explained.

When you base a form on one table, you simply identify that table when in the Form Wizard setup. The form will have all the fields from that table, and only those fields. When data is entered into the form, a complete new record is automatically added to the table.

But what if you need a form that includes the data from two (or more) tables? Begin (unintuitively) with a query. Bring all tables you need in the form into the query. Bring down the fields you need from each table. (For data entry purposes, this probably means bringing down *all* the fields from each table.) All you are doing is selecting fields that you want to show up in the form, so you make *no criteria* after bringing fields down in the query. Save the query. When making the form, tell Access to base the form on the query. The form will show all the fields in the query; thus, you can enter data into the tables all at once.

Suppose you want to make one form that would, at the same time, enter records into the Employee table and the Wage Data table. The first table holds relatively permanent data about an employee. The second table holds data about the employee's starting wage rate, which will probably change.

The first step is to make a query based on both tables. Bring all the fields from both tables down into the lower area. Basically the query just acts as a way to gather up all the fields from both tables into one place. No criteria are needed. Save the query.

The second step is to make a form based on the query. This works because the query knows about all the fields. Tell the form to display all fields in the query. (Common fields—here, SSN—would appear twice, once for each table.)

❧ Errors, Pitfalls, and Cautions

Access beginners (and veterans!) sometimes create databases that have problems. Common problems are described here, along with causes and corrections.

1. *"I saved my database file, but it is not on my diskette! Where is it?"*

   You saved to a fixed disk. Use the Find option of the Windows Start button. Search for all files ending in ".mdb" (search for *.mdb). If you did save it, it is on the hard drive (C:\) or on some network drive. (Your site assistant can tell you the drive designators.) Once you have found it, use Windows Explorer to copy it to your diskette in drive A:. Click on it, and drag to drive A:.

   Reminder: Your first step with a new database should be to Open it on the intended drive, which is usually drive A: for a student. Don't rush this step. Get it right. Then, for each object made, save it *within* the current database file.

2. *"What is a 'duplicate key field value'? I'm trying to enter records into my Sales table. The first record was for a sale of product X to customer #101, and I was able to enter that one. But when I try to enter a second sale for customer #101, Access tells me I already have a record with that key field value. Am I only allowed to enter one sale per customer!?"*

   Your key field needs work. You may need a compound key—customer number and some other field or fields. In this case, customer number, product number, and date of sale might provide a unique combination of values—or consider using an invoice number field as a key.

3. *"My query says 'Enter Parameter Value' when I run it. What is that?"*

   This symptom, 99 times out of 100, indicates you have an expression in a Criteria or a Calculated Field and *you misspelled a field name in the expression*. Access is very fussy about spelling. For example, Access is case sensitive. Furthermore, if you put a space in a field name when you define the table, then you must put a space in the field name when you reference it in a query expression. Fix the typo in the query expression.

   This symptom infrequently appears when you have a calculated field in a query, and you elect *not* to show the value of the calculated field in the query output. (You clicked off the Show box for the calculated field.) To get around this problem, click Show back on.

4. *"I'm getting a fantastic number of rows in my query output—many times more than I need. Most of the rows are dupes!"*

   This symptom is usually caused by a failure to link together all tables you brought into the top half of the query generator. The solution is to use the manual click-and-drag method. Link the fields (usually key fields) with common *values* between tables. (Spelling of the field names is irrelevant because the link fields need not be spelled the same.)

5. *"For the most part, my query output is what I expected, but I am getting one or two dupe rows."*

   You may have linked too many fields between tables. Usually only a single link is needed between two tables. It's unnecessary to link each common field in all combinations of tables; usually it's enough to link the keys. A layman's explanation for why overlinking causes problems is that excess linking causes Access to "overthink" the problem and repeat itself in its answer.

   On the other hand, you might be using too many tables in the query design. For example, you brought in a table, linked it on a common field with some other table, but then made no use of the table. You brought down none of its fields and/or you used none of its fields in query expressions. Therefore, get rid of the table, and the query should still work. Try doing this to see if the few duplicate rows go away: click on the unneeded table's header in the top of the QBE area and press the Delete key.

6. *"I expected six rows in my query output, but I only got five. What happened to the other one?"*

   Usually this indicates a data entry error in your tables. When you link together the proper tables and fields to make the query, the linking operation joins records from the tables *on common values* (*equal* values in the two tables). Assume a key in one table has the value "123." The key in the other table should be the same to allow linking. Note that the text string "123" is not the same as the text string "123 " —the space in the second string is a character, too! Access does not see unequal values as an error: Access moves on to consider the rest of the records in the table for linking. Solution: Look at the values entered into the link fields in each table and fix any data entry errors.

7. *"I linked correctly in a query, but I'm getting the empty set in the output. All I get are the field name headings!"*

   You probably have zero common (equal) values in the link fields. For example, suppose you are linking on Part Number (which you declared as text): in one field you have part numbers "001", "002", "003" and in the other table part numbers "0001", "0002", "0003". Your tables have no common Part Number values, which means no records are selected for output. You'll have to change the values in one of the tables.

8. *"I'm trying to count the number of today's sales orders. A sigma query is called for. Sales are denoted by an invoice number, and I made this a text field in the table design. However, when I ask the sigma query to 'Sum' the number of invoice numbers, Access tells me I cannot add them up! What is the problem?"*

   Text variables are words! You cannot add up words, but you can count them. Use the Count sigma operator (not the Sum operator): count the number of sales, each being denoted by an invoice number.

9. *"I'm doing Time arithmetic in a calculated field expression. I subtracted the Time In from the Time Out and I got a decimal number! I expected 8 hours, and I got the number .33333. Why?"*

   [Time Out] - [Time In] yields the decimal percentage of a 24-hour day. In your case, 8 hours is a third of a day. You must complete the expression by multiplying by 24: ([Time Out] - [Time In]) * 24. Don't forget the parentheses!

10. *"I formatted a calculated field for currency in the query generator, and the values did show as currency in the query output; however, the report based on the query output does* not *show the dollar sign in its output. What happened?"*

Go into the report Design View. There is a box in one of the panels representing the calculated field's value. Click on the box and drag to widen it. That should give Access enough room to show the dollar sign, as well as the number, in output.

11. *"I told the Report Wizard to fit all my output to one page. It does print to just one page. But some of the data is missing! What happened?"*

Access makes the output all fit on one page by *leaving data out*! If you can stand to see the output on more than one page, click off the "Fit to a Page" option in the Wizard. One way to tighten output is to go into the Design View and remove space from each of the boxes representing output values and labels. Access usually provides more space than needed.

12. *"I grouped on three fields in the Report Wizard, and the Wizard prints the output in a staircase fashion. I want the grouping fields to be on one line! How can I do that?"*

Make adjustments in the Design View. See the Reports part of this tutorial for instruction.

1

CASE

Preliminary Case
The Mrs. Grey Rooming
House Database

SETTING UP A RELATIONAL DATABASE TO CREATE TABLES AND REPORTS

⋗ PREVIEW

In this case, you will create a relational database for a rooming house in a college town. First, you'll create four tables and populate them with data. Next, you'll create two reports: one will track the frequency of rentals; the other will generate occupants' bills.

⋗ PREPARATION

- Before attempting this exercise, you should have experience using Microsoft Access.
- Complete any part of the previous Access tutorial your instructor assigns, or refer to the tutorial as necessary.

↬ BACKGROUND

Your instructor has just received the following letter from a former student.

Dear Professor Sanchez,

I have been asked to finish a database project that I began last year. Because I will be traveling so much with my new job, I won't have time to complete it. I hope some of your students might be able to help me. Here are the details.

Mrs. Grey owns a rooming house in College Town, Missouri. Students' visitors often stay at Mrs. Grey's because it is cheap, clean, and almost always available. Students attending the university often spend a few weeks at Mrs. Grey's before finding permanent accommodations.

The rooming house has seven rooms, some of which are double rooms, i.e., have two twin beds, and some are single rooms. In addition, some rooms have a bathroom.

When I stayed at Mrs. Grey's Rooming House, I convinced her that instead of paying my rent, I could develop an Access database system for her to streamline her operation. I started the project but then was so busy with final exams and job hunting that I couldn't finish the database. Mrs. Grey has called me to complete the database system—or else find someone who could.

The database management system will be used to do the following:

1. Keep track of customers and their permanent address.
2. Keep track of the rooms in the house and their room type.
3. List the price of each room type.
4. Record the length of a stay in a specific room by a customer.
5. Rank the popularity of each room.
6. Generate monthly bills for customers.

I have designed the tables on the next page (in Microsoft Access) to do the first four tasks.

In addition to having these tables, Mrs. Grey requested two reports: the first report should show her how often each type of room is rented, with the most popular room being noted first, sorted to the least popular. Next, she would like a report from which she can generate her occupants' end-of-month bills. This report should include the occupant's name, address, date first rented, and total amount due.

I hope some of your students can help me with this project.

Thank you.

Yours truly,

Amy Patterson

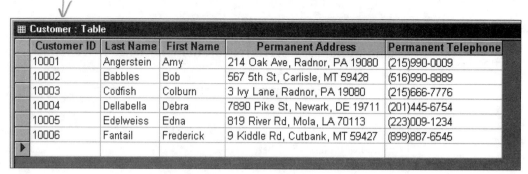

Customer : Table

Customer ID	Last Name	First Name	Permanent Address	Permanent Telephone
10001	Angerstein	Amy	214 Oak Ave, Radnor, PA 19080	(215)990-0009
10002	Babbles	Bob	567 5th St, Carlisle, MT 59428	(516)990-8889
10003	Codfish	Colburn	3 Ivy Lane, Radnor, PA 19080	(215)666-7776
10004	Dellabella	Debra	7890 Pike St, Newark, DE 19711	(201)445-6754
10005	Edelweiss	Edna	819 River Rd, Mola, LA 70113	(223)009-1234
10006	Fantail	Frederick	9 Kiddle Rd, Cutbank, MT 59427	(899)887-6545

Fig. 1-1

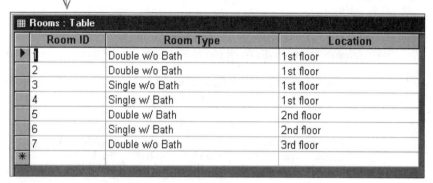

Rooms : Table

Room ID	Room Type	Location
1	Double w/o Bath	1st floor
2	Double w/o Bath	1st floor
3	Single w/o Bath	1st floor
4	Single w/ Bath	1st floor
5	Double w/ Bath	2nd floor
6	Single w/ Bath	2nd floor
7	Double w/o Bath	3rd floor

Fig. 1-2

Room Charges : Table

Room Type	Price per Night
Double w/ Bath	$30.00
Double w/o Bath	$20.00
Single w/ Bath	$20.00
Single w/o Bath	$10.00
	$0.00

Fig. 1-3

Rentals : Table

Customer ID	Room ID	Date In	Date Out
10001	1	9/1/99	9/10/99
10002	5	9/12/99	9/30/99
10003	6	9/5/99	9/6/99
10004	3	9/6/99	9/12/99
10005	4	9/4/99	9/30/99
10006	7	9/15/99	9/30/99
10007	2	9/1/99	9/10/99

Fig. 1-4

➤ ASSIGNMENT 1   CREATING TABLES

Use Microsoft Access to create the four tables requested in the letter to Professor Sanchez. Use the data provided in the letter. Add your name and address to the Customer Table, using a Customer ID of 10007.

➤ ASSIGNMENT 2   CREATING REPORTS

Assignment 2A: Generating a Report that Ranks Data

Create a report that lists the number of nights each room is rented, listing the most popular room at the top and the least popular room at the bottom.

- You must create a sigma query and sort the output on the Number of Nights.
- Title the report *Number of Nights Rooms Were Rented.*
- Headings for the report are as follows:

  Room Type   Number of Nights

- Make sure you view the Print Preview of the report to make sure that it looks good. Your report should resemble the one that follows.

Number of Nights Rooms Were Rented

Room Type	Number of Nights
Double w/o Bath	33
Single w/ Bath	27
Double w/ Bath	18
Single w/o Bath	6

Fig. 1-5

Assignment 2B: Generating a Billing Report

Generate a report that shows each customer's bill for September.

- You must create a query with a calculated field to figure the charges for each person.
- Title the report *September Bills*.
- Use the following headings in the order given: First Name, Last Name, Permanent Address, Date In, Charges.
- Make sure all fields are formatting properly; for example, check Charges—it should be in currency format. If not, find the object in Report Design, select it (handles appear around it), click the RIGHT mouse button—Properties—Format—Currency.
- Preview the report to make sure it will print correctly. Your report should resemble the one that follows.

September Bills

First Name	Last Name	Permanent Address	Date In	Charges
Your Name	Your Name	Your Address	9/1/99	$180.00
Edna	Edelweiss	819 River Rd, Mola, LA 70113	9/4/99	$520.00
Frederick	Fantail	9 Kiddie Rd, Cutbank, MT 59427	9/15/99	$300.00
Amy	Angerstein	214 Oak Ave, Radnor, PA 19080	9/1/99	$180.00
Bob	Babbles	567 5th St, Carlisle, MT 59428	9/12/99	$540.00
Colburn	Codfish	3 Ivy Lane, Radnor, PA 19080	9/5/99	$20.00
Debra	Dellabella	7890 Pike St, Newark, DE 19711	9/6/99	$60.00

Fig. 1-6

➤ DELIVERABLES

1. Four tables
2. Report: *Number of Nights Rooms Were Rented*
3. Report: *September Bills*
4. Diskette with database file
5. Any other required tutorial printouts or tutorial diskette

Staple all pages together. Put your name and class number at the top of each page. Make sure your diskette is labeled.

Preliminary Case
The Purple and Green
Faculty Club Database

SETTING UP A RELATIONAL DATABASE TO CREATE TABLES AND REPORTS

➤ PREVIEW

In this case, you'll create a relational database for a faculty club that serves food and drinks to members. First, you'll create four tables and populate them with data. Next, you'll create two reports: one will track the frequency of types of food and drink ordered; the other report will generate members' bills.

➤ PREPARATION

- Before attempting this exercise, you should have experience using Microsoft Access.
- Complete any part of the previous Access tutorial your instructor assigns, or refer to the tutorial as necessary.

BACKGROUND

Your instructor recently encountered an old friend who now manages the Purple and Green Faculty Club. During their conversation, your instructor described teaching Microsoft Access to your class. Several days later, your instructor received the following letter.

Dear Buddy,

It was great to see you the other day! After we spoke about your teaching Microsoft Access to your students, I thought they might be able to help me out. I manage the Purple and Green Faculty Club here at the University of Squeedunk, and we have a very antiquated system for recording orders and sending out bills. Believe it or not, all transactions and bills are prepared by hand. Our system is not too complex, so I thought updating our operation might be a great project for your students. Let me explain how it all works and how I would like things set up.

The Purple and Green Faculty Club contains a bar and restaurant. Faculty members from the university can join the club and have dinner or drinks during the academic year. The club charges the members a yearly fee for joining.

The Purple and Green staff do not handle any cash on the premises. All meals and drinks are charged to the member, using a plastic card similar to a credit card. Prices include gratuity, and extra tipping is prohibited. Members must pay for nonmember guests.

Each member gets a monthly bill from the club, itemizing charges by the type of food and drink bought on each date. For example, charges on a member's bill for a month could look like the following:

Date	Type of food/drink	Charge
~~September 10, 1999~~	~~Dinner~~	~~$45.00~~
September 10, 1999	Soft Drink	$20.00
September 15, 1999	Dinner	$65.00

I'd like to have a database management system do the following tasks:

1. List faculty members and their campus addresses
2. List the type of food and drink
3. List the prices of food and drink
4. Record individual members' purchases of food and drink
5. Rank the frequency of purchase of food and drink types
6. Generate monthly bills for individual members

So far, I have sketched out four tables that do the first four tasks: list members, list food and drink available, list prices, and record charges members have incurred. Here is what they look like.

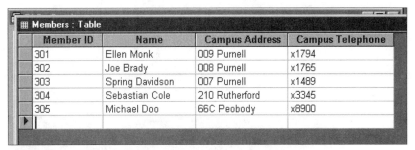

Members : Table

Member ID	Name	Campus Address	Campus Telephone
301	Ellen Monk	009 Purnell	x1794
302	Joe Brady	008 Purnell	x1765
303	Spring Davidson	007 Purnell	x1489
304	Sebastian Cole	210 Rutherford	x3345
305	Michael Doo	66C Peobody	x8900

Fig. 2-1

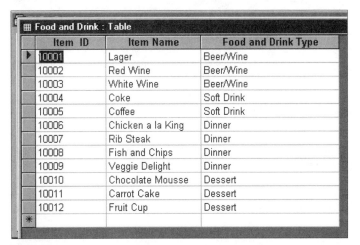

Food and Drink : Table

Item ID	Item Name	Food and Drink Type
10001	Lager	Beer/Wine
10002	Red Wine	Beer/Wine
10003	White Wine	Beer/Wine
10004	Coke	Soft Drink
10005	Coffee	Soft Drink
10006	Chicken a la King	Dinner
10007	Rib Steak	Dinner
10008	Fish and Chips	Dinner
10009	Veggie Delight	Dinner
10010	Chocolate Mousse	Dessert
10011	Carrot Cake	Dessert
10012	Fruit Cup	Dessert

Fig. 2-2

Prices : Table

Type of Meal	Price
Beer/Wine	$5.00
Dessert	$5.00
Dinner	$15.00
Soft Drink	$2.00
	$0.00

Fig. 2-3

Date	Member ID	Item ID	Quantity	Order Number
9/10/99	306	10001	10	1
9/11/99	306	10010	1	2
9/13/99	301	10012	1	3
9/13/99	301	10002	1	4
9/20/99	303	10007	2	5
9/21/99	304	10004	3	6
9/29/99	302	10001	5	7
9/29/99	302	10009	5	8
9/30/99	305	10008	2	9
9/30/99	305	10001	2	10
			0	0

Fig. 2-4

Examples of orders are noted here.

1) Order 1, charged to member 306, was for ten orders of lager (see Food and Drink Table) ordered by the member's party on 9/10.
2) Order #6, charged to member 304, was for three Cokes ordered by the member's party on 9/21.
3) Order #9 was for two fish and chip dinners on 9/30.

In addition to these tables, I'd like two reports: one report should show the frequency of types of food and drink ordered, sorted by most popular item to least popular item. (I have a bet with a friend that I sell more beer and wine than dessert.) I would also like a report that generates the monthly charges of each member, listing each person's name, address, the date he or she came, the type of food or drink ordered, its price, and the total bill for the month.

I certainly hope you can help me. Thanks.

Yours truly,

Maria

☞ ASSIGNMENT 1 CREATING TABLES

Use Microsoft Access to create the output outlined in the letter from the faculty club manager. Use the data provided in the letter. Add your name and address to the Member Table, using Member ID 306. Do not add any additional records to the other tables.

Assignment 2A: Generating a Report that Ranks Data

Create a report that ranks in descending order the frequency of food and drink type purchased.

- You will need to create a sigma query and sort the output by the number by times ordered.
- Title the report *Frequency of Food and Drink Ordered in September*
- Headings should be as follows:

  Food and Drink Type   *Number of Times Ordered*

  (For example, if 17 beers and 1 glass of wine were ordered in the month, then under the Food and Drink Type column, you would have Beer/Wine; the number 18 would show under the column Number of Times Ordered.)
- Make sure you view Print Preview to make sure the report looks good. Your report should resemble the following report.

Frequency of Food and Drink Ordered in September

Food and Drink Type	Number of Times Ordered
Beer/Wine	18
Dinner	9
Soft Drink	3
Dessert	2

Fig. 2-5

Assignment 2B: Generating a Billing Report

Generate a report that shows each member's bill for September.

- You must create a query with a calculated field to figure the amount due for each date and food/drink type.
- Title the report *September Bills*.
- Use the following headings in the order given: Name, Address, Date, Food and Drink Type, Amount Due.
- Make sure you total the amount due for each member. First, while you're in Report Wizard, group on Name and Address. Sum the total dollars owed under the Summary Options button. Then go into the report design after completing the Wizard's questions, and move the Address object into the Name header band. This will make the report more attractive. Delete any italicized lines and duplicate sums. (See Creating Reports in the Access tutorial.)

- Make sure all fields are formatting properly; for example, check Amount Due—it should be in currency format. If not, find the object in Report Design, select it (handles appear around it), click the RIGHT mouse button—Properties—Format—Currency.
- Change the word "Sum" to "Owed for Month," as shown below.
- Preview the report to make sure it will print correctly.
- Your report should resemble the portion of the one that follows.

September Bills

Name	Address	Date	Food and Drink Type	Amount Due
Ellen Monk	009 Purnell			
		9/13/99	Beer/Wine	$5.00
		9/13/99	Dessert	$5.00
Owed for Month				*$10.00*
Joe Brady	008 Purnell			
		9/29/99	Dinner	$75.00
		9/29/99	Beer/Wine	$25.00
Owed for Month				*$100.00*
Michael Doo	66C Peobody			
		9/30/99	Beer/Wine	$10.00
		9/30/99	Dinner	$30.00
Owed for Month				*$40.00*

Fig. 2-6

☞ DELIVERABLES

1. Four tables
2. Report: *Frequency of Food and Drink Type Ordered in September*
3. Report: *September Bills*
4. Diskette with database file
5. Any other required tutorial printouts or tutorial diskette

Staple all pages together. Put your name and class number at the top of the page. Make sure your diskette is labeled.

The Pest-B-Gone Exterminator Service Database

DESIGNING A RELATIONAL DATABASE TO CREATE FORMS AND REPORTS

✦ PREVIEW

In this case, you will design a database for a small extermination business. After the design is complete and correct, you will create tables in the database, a form for data input, a list, and two other reports. The list identifies customers who want outside treatment only. The first report shows income generated by each technician. The second report generates customers' bills.

✦ PREPARATION

- Before attempting this exercise, you should have some experience in database design and Microsoft Access.
- Complete any part of Database Design Tutorial A your instructor assigns.
- Complete any part of Access Tutorial B your instructor assigns, or refer to the tutorial as necessary.

➤ BACKGROUND

Your instructor has invited a friend to ask your class for help. Here's the letter you receive.

Pest-B-Gone Exterminators

Dear Students,

I own a small pest-extermination business, and I need your help designing a database. Since the start of my company in 1995, my business has grown rapidly through word-of-mouth advertising. I have been doing all my own bookkeeping by hand, but it's becoming increasingly difficult as my business grows. I would like to implement a computerized billing system this winter, while the business is a little slow.

Here's how my business works. I have five technicians who travel to customers' homes to exterminate pests, such as roaches, termites, ants, and rats. Each technician has an area defined by Zip Code. The technician travels to a customer's home, inspects the job, and then decides which chemicals to apply. The customer is charged only for the chemicals used that day, so the bills to individual customers vary month by month. The charge for each chemical applied depends on the price and quantity applied. Each is priced and applied by the pound.

A few of my customers request that I treat only the exterior of their house. This is noted on the customer's record, so the technician can, at a time when it's convenient for the technician to visit, complete the monthly treatment without being let into the house.

When technicians return to the office after a day's work, I want them to log all the chemicals and the quantities used for each customer. Then I will take that information and generate a report that shows my total monthly billing by individual customer in each Zip Code area. This will help me to identify which technicians are generating the most business. I also want to generate individual bills for each customer, itemizing the chemicals used and their price.

I hope you can help me set up my system.

Thank you.

Mary "Pest-B-Gone" Rodriquez

➤ ASSIGNMENT 1   CREATING THE DATABASE DESIGN

In this assignment, you will design your database tables on paper. Focus on the logic and structure of your tables. Do not start your Access code (Assignment 2) before getting feedback from your instructor on Assignment 1.

- Design the tables you'll need on paper, avoiding data redundancy. Do not create a field if it could be created by "calculated field" in a query.
- You'll need a transaction table. If you avoid duplicating data contained within other tables, the transaction table should be pretty sparse.

- One of your tables should contain a logical (yes/no) field. (Remember, each chemical is priced and applied by the pound.)
- Create your tables using the Table facility of your word processor. Your word-processed tables should look something like the one that follows.

Table name

Field name	**Data type (text, numeric, currency, etc.)**
…	…

- You must mark the appropriate key field(s). You can denote a key field by an asterisk (*) next to the field name. Keep in mind that some tables need a compound field key to uniquely identify a record within a table.
- Print out the database design.

Note: Have this design approved before beginning Assignment 2; otherwise, you may need to redo Assignment 2.

➤ ASSIGNMENT 2   CREATING THE DATABASE WITH FORMS AND REPORTS

Assignment 2A: Creating Tables in Access

Type in your records, using the following list of customers. All customers live in New York State (NY). After each customer's Zip Code, you'll see the name of the Pest-B-Gone technician who treats the person's home.

Greg Hapless	10 15th Ave., Rochester	14566 (Michael Fredricks)
Mary Morris	108 Main St, Rochester	14566 (Michael Fredricks)
Joe Brady	008 Purnell, Newark	14899 (Jack Moore)
Ellen Monk	009 Purnell, Newark	14899 (Jack Moore)
Maria Ortez	16 E. 5th Ave., Potsdam	14666 (Sandra Locke)
Larry Goldstein	217 Oak Ave., Potsdam	14666 (Sandra Locke)
Patricia Buckley	27 DePue, Pensville	14665 (Philip Brenche)
Your Name	**Your Address**	**Your Zip Code (your technician)**

Fig. 3-1

- Add your name and address as a customer. Make up your technician's name.
- Choose any three customers to have "outside treatment only."
- Use five chemical names (for example, DDT, Dursban, Arsenic, Ant Killer, and Chlordane).

- All visits occur in one month. Show each customer as having one visit per month, but show multiple chemicals as being applied to at least five customers' homes.
- Charge a different price per pound for each chemical.
- Appropriately limit the size of the text fields; for example, a Zip Code field does not need to be the default setting of 50 characters in length.
- Print all tables.

Assignment 2B: Creating Forms, Queries, and Reports

Form

Create a form that technicians can fill out at the end of the day. Base this form on your transaction table.

List Report

Create a list of those customers who want only their home's exterior treated. Show each customer's name and address. To do this, first create a query to find those specific records, and then feed that query into a report. If you group the report on Zip Code, it will be easier for the technicians to find their individual work. Your report will resemble the portion of the report that follows. Your report will include more and different data.

Customers Treated Outside Only

Zip	Name	Address
14566		
	Greg Hapless	1015th Ave, Rochester NY
14899		
	Joe Brady	008 Purnell Rd, Newark NY
	Ellen Monk	009 Purnell Rd, Newark NY

Fig. 3-2

Report 1

Create a report that shows all money brought in by each technician, so the sales manager can see who is bringing in the most business.

- Because each technician covers an area designated by Zip Code, the report needs to be grouped by Zip Code, with a total dollar value of chemicals charged to that Zip Code. To accomplish this, you must create a query with a calculated field that computes the total dollar amount of chemicals for each customer's service. Also include the customer's name, address, and date of service. (Hint: use the summation button on the query and sum the total money owed by each customer.) Bring that query into a report, group the report on Zip Code, group on technician, and while in the Report Wizard, choose the Summary Options button on the Sort dialog box. (You will not need to sort.) This will allow you to sum within Zip Code.

- Make sure that all totals are in currency format. If they are not, go to the Design View of the report, click on the object that represents the totals to select it (handles will appear), click on the RIGHT mouse button—Properties—General Properties—Format—Currency. You will need to go into the report design and move the Technician object from the Technician Name header to the Zip Code header. This makes for a neater report. (See Creating Reports in the Access tutorial.)
- Your report, after all the adjustments, should resemble the portion of the report that follows. (Treatment dates and dollar values will differ.)

Dollars Brought in by Technician

Zip	Technician Name	Name	Address	Date	Dollar Value
14566	Michael Fredricks				
		Greg Hapless	10 15th Ave, Rochester NY	2/26/99	$150.00
		Mary Morris	108 Main St, Rochester NY	2/26/99	$110.00
Sum					$260.00

Fig. 3-3

Report 2

Create an itemized bill for each customer.

- The itemized bill should include the customer's name, address, Zip Code, date of service, the name and amount of each chemical applied, and total cost of each chemical applied (quantity times price). Total cost for all chemicals should also show on each customer's bill.
- Adjust the report's design to make it look correct. Make sure that when you are in the Report Wizard, you group the report on Customer, Address, and Zip Code. After the report is created, go to the Design View and take the Address object and move it up to the Customer header, and take the Zip Code object and move it up to the Customer header. If you do this, the report will have the customer name, address, and Zip Code all on the same grouping line, which will look better than if you had left the report as the Wizard makes it. (See Creating Reports in the Access tutorial.)
- Delete any italicized lines or duplicate sum objects in the report design view. (See Creating Reports in the Access tutorial.)
- Check formatting to make sure that money is expressed in currency format.

Your finished report will be similar in format to the portion of the report that follows.

Customer's Bill

Name	Address	Zip	Date	Chemical	Quantity	Cost
Ellen Monk	009 Purnell Rd, Newark NY	14899				
			2/26/99	Dursban	3	$45.00
			2/26/99	DDT	1	$20.00
Sum						$65.00
Greg Hapless	10 15th Ave, Rochester NY	14566				
			2/26/99	Arsenic	10	$150.00
Sum						$150.00
Joe Brady	008 Purnell Rd, Newark NY	14899				
			2/26/99	DDT	4	$80.00
Sum						$80.00

Fig. 3-4

❧ DELIVERABLES

1. Word-processed design of tables
2. Tables created in Access
3. Form: Print only 1 record
4. List Report
5. Report 1
6. Report 2
7. Diskette
8. Any other required tutorial printouts or tutorial diskette

Staple all pages together. Put your name and class number at the top of the page. Make sure your diskette is labeled.

The Dentist's Office Database

Designing a Relational Database to Create Forms and Reports

➤ Preview

In this case, you will design a database for a dentist's office that employs a dental assistant. After your design is complete and correct, you will create tables, a form for recording appointments, and two reports. The first report calculates and lists payment for the dental assistant. The second report calculates patients' bills.

➤ Preparation

- Before attempting this exercise, you should have some experience in database design and Microsoft Access.
- Complete any part of Database Design Tutorial A your instructor assigns.
- Complete any part of Access Tutorial B your instructor assigns, or refer to the tutorial as necessary.

➥ BACKGROUND

While at the dentist's office, your instructor overheard the receptionist complain about all the handwritten paperwork required to run the office. Your instructor mentioned that your class is learning Microsoft Access database design and could set up a system for the dentist's office. Here's the letter that followed the conversation.

Dear Professor,

I am the receptionist and manager of your dentist's office, and I would be delighted for you to assist me in setting up a computerized database billing system.

Our office has one dental assistant and one dentist. Each performs various procedures, and each procedure has a specific cost.

We want the database system to do several things. First, we'd like the receptionist, that's me, to be able to enter the name of the procedure (or procedure ID) performed on each patient. For example, let's say Mrs. Young comes in to have a root canal (which we might call Procedure 7). When she leaves the office, I'd check her out, logging her name or patient ID, the time in and the time out, the name or ID of the procedure performed (in this case, a root canal), and the date of service. Note that multiple procedures might be performed on a patient during one visit. For example, Mrs. Young might have her teeth filled and cleaned during one visit.

Second, we need to track the number of hours the dental assistant works. Even though we charge the patient a set fee per procedure, the dental assistant is paid by the hour. So we'll need to record the start and finish times of each appointment, so the time the dental assistant spends with each patient can be calculated.

Third, we want to generate monthly bills to send to our patients who do NOT have dental insurance. These bills should show the name and address of the patient, the procedures performed, the date of service, the service provider, the cost for each procedure, and the total bill.

I hope you can help me set up my system.

Thank you.

Mavis Walker

➥ ASSIGNMENT 1   CREATING THE DATABASE DESIGN

In this assignment, you will design your database tables on paper. Focus on creating tables that have good logic and structure. Do not start your Access code (Assignment 2) before getting feedback from your instructor on Assignment 1.

- Design the tables you'll need on paper, avoiding data redundancy. Do not create a field if it could be created by "calculated field" in a query.
- You'll need a transaction table. If you avoid duplicating data contained within other tables, the transaction table should be pretty sparse.

- One of your tables should contain a logical (yes/no) field.
- Remember to design fields to record the start and finish time for each office visit.
- Create your tables using the Table facility of your word processor. Your word-processed tables should look something like this:

Table name	
Field name	**Data type (text, numeric, currency, etc.)**
...	...

- You must mark the appropriate key field(s). You can denote a key field by an asterisk (*) next to the field name. Keep in mind that some tables need a compound field key to uniquely identify a record within a table.
- Print out the database design.

Note: Have this design approved before beginning Assignment 2; otherwise, you may need to redo Assignment 2.

➥ ASSIGNMENT 2   CREATING THE DATABASE WITH FORMS AND REPORTS

Assignment 2A: Creating Tables in Access

Type in your records. Use this patient data.

Greg Hapless	10 15th Ave., Rochester NY	14566
Mary Morris	108 Main St, Rochester NY	14566
Joe Brady	008 Purnell, Newark NY	14899
Ellen Monk	009 Purnell, Newark NY	14899
Maria Ortez	16 E. 5th Ave., Potsdam NY	14666
Larry Goldstein	217 Oak Ave, Potsdam NY	14666
Patricia Buckley	27 DePue, Pensville NY	14665
Your Name	**Your Address**	**Your Zip Code**

Fig. 4-1

- Add your name and address as a patient.
- Use these five different dental procedures: cleaning, crown, filling, root canal, and x-ray.
- Make up a different cost for each procedure.
- Half of the patients should NOT have dental insurance; you choose who they are.
- Have all office visits occur in one month, and make each patient go to the dentist at least once, with some patients visiting twice or more. Be sure to add the start and finish time of each visit.
- Show some patients as having multiple procedures on the same day.

- Appropriately limit the size of the text fields; for example, a Zip Code field does not need to be the default setting of 50 characters in length.
- Print all tables.

Assignment 2B: Creating Forms, Queries, and Reports

Form

Create a form the receptionist can use when checking out a patient. The information on the form should correspond to a table created for the database. Base this form on your transaction table.

Report 1

Create a report that displays the total pay for the dental assistant.

- Begin with a query, and calculate the total hours worked times the hourly pay, which should be $30 per hour. Bring this query into a report to list the dental assistant's pay per procedure and date. (See Time Arithmetic in Tutorial B.) Using the Report Wizard, group on Procedure and sum the pay by clicking the Summary Options button appearing after the grouping question. You should format the Pay calculated field in either the query or in the report. To do this in the report, click on field, then click the RIGHT mouse button, then Properties—Format—Currency.
- Preview the report, go to the Design View, and remove any italicized lines. (See Creating Reports in the Access tutorial.)
- The format of your report will look similar to the portion of the one that follows. (Actual dates and pay depend on the data typed in.)

Dental Assistant's Pay

Procedure	Date	Pay
cleaning		
	2/28/99	$15.00
	2/28/99	$30.00
Total for Procedure		$45.00
crown		
	2/28/99	$90.00
Total for Procedure		$90.00
filling		
	2/28/99	$15.00
Total for Procedure		$15.00

Fig. 4-2

Report 2

Create an itemized bill for each customer who is NOT insured. Again, a query needs to be generated before the report can be processed.

- The itemized bill should include patient's name, address, date of procedure, type of procedure, and cost of procedure.

- Total cost for each patient should also show on the bill. To do this, use the Summary Options button on the Report Wizard after you group the report. Group the report by patient, address, and Zip Code to get the total cost. You will have to adjust the design of the report once the Wizard is complete to make the grouping look professional.
- After previewing the report, go to the Design View and move the Address object and the Zip Code object to the Patient header band. (See Creating Reports in the Access tutorial.)
- Make sure all money is formatted as currency, and delete any italicized lines and duplicate sums (See Creating Reports in the Access tutorial.)
- After your adjustments, the format of your report will look similar to the portion of the report that follows.

Patient's Bill

Name	Address	Zip	Date	Procedure	Price
Ellen Monk	*009 Purnell Rd, Newark NY*	14899			
			2/28/99	crown	$450.00
			2/24/99	x-ray	$20.00
Total Bill					$470.00
Greg Hapless	*10 15th Ave, Rochester NY*	14566			
			2/28/99	x-ray	$20.00
			2/28/99	filling	$45.00
			2/28/99	cleaning	$25.00
Total Bill					$90.00

Fig. 4-3

➤ DELIVERABLES

1. Word-processed design of tables
2. Tables created in Access
3. Form: Print 1 record from the form only
4. List Report
5. Report 1
6. Report 2
7. Diskette
8. Any other required tutorial printouts or tutorial diskette

Staple all pages together. Put your name and class number at the top of each page. Make sure your diskette is labeled.

5
CASE

The Gourmet Chocolate Company Database

DESIGNING A RELATIONAL DATABASE TO CREATE FORMS AND REPORTS

➤ PREVIEW

In this case, you will design a database for a small mail-order business that sells chocolate candy. After your design is complete and correct, you will create tables in the database and populate them with data, create a form for order entry, generate a mailing list, and produce two reports. The first report shows the frequency of sales, and the second report generates customers' bills.

➤ PREPARATION

- Before attempting this exercise, you should have some experience in database design and Microsoft Access.
- Complete any part of Database Design Tutorial A your instructor assigns.
- Complete any part of Access Tutorial B your instructor assigns, or refer to the tutorial as necessary.

Your instructor's mother recently retired from a long career with the government. To keep herself busy, she began selling her homemade candy to relatives and friends. The candy was so delicious, word quickly spread, and the hobby became a business called The Gourmet Chocolate Company. Until now, all recordkeeping has been done by hand. Now your instructor's mother wants help to create a database for her company. Here is what she wrote in a recent letter.

Dear Students,

Years ago, I began making chocolates for holiday gifts. It started out as just a hobby; I would give boxes of my homemade truffles or chocolate-covered cherries to friends and relatives at Christmas and for birthdays. Everyone always raved about how delicious they were and persuaded me to go into business for myself. I started a small mail-order business to sell specialty chocolates.

Initially, my thoughts were to keep the business small, and do all the paperwork by hand (filling orders, sending bills, computing statistics on sales, etc.). Well, luckily for me, my business has grown rapidly, and now I have a small factory operation and employ five workers. I need your help setting up a computer database that can help me to manage my growing business.

I would like the database to do several things. First, I'd like it to record the details of incoming orders. When customers phone our company, they order one or more of our products by product number, in order quantities per pound. (Everything is priced per pound—there are no quantities less than one pound.) It is noted on a customer's record whether he or she wants to receive monthly catalogs. The catalog mailing is quite expensive, so I send catalogs to those who request them. (I also need a mailing list of those who want the monthly catalogs.)

I'd also like to know which items are my most popular. Each month I'd like to generate a report that shows sales volume by item. I'd appreciate it if the report could rank the items from highest-volume sales to lowest.

Finally, I'd like to generate the bill to accompany each customer's order. This information should appear on each customer's bill: the customer's name and address, the date of the order, item(s) ordered, cost of each item, and a grand total due.

I hope you can help me set up my system.

Thank you.

Anne Bean

✤ ASSIGNMENT 1 CREATING THE DATABASE DESIGN

In this assignment, you will design your database tables on paper. Pay close attention to their logic and structure. Do not start your Access code (Assignment 2) before getting feedback from your instructor on Assignment 1.

- Design the tables you'll need on paper, avoiding data redundancy. Do not create a field if it could be created by "calculated field" in a query.

- You'll need a transaction table. If you avoid duplicating data contained within other tables, the transaction table should be pretty sparse.
- One of your tables should contain a logical (yes/no) field.
- You'll need to note the date on which each order is shipped.
- Create your tables using the Table facility of your word processor. Your word-processed tables should look something like the table that follows.

Table name	
Field name	**Data type (text, numeric, currency, etc.)**
...	...

- You must mark the appropriate key field(s). You can denote a key field by an asterisk (*) next to the field name. Keep in mind that some tables need a compound field key to uniquely identify a record within a table.
- Print out the database design.

Note: Have this design approved before beginning Assignment 2; otherwise, you may need to redo Assignment 2.

ASSIGNMENT 2 CREATING THE DATABASE WITH FORMS AND REPORTS

Assignment 2A: Creating Tables in Access

Type in your records using these customers; all are from Newark, DE 19711. Add your name and address to the table.

Name	Address
Ellen Monk	009 Purnell Road
Joe Brady	008 Purnell Road
Spring Davidson	007 Purnell Road
Paula Brienza	3 Engle Way
Jasper Downs	9 10th Street
Cookie Pugglie	101 E. Freemont Ave
Darla Green	1601 French Street
Peter Weigh	9 Main Street
Jacob Harriet	9000 W. 5th Ave
Sandy Roth	8213 Mulberry Lane
Your Name	**Your Address**

Fig. 5-1

- The products sold are turtles, truffles, chocolate bark, chocolate ants, white chocolate, caramels, chocolate popcorn, and chocolate raisins.
- Make up a cost per pound for each item.
- Each customer should order at least once, some twice or more; some customers should order multiple quantities of the same item (e.g., 3 pounds of chocolate turtles).
- Make all the orders be filled within one month.
- Choose any three customers to request monthly catalogs.
- Appropriately limit the size of the text fields; for example, a Zip Code field does not need to be the default setting of 50 characters in length.
- Print all tables.

Assignment 2B: Creating Forms, Queries, and Reports

Form

Create a form in which a clerk can type the order as it is taken on the telephone. Base this form on your transaction table.

List Report

Generate a mailing list report for those customers who want a monthly catalog. First, make a query to identify those customers, and then bring that query into a report. Using the Report Wizard, create a report that shows the name and address of these customers. Your report should display the list of customers in alphabetical order. Your report should be similar in format to the portion of the report that follows. (Records will vary depending on who orders the catalog.)

Mailing List for Catalogs

Customer Name	Customer Address
Paula Brienza	3 Engle Way, Newark, DE 19711
Jasper Downs	9 10thSt, Newark, DE 19711
Darla Green	1601 FrenchSt, Newark, DE 19711

Fig. 5-2

Report 1

Calculate how many dollars of each product has been sold this month. Display the data from the highest sales down to the lowest sales.

- You will need to generate a query before creating the report. The query will need to sum each individual product and its dollar value. Make sure you give the sum an appropriate heading (not "Sum of" etc., which is automatically generated.)
- Sort the Sum field in descending order to get the high-to-low sales structure. Then bring that query into a report, as shown here.

High/Low Sales

Product Name	Dollar Value Sold
turtles	$49.50
truffles	$20.00
choc bark	$14.00
choc ants	$12.00
white choc	$10.00
caramels	$10.00
choc popcorn	$5.00
choc raisins	$3.00

Fig. 5-3

Report 2

Create a report that itemizes customers' bills. Again, a query needs to be generated before the report can be processed.

- The itemized bill should include the customer's name and full address, each individual item ordered, and the cost of the item. (Hint: Make a calculated field in the query to calculate the dollar amount of each item purchased. Also calculate the grand total owed for the order. Assume all customers pay by check.

- After you create your report, you will need to adjust the design. First, while you're in Report Wizard, group on Name and Address. Sum the total dollars owed under the Summary Options button. Then, after completing the Wizard's questions, go into the report design and move the Address object into the Name header band. This will make the report more attractive. Delete any italicized lines and duplicate sums. (See Creating Reports in the Access Tutorial.)

- Make sure all fields are formatting properly; for example, check the grand total—it should be in currency format. If not, find the object on Report Design, select it (handles appear around it), click the RIGHT mouse button—Properties—Format—Currency. The format of your report should resemble the one that follows.

Customer's Bill

Customer Name	Customer Address	Product Name	Cost
Darla Green	1601 French St, Newark, DE 19711		
		white choc	10.00
		truffles	20.00
		caramels	10.00
Total Amount Owed			$40.00
Ellen Monk	009 Purnell Rd, Newark, DE 19711		
		choc raisins	$3.00
		choc bark	$4.00
		choc ants	12.00
Total Amount Owed			$19.00

Fig. 5-4

➤ DELIVERABLES

1. Word-processed design of tables
2. Tables created in Access
3. Form: Print only 1 record from the form
4. List Report
5. Report 1
6. Report 2
7. Diskette
8. Any other required tutorial printouts or tutorial diskette

Staple all pages together. Put your name and class number at the top of each page. Make sure your diskette is labeled.

The Rent-a-Computer Company Database

DESIGNING A RELATIONAL DATABASE TO CREATE FORMS AND REPORTS

➤ PREVIEW

In this case, you will design a database for a small company that rents computer equipment. After your design is complete and correct, you will create tables in a database and populate them with data. Then you will create a form for recording rental reservations, generate a mailing list, and produce two reports. The first report shows the number of days each type of equipment was rented for the past month. The second report calculates customers' bills.

➤ PREPARATION

- Before attempting this exercise, you should have some experience in database design and Microsoft Access.
- Complete any part of Database Design Tutorial A your instructor assigns.
- Complete any part of Access Tutorial B your instructor assigns, or refer to the tutorial as necessary.

Your instructor's younger brother, Chip, who majored in business and minored in information systems, just started a new computer-equipment rental business. Surprisingly, Chip does all his paperwork by hand, even though he owns many computers and peripherals! His business has grown rapidly, and now he's decided he must computerize equipment reservations and his billing system. Knowing his older sibling teaches database design and Microsoft Access, Chip asks for help. Your instructor decides to make helping Chip a class project. Here's Chip's letter to you.

Dear Students,

I own a company called The Rent-a-Computer Company, and we rent computer equipment to individuals and business customers. Since our inception in 1998, we have remained a small, local company with a staff of about 12 people, depending on the season. As the busy academic year approaches, however, our bookkeeping practices make me uneasy. Customers place orders by phone, and we log them in a notebook. Recently I've noticed some of my staff have been double-booking certain items, such as our only Sun Workstation 2000. I really feel that we need a database system to help us sort out all our paperwork.

First, I would like the database system to log rental information, so I can easily see which items have been rented and for which dates. I'd like my staff to be able to pull up a Rentals screen and type the rental information directly into the computer. Information on the screen should appear in this order: customer (or their ID number), date out, date returned, and the name or ID of the item(s) rented.

Next, I would like to have a list of my business customers. These customers rent at the highest volume, and such a list would allow me to target these customers for additional marketing. Because business customers often rent in bulk, they get a 10% discount.

In addition, I would like to be able to track the frequency of equipment rentals each month. If I could generate a monthly report that displays rental items from the most popular item down to the least popular, I could make better marketing decisions in the future.

Finally, I would like to send each customer a monthly computer-generated bill. Each piece of equipment is rented by the day and is priced at a certain dollar rate per day. The bill should include the date of rental, the total number of days, and the total amount due.

I hope you can help me set up my system.

Thank you.

Chip Morris

➤ Assignment 1 Creating the Database Design

In this assignment, you will design your database tables on paper. Pay close attention to their logic and structure. Do not start your Access code (Assignment 2) before getting feedback from your instructor on Assignment 1.

- Design the tables you'll need on paper, avoiding data redundancy. Do not create a field if it could be created by "calculated field" in a query.
- You'll need a transaction table. If you avoid duplicating data contained within other tables, the transaction table should be pretty sparse.
- One of your tables should contain a logical (yes/no) field.
- Create your tables using the Table facility of your word processor. Your word-processed tables should look something like the table that follows.

Table name	
Field name	**Data type (text, numeric, currency, etc.)**
...	...

- You must mark the appropriate key field(s). You can denote a key field by an asterisk (*) next to the field name. Keep in mind that some tables need a compound field key to uniquely identify a record within a table.
- Print out the database design.

Note: Have this design approved before beginning Assignment 2; otherwise, you may need to redo Assignment 2.

➤ Assignment 2 Creating the Database with Forms and Reports

Assignment 2A: Creating Tables in Access

- Type in your records using these customers, all of whom are in Newark, DE 19711. Add your name and address to the table.

Name	Address
Ellen Monk	009 Purnell Road
Joe Brady	008 Purnell Road
Spring Davidson	007 Purnell Road
Paula's Hair Style	3 Engle Way
Jasper's Shoppe	9 10th Street
Cookie Pugglie	101 E. Freemont Ave
Darla Green	1601 French Street
Sam's Insurance	9 Main Street
Jacob Harriet	9000 W. 5th Ave
Sandy Roth	8213 Mulberry Lane
Your Name	**Your Address**

Fig. 6-1

Case 6

- The rental items are HP LaserWriter, Pentium II, Sharp Digicam, Sun Workstation 2000, Gateway Solo, and HP Colorjet.
- Each customer should rent at least one item; several customers should rent more than one item. Business customers should be obvious.
- Make up rental data for each customer and daily prices for each item. Make all rentals occur in one month.
- Appropriately limit the size of the text fields; for example, a Zip Code field does not need to be the default setting of 50 characters in length.
- Print all tables.

Assignment 2B: Creating Forms, Queries, and Reports

Form

Create a form for taking telephone orders. Base the form on your transaction table.

List Report

Generate a mailing list of business customers. First, create a query to find those specific records, and then bring that query into a report that lists the names and addresses. Your list will resemble the one that follows.

Business Customers

Customer Name	Customer Address
Sam's Insurance	10 W. Main St, Newark, DE 19711
Paula's Hair Style	3 Engle Way, Newark, DE 19711
Jasper's Shoppe	9 10th St, Newark, DE 19711

Fig. 6-2

Report 1

Calculate how many days each item of equipment has been rented this month. Display equipment rentals from the most number of days rented down to least number of days rented.

- You will need to generate a query before creating the report. The query will simply sum the number of days for each item. Make sure that you give the summed field an appropriate heading, such as Frequency of Rental or Number of Times Rented. Also, sort that field in descending order, so that the most frequently rented item will be first, and the least frequently rented item will be last. Bring the query into a report.

- Don't group or sum the report. The format of your report will resemble the portion of the report that follows.

Frequency Report

Item Name	Total Days
HP LaserWriter	20
Pentium II	15
Sharp Digicam	11
Sun Workstation 2	7
Gateway Solo	5
HP Colorjet	1

Fig. 6-3

Report 2

This report involves creating an itemized bill for a customer. Again, a query needs to be generated before the report can be processed.

- The itemized bill should include the customer's name and address, each item rented and its cost. (Hint: Make a calculated field in the query to calculate the dollar amount of each item rented; this will involve time arithmetic.) Also show the grand total owed for the rental. Assume that all customers pay by check when they receive their bill. Remember that business customers get a 10% discount.

- To make your calculated field include the discount for business customers, try to make a calculated field that includes an "if" statement (similar in logic and syntax to the Excel "if" statement). For example, it might look something like this:

  Total Bill: Iif([Business Customer?]=yes,([End Time]-[Start Time])*[Cost]*.9,

  ([End Time]-[Start Time])*[Cost])

- It might be easier to build this calculated field in the Expression Builder window. Go to a blank field in the qbe grid. Click on the button that looks like a magic wand. Type in a calculated field that's similar to the example above.

- Using the Report Wizard, group on name and address. Click on the Report Summary options button in the Report Wizard and Sum on Total.

- You will need to format the calculated field to currency format. Click in the new field, click the RIGHT mouse button — Properties — Format — Currency. When you make your report, you may want to adjust the design to make the report look good. Move the Address object into the Name header to make it appear all on one line. Delete any italicized lines and duplicate sums. (See Creating Reports in the Access tutorial.)

Case 6

The Rent-a-Computer Company Database   77

The format of your report will resemble the portion of the report that follows.

Customer's Bill

Customer Name	Customer Address	Item Name	Cost
Ellen Monk	009 Purnell Rd, Newark, DE 19711		
		HP Colorjet	$14.00
		Sun Workstation 2	$20.00
Sum			$34.00
Jasper's Shoppe	9 10th St, Newark, DE 19711		
		Gateway Solo	$43.20
Sum			$43.20
Joe Brady	008 Purnell Rd, Newark, DE 19711		
		HP LaserWriter	$320.00
		Sharp Digicam	$275.00
Sum			$595.00

Fig. 6-4

✦ DELIVERABLES

1. Word-processed design of tables
2. Tables created in Access
3. Form: Print out only 1 record.
4. List Report
5. Report 1
6. Report 2
7. Diskette
8. Any other required tutorial printouts or tutorial diskette

Staple all pages together. Put your name and class number at the top of each page. Make sure your diskette is labeled.

The Information Systems Temp Agency Database

DESIGNING A RELATIONAL DATABASE TO CREATE REPORTS

➤ PREVIEW

In this case, you will design a database for The Information Systems Temp Agency, a small company that places temporary information systems (IS) employees with other companies. Once your design is complete and correct, you will create tables in the database and populate them with data. Then you will create three reports. The first report shows employees matched with their current jobs. The second report calculates and displays the potential total salary for each employee. The third report computes the fee charged to each company that uses The Information Systems Temp Agency.

➤ PREPARATION

- Before attempting this exercise, you should have some experience in database design and Microsoft Access.
- Complete any part of Database Design Tutorial A your instructor assigns.
- Complete any part of Access Tutorial B your instructor assigns, or refer to the tutorial as necessary.

A former business administration student contacted your instructor for help in setting up a database. This is what he wrote.

Dear Professor,

I run a temporary employment agency that matches companies with temporary employees for a predetermined length of time. My agency specializes in providing COBOL programmers to companies that need help revising their codes for the year 2000. My business started with just a few client companies and a handful of temporary employees. Since then, the business has grown rapidly, mostly due to the explosive demand for competent IS workers. I need a database system to match employees with jobs, to send out job offers displaying potential earnings, and to bill the companies for my headhunting fee.

I would like you to set up an Access database with three reports that I can run weekly. Report 1 needs to show me the jobs that have had employees assigned to them.

Once that report is generated, I should be able to run Report 2, which should display employees matched with job openings, the start date, and total potential salary. This report will be used by the secretaries to type up the position offers for my employees. (Keep in mind that employees can only work on one job at a time.)

The final report, Report 3, will calculate the amount of money I will bill the companies that use my agency for hiring temporary employees. The client companies pay employees directly, and I bill the client companies for my fee, which is 15% of the total salary paid to the employee. Here is an example of my Report 3 headings:

Agency Fees from Headhunting

Company Name	Contact Person	Job Type	Agency Fee

In order to produce these reports, you will need to set up the database to log all my client companies, their contact people, jobs available, established fees for jobs, employees' names, and each employee's field of expertise. In the table that lists positions available, I need to be able to mark whether a position is "filled" or not. "Filled" can mean either that the job is currently filled, or that a specific person will fill it in the future. So, if an employee has been assigned to a future job, you can consider that job "filled."

I certainly hope you can help me with my problem, and I wish you the best of luck for a good database design.

Yours truly,

Tom Watson

❧ ASSIGNMENT 1   CREATING THE DATABASE DESIGN

In this assignment, you will design your database tables on paper. Pay close attention to their logic and structure. Do not start your Access code (Assignment 2) before getting feedback from your instructor on Assignment 1. Keep in mind, however, that you need to look at the requirements for Assignment 2 to determine what tables you need and what fields are required in each table. In other words, good programming practice says you should work backwards from your desired output.

- Design the tables you'll need on paper, avoiding data redundancy. Do not create a field if it could be created by "calculated field" in a query.
- You'll need a transaction table. If you avoid duplicating data contained within other tables, the transaction table should be pretty sparse. Consider using the logical field "filled."
- Create your tables using the Table facility of your word processor. Your word-processed tables should look something like the table that follows.

Table name	
Field name	Data type (text, numeric, currency, etc.)
...	...

- You must mark the appropriate key field(s). You can denote a key field by an asterisk (*) next to the field name. Keep in mind that some tables need a compound field key to uniquely identify a record within a table.
- Print out the database design.

Note: Have this design approved before beginning Assignment 2; otherwise, you may need to redo Assignment 2.

❧ ASSIGNMENT 2   CREATING THE DATABASE WITH REPORTS

Assignment 2A: Creating Tables in Access

In this part of the assignment, you will create your tables in Access. Type in your records. There should be about 6 companies that use this agency, with a total of 11 employees. Use the data that follows. Add your name to the employee list with your address.

Employee Name	Address
Marie Sanchez	101 E. Main St.
John Short	16 French St.
Paul Satchel	123 5th Ave.
Quinn Koala	5 Amy Lane
Mark Philips	45 W. Main St.
Juan Carlos	6700 4th Ave.
Jacques Samm	23 Fifer Blvd.
Herman Fish	2456 9th St.
Christie Keller	5 W. George St.
Wanda Ball	9 Oak Ave.
Your Name	**Your Address**

Fig. 7-1

Company Name	Contact Person
Acme Insurance	George Acme
Shopper's Paradise	Anne Paradise
Quincy's Pens	Harry Quincy
Ace Chemicals	Allen Ace
Fresh Grocers	Joal Manstein
Harlan's Publishing	Mandy Harlan

Fig. 7-2

- Limit the different types of jobs to 5. Make up this data with ideas you have from your information systems class.
- Some companies should have openings for more than one employee. Make at least 15 job openings, all of which should already be "filled" and matched with an appropriate employee.
- Appropriately limit the size of the text fields; for example, a Zip Code field does not need to be the default setting of 50 characters in length.
- Print all tables.

Assignment 2B: Creating Queries and Reports

There are three reports to create, as outlined in the letter to the professor. You'll need to generate a query to produce each report.

Report 1

This report matches employees with their jobs. Include information such as employee name, position name, company name, and dates of job—beginning and ending. Group the report on company name. Your report will resemble the portion of the one that follows.

Job Matching

Company Name	Employee Name	Job Name	Start Date	End Date
Ace Chemicals				
	Christie Keller	SAP	4/5/99	6/7/99
Acme Insurance				
	John Short	WindowsNT	3/2/99	3/30/99
	Marie Sanchez	COBOL	3/15/99	3/30/99
Fresh Grocers				
	Quinn Koala	SAP	7/1/99	7/1/99
	Paul Satchel	COBOL	7/1/99	8/1/99
Harlan's Publishing				
	Herman Fish	Networking	3/2/99	6/2/99
Quincy's Pens				
	Wanda Ball	SAP	3/15/99	3/17/99

Fig. 7-3

Report 2

The purpose of this report is to entice an employee to accept a job offer. This report should include a calculation of the total potential salary earned for the entire job.

- Assume employees work only 5 days per week, and only 8 hours per day.
- A calculated field is required. Other fields required for this report are employee name, position, company name, contact person in the company, the beginning date of the job, and the total potential salary.
- There shouldn't be any grouping on this report. The beginning of your report should resemble the following:

Case 7

Salary Enticement

Employee Name	Job Name	Company Name	Contact Person	Start Date	Potential Salary
Marie Sanchez	COBOL	Acme Insurance	George Acme	3/15/99	$2,142.86
Paul Satchel	COBOL	Fresh Grocers	Joal Manstein	7/1/99	$4,428.57
John Short	WindowsNT	Acme Insurance	George Acme	3/2/99	$4,160.00
Jacques Samm	Networking	Shopper's Paradise	Anne Paradise	3/4/99	$1,508.57
Herman Fish	Networking	Harlan's Publishing	Mandy Harlan	3/2/99	$12,617.14
Wanda Ball	SAP	Quincy's Pens	Harry Quincy	3/15/99	$342.86
Christie Keller	SAP	Ace Chemicals	Allen Ace	4/5/99	$10,800.00

Fig. 7-4

Report 3

This report highlights how much money The Information Systems Temp Agency can make from its headhunting.

- Again, a calculated field is required to calculate 15% of the total potential salary. Other fields to include are client company name, contact person, job name, and of course, agency fee. Group on company name and contact person.

- Sum the fee for each group by clicking on the Summary Options button after the grouping screen.

- You will need to adjust the report design to make this look good. Move the Contact Person field to the Company Name header to make both of those appear on the same line in the report. (See Creating Reports in the Access tutorial.)

- Get rid of extra totals and italicized total lines.

- A note on formatting: To make the reports look professional, you should format the calculated fields in Currency format. If you haven't formatted your Agency Fee field in the query, you can do so in the report Design View. To do this, you can click on the field in the report design, right-click Properties and set it to Currency there. Your report should resemble the portion of the report that follows.

Agency Fees from Headhunting

Company Name	Contact Person	Job Name	Agency Fee
Ace Chemicals	Allen Ace		
		SAP	$1,620.00
	Sum		$1,620.00
Acme Insurance	George Acme		
		WindowsNT	$624.00
		COBOL	$321.43
	Sum		$945.43

Fig. 7-5

ꙮ DELIVERABLES

1. Word-processed design of tables
2. Tables created in Access
3. Report 1
4. Report 2
5. Report 3
6. Diskette
7. Any other required tutorial printouts or tutorial diskette

Staple all pages together. Put your name and class number at the top of each page. Make sure your diskette is labeled.

Case 7

8 CASE

The Baby-sitting Co-op Database

DESIGNING A RELATIONAL DATABASE TO CREATE REPORTS

➤ PREVIEW

In this case, you will design a database for a group of college graduate students who have formed a baby-sitting cooperative. Once your design is complete and correct, you will create tables in the database and populate them with data. Then you will produce three reports. The first report calculates and displays the credits each family in the cooperative has accumulated. The second report calculates and displays the debits each family has accumulated. The third report creates a mailing list that shows each family's children's names, address, and birthdays.

➤ PREPARATION

- Before attempting this exercise, you should have some experience in database design and Microsoft Access.
- Complete any part of Database Design Tutorial A your instructor assigns.
- Complete any part of Access Tutorial B your instructor assigns, or refer to the tutorial as necessary.

✈ BACKGROUND

A graduate assistant who works for your professor has asked your class to develop a database to help her keep track of a baby-sitting cooperative that she is running with some friends. Here's the e-mail she sends to you.

TO: Class101@youruniversity.edu

FROM: lucky@youruniversity.edu

Dear Class,

A group of married graduate students here at the university have formed a baby-sitting co-op. Most of us are on very tight budgets and cannot afford to pay baby-sitters, so we baby-sit for one another's children. Each of us builds up credits when we baby-sit, and then we use those credits toward having other grad students baby-sit for us.

Since we began this baby-sitting co-op five years ago, it has grown so much that I can't take care of the paperwork without the help of the computer. I would like you to design and create a database for me to keep track of debits and credits of our members.

I need to keep track of our members, who their children are, and each child's birthday. I also need to log how many hours each person baby-sits (the start and finish times and the date) and for whom. We calculate credits based on the number of hours a family baby-sits. The credits and debits of baby-sitting are based on the family as a unit. So, one time the dad could baby-sit, and the next time the mom might baby-sit, but both times are credited to their family account.

With the new database system, I would like to have a table where I can keep track of the future baby-sitting appointments and also keep track of past appointments. Then each week, I will generate a report of the credits people have earned and the credits they have used up for having a sitter for their own children. Finally, I would like to have a mailing list of all the children, sorted by their birth date, so I can send each of them a card at the appropriate time.

I hope you can help me with my problem. Thank you and good luck.

Candace Lucky

✈ ASSIGNMENT 1   CREATING THE DATABASE DESIGN

In this assignment, you will design your database tables on paper. Pay close attention to their logic and structure. Do not start your Access code (Assignment 2) before getting feedback from your instructor on Assignment 1. Keep in mind that you will need to look at what is required in Assignment 2 to design your fields and tables properly. It's good programming practice to look at the required outputs before designing your database.

- Design the tables you'll need on paper, avoiding data redundancy. Do not create a field if it could be created by "calculated field" in a query.

- You'll need a transaction table. If you avoid duplicating data contained within other tables, the transaction table should be pretty sparse.
- Include a logical field that answers the question, "baby-sitting completed?"
- Create your tables using the Table facility of your word processor. Your word-processed tables should look something like the table that follows.

Table name	
Field name	Data type (text, numeric, currency, etc.)
...	...

- You must mark the appropriate key field(s). You can denote a key field by an asterisk (*) next to the field name. Keep in mind that some tables need a compound field key to uniquely identify a record within a table.
- Print out the database design.

Note: Have this design approved before beginning Assignment 2; otherwise, you may need to redo Assignment 2.

➤ ASSIGNMENT 2   CREATING THE DATABASE WITH REPORTS

Assignment 2A: Creating Tables in Access

In this part of the assignment, you will create your tables in Access.

- Type in your records. You should have the following families. (Add your family name and address as the last record.)

Family Name	Address
Sanchez	101 E. Main St.
Short	16 French St.
Satchel	123 5th Ave.
Koala	5 Amy Lane
Philips	45 W. Main St.
Carlos	6700 4th Ave.
Samm	23 Fifer Blvd.
Fish	2456 9th St.
Keller	5 W. George St.
Ball	9 Oak Ave.
Your Name	**Your Address**

Fig. 8-1

- Assign children to each family, with some families having more than one child. Make up names.

- Make up baby-sitting appointments.
- Three families should baby-sit twice, and two families should baby-sit at least three times.
- Have all but one or two of the jobs be in the past. (In other words, the logical field "completed" should be checked for all but two jobs.)
- Appropriately limit the size of the text fields; for example, a Zip Code field does not need to be the default setting of 50 characters in length.
- Print all tables.

Assignment 2B: Creating Queries and Reports

There are three reports to generate (including the mailing list), as outlined in the letter. You'll need to generate a query to produce each report.

Report 1

Form a query to calculate the number of credits each family has. Include the member ID, member's name, date of the job, and the credit calculation (finish time - start time).

- Note: When doing "time arithmetic" in Access, you must multiply the expression by 24. You will need to make a query (a sigma-type query) first, before going into the Report Wizard. (Hint: Link the family ID field on those who have done the baby-sitting.) Once in the Report Wizard, group on Family ID and Name. Sum the total number of hours accumulated.
- You will need to go into the Report Design and adjust it so the family ID field and the family name are all on the same line. (See Creating Reports in the Access tutorial.)
- Delete any extra totals and italicized total lines.
- Your report should resemble the portion of the report that follows.

Babysitting Credits

Family ID - Sitter	Family Name	Date	Credit Hours
101	Sanchez		
		5/4/98	8
		2/12/99	2.5
Total Hours Credited			10.5
102	Short		
		3/4/99	4
Total Hours Credited			4
103	Satchel		
		3/15/99	3
		3/17/99	3
Total Hours Credited			6

Fig. 8-2

Report 2

Do the same type of query as you did in Report 1 to calculate the debits for each family. Each report will be very similar in layout, data fields, and arrangement, except one report shows credits, and one shows debits.

- You will need to change the link line on the query to link the family that has been baby-sat for with the family ID in the other table.
- The requirements for this report are the same as those for Report 1.
- Your report will resemble the portion of the one that follows.

Babysitting Debits

Family ID - Sat for	Family Name	Date	Debit Hours
101	Sanchez		
		3/15/99	3
		3/17/99	3
Total Hours Debited			6
102	Short		
		5/4/98	8
Total Hours Debited			8
103	Satchel		
		2/12/99	2.5
Total Hours Debited			2.5

Fig. 8-3

Report 3

Finally, do the mailing list. You need to make a query for this list that includes the child's first name, last name, address, and birthday. Sort on date of birth. Your completed list should resemble the following list.

Birthday List

Child Name	Family Name	Address	Birth date
John	Sanchez	101 E. Main St	4/5/89
Katie	Sanchez	101 E. Main St	3/9/90
Jorge	Koala	5 Amy Lane	5/6/93
Peter	Short	16 French St	12/18/93
Paul	Short	16 French St	3/4/94
Sammie	Satchel	123 5th Ave	4/5/98
Juanita	Koala	5 Amy Lane	1/2/99

Fig. 8-4

✤ DELIVERABLES

1. Word-processed design of tables
2. Tables created in Access
3. Report 1
4. Report 2
5. Report 3
6. Diskette
7. Any other required tutorial printouts or tutorial diskette

Staple all pages together. Put your name and class number at the top of each page. Make sure your diskette is labeled.

9
CASE

The Forever-Green Lawn Care Company Database

DESIGNING A RELATIONAL DATABASE TO CREATE FORMS AND REPORTS

➤ PREVIEW

In this case, you will design a database for a lawn care business. After the design is complete and correct, you will create tables in the database and populate them with data. Then you will create a data entry form, a list report, and two other reports. The list identifies customers who want only organic treatments for their lawns. The first report shows the chemicals applied and the dollar amount of income generated by each technician. The second report generates customers' bills.

➤ PREPARATION

- Before attempting this exercise, you should have some experience in database design and Microsoft Access.
- Complete any part of Database Design Tutorial A your instructor assigns.
- Complete any part of Access Tutorial B your instructor assigns, or refer to the tutorial as necessary.

One of the maintenance personnel at your university has sent your instructor an e-mail message, asking for help designing a database for his business. Here's what he wrote.

TO: professor@youruniversity.edu

FROM: joe.green@youruniversity.edu

I own a small lawn care business, and I need your help designing a database. Since the start of my company in 1995, business has grown rapidly due to a core of good customers who have recommended me to friends. I have been doing all my own bookkeeping by hand, but it's becoming a difficult task with the expansion of my business. I would like to implement a computerized billing system this winter, while business is a little slow.

Here's how my business works. I have four technicians who travel to customers' homes to apply chemicals to treat lawns. Each technician has an area defined by Zip Code. The technician travels to the customer's home, inspects the lawn, and then decides which chemicals to apply. The customer is only charged for the chemicals used that day, so the bills to individual customers vary month by month. The charge for each chemical applied depends on the quantity applied. All of my lawn chemicals are charged by the gallon.

A few of my customers require that I use only organic products on their lawn. This is noted on their customer records. When technicians go to the customer's home, they know from the list whether to apply only organic products. Since the products carried on the truck are normally synthetic chemicals, I need a list of those customers who prefer "organic only," so their lawns can be treated at a separate time.

I would like a system that is easy enough for my technicians to use, so when they return to the office after a day's work, they can log the chemical names and quantities used for each customer. Then I will take that information and generate a report which will show my total monthly billing by each technician in each Zip Code area. This will help me to identify which technicians are generating the most income. I also want to be able to produce individual bills for each customer that will itemize the chemicals used and their price.

I hope you can help me set up my system.

Thank you.

Joe Green

➤ ASSIGNMENT 1   CREATING THE DATABASE DESIGN

In this assignment, you will design your database tables on paper. Focus on the logic and structure of your tables. Do not start your Access code (Assignment 2) before getting feedback from your instructor on Assignment 1.

- Design the tables you'll need on paper, avoiding data redundancy. Do not create a field if it could be created by "calculated field" in a query.

Case 9

- You'll need a transaction table. If you avoid duplicating data contained within other tables, the transaction table should be pretty sparse.
- One of your tables should contain a logical (yes/no) field. (Remember, each chemical is priced and applied by the gallon.)
- Create your tables using the Table facility of your word processor. Your word-processed tables should look something like the one that follows.

Table name	
Field name	**Data type (text, numeric, currency, etc.)**
...	...

- You must mark the appropriate key field(s). You can denote a key field by an asterisk (*) next to the field name. Keep in mind that some tables need a compound field key to uniquely identify a record within a table.
- Print out the database design.

Note: Have this design approved before beginning Assignment 2; otherwise, you may need to redo Assignment 2.

➣ ASSIGNMENT 2 CREATING THE DATABASE WITH FORMS AND REPORTS

Assignment 2A: Creating Tables in Access

Type in your records. There should be customers in four different Zip Codes. Make three customers use organic products only. (You choose which three.) Use the data that follows. All customers live in Newark, DE. (The technician who treats the lawn is noted after the Zip Code.) Add your own name and address. Use one of the given Zip Codes and it's corresponding technician.

Customer Name	Address	Zip
Beth Schwander	101 W. Park	19711 (Stephen Jay)
Chris Prescott	700 Oak	19713 (Dylan Dreyfus)
Natalie Walsh	23 Amsterdam	19710 (Martha Ruben)
Mark Knightly	23 Crofton	19711 (Stephen Jay)
Samuel Smoth	180 Elm	19713 (Dylan Dreyfus)
Sally Brennan	15 E. 5th	19714 (Barry Henry)
Patti Fredricks	450 Maple	19713 (Dylan Dreyfus)
Tom Bell	5 Rt 52	19714 (Barry Henry)
Your Name	**Your Address**	**Zip (Technician)**

Fig. 9-1

- Create the names of five different chemicals to be used.
- All visits occur in one month. Show each customer as having one visit per month, but show multiple chemicals as being applied to at least five customers' homes.

- Charge a different price per gallon for each chemical.
- Appropriately limit the size of the text fields; for example, a Zip Code field does not need to be the default setting of 50 characters in length.
- Print all tables.

Assignment 2B: Creating Forms, Queries, and Reports

Form

Create a form that technicians can fill out at the end of the day. Base your form on the transaction table.

List Report

Create a list of those customers who use organic products only. This list should be grouped by Zip Code and technician name and should show the customer's name and full address. To do this, first create a query to find those specific records, and then feed that query into a report. If you group the report on Zip Code, it will be easier for the technicians to find their individual work. You will need to adjust the report design after using the Report Wizard to bring the Technician Name and Zip Code on to the same line. (See Creating Reports in the Access tutorial.)

Your report will resemble the portion of the report that follows. Your report will include more and different data.

Organic Only

Technician Name	Zip	Customer Name	Address
Dylan Dreyfus	19713		
		Patti Fredricks	450 Maple, Newark, DE
		Samuel Smoth	180 Elm, Newark, DE
Martha Ruben	19710		
		Natalie Walsh	35 Amsterdam, Newark, DE
Stephen Jay	19711		
		Beth Schwander	101 W. Park, Newark, DE

Fig. 9-2

Report 1

Create a report that calculates the total value of chemicals applied by each technician this month.

- Because each technician covers an area designated by Zip Code, the report needs to be grouped by Zip Code, with a total dollar value of chemicals charged to that Zip Code. To accomplish this, you must create a query with a calculated field that computes the total dollar amount of chemicals for each customer's lawn. (Also include each chemical's name.) Then bring that query into a report, group the report on Zip Code and Technician Name, and while in the Report Wizard, choose the Summary Options button on the Sort dialog box. (You will not need to sort.) This will allow you to sum the dollar value of chemicals within Zip Code.

- Make sure that all totals are in currency format. If they are not, go to the Design View of the report, click on the object that represents the totals to select it (handles will appear), click on the RIGHT mouse button—Properties—Format—Currency.
- Adjust the report's design to make related information appear on one line, as is appropriate.
- Make sure that all italicized lines or duplicate sum objects are deleted from your report design. (See Creating Reports in the Access tutorial.)
- Your report, after all the adjustments, should resemble the portion of the report that follows. (Treatment dates and dollar values will differ.)

Chemicals by Technician

Technician Name	Zip		Chemical Name	Money
Dylan Dreyfus	19713			
			Lyme	$60.00
			Weed-b-gone	$12.00
Sum				$72.00
Martha Ruben	19710			
			Nitrogen	$10.00
			Weed-b-gone	$16.00
Sum				$26.00

Fig. 9-3

Report 2

Create an itemized bill for a customer. Again, a query needs to be generated before the report can be processed.

- The itemized bill should include the customer's name, address, Zip Code, date of service, name of each chemical applied, and total cost of each chemical applied (quantity times price). Total cost for all chemicals should also show on each customer's bill.
- Adjust the report's design to make it look correct. Make sure that when you are in the Report Wizard, you group the report on Customer, Address, and Zip Code. After the report is created, go to the Design View and take the Address object and move it up to the Customer header, and take the Zip Code object and move it up to the Customer header. If you do this, the report will have the customer name, address, and Zip Code all on the same grouping line, which will look better than if you had left the report as the Wizard makes it. (See Creating Reports in the Access tutorial.)

- Delete any italicized lines or duplicate sum objects in the report Design View. (See Creating Reports in the Access tutorial.)
- Check formatting to make sure that money is expressed in currency format.

Your finished report will be similar in format to the portion of the report that follows.

Customer's Bill

Customer Name	Address	Zip	Date	Chemical Name	Cost
Beth Schwander	101 W. Park, Newark, DE	19711			
			3/23/99	Sure-Grow	$27.50
			3/23/99	Lyme	$30.00
Total Cost					*$57.50*
Chris Prescott	700 Oak, Newark, DE	19713			
			3/4/99	Weed-b-gone	$12.00
			3/4/99	Lyme	$60.00
Total Cost					*$72.00*

Fig. 9-4

➤ DELIVERABLES

1. Word-processed design of tables
2. Tables created in Access
3. Form: Print only 1 record
4. List Report
5. Report 1
6. Report 2
7. Diskette
8. Any other required tutorial printouts or tutorial diskette

Staple all pages together. Put your name and class number at the top of the page. Make sure your diskette is labeled.

10

The Rent-an-Event Party Rentals Database

DESIGNING A RELATIONAL DATABASE TO CREATE FORMS AND REPORTS

⇥ PREVIEW

In this case, you will design a database for a small company that rents equipment for parties. After your design is complete and correct, you will create tables in a database and populate them with data, create a data entry form, and generate three reports. The first report lists customers in alphabetical order. The second report shows the number of days each type of equipment was rented. The third report generates a bill for each customer.

⇥ PREPARATION

- Before attempting this exercise, you should have some experience in database design and Microsoft Access.
- Complete any part of Database Design Tutorial A your instructor assigns.
- Complete any part of Access Tutorial B your instructor assigns, or refer to the tutorial as necessary.

✤ BACKGROUND

One of your friends who graduated last year has heard that you are taking a class in database design and implementation. She desperately needs help in her business and has come to you for help. Here is what she has written to you.

Dear Friend,

How are things down at the U? I sure miss those fun days. Since I left the university, I started a company called "Rent-an-Event Party Rentals." We rent party equipment, such as tents, canopies, tables, chairs, china, linens, glassware, and flatware. Private individuals make up most of our customers, but we also have a few business customers.

Ever since our inception in 1998, we have remained a small, local company with a staff of about 12 people, depending on the season. As the busy summer approaches, however, I am uneasy about how we've been managing our bookkeeping. All orders are placed by telephone and written in a notebook. Recently, I noticed that some of our staff has been double-booking certain items, such as our only 20' × 14' tent. I feel that we need a computer system to sort out all our paperwork. I wish I had taken a computer class in school, but now I hope I can rely on your expertise.

First, I would like the database system to log rental information so I can easily see which items have been rented and for which dates. I'd like my staff to be able to pull up a Rentals screen and type telephone orders for rentals directly into the computer. Information on the screen should include the customer's name or their ID number, the date and time desired, and the rental item name or ID number.

My plan for the business is to expand into the business-customer market. These clients seem to rent at the highest volume. I would like to have a listing of my local business customers, so I can further market to them and others like them.

In addition, I would like to be able to track the frequency of equipment rentals each month. If I could generate a monthly report that ranks my most popular item down to the least popular, I could make better marketing decisions in the future.

Finally, I would like to send my customers a computer-generated bill after we have successfully rented our party goods. Most of our rentals are by the hour, so the bill would have to calculate the total cost for each item rented. Include the date of rental, the number of hours, and the total bill.

I hope you can help me set up my system.

Thank you.

Sarah Wellington

☙ ASSIGNMENT 1 CREATING THE DATABASE DESIGN

In this assignment, you will design your database tables on paper. Pay close attention to their logic and structure. Do not start your Access code (Assignment 2) before getting feedback from your instructor on Assignment 1.

- Design the tables you'll need on paper, avoiding data redundancy. Do not create a field if it could be created by "calculated field" in a query.
- You'll need a transaction table. If you avoid duplicating data contained within other tables, the transaction table should be pretty sparse.
- One of your tables should contain a logical (yes/no) field.
- Create your tables using the Table facility of your word processor. Your word-processed tables should look something like the table that follows.

Table name	
Field name	**Data type (text, numeric, currency, etc.)**
...	...

- You must mark the appropriate key field(s). You can denote a key field by an asterisk (*) next to the field name. Keep in mind that some tables need a compound field key to uniquely identify a record within a table.
- Print out the database design.

Note: Have this design approved before beginning Assignment 2; otherwise, you may need to redo Assignment 2.

☙ ASSIGNMENT 2 CREATING THE DATABASE WITH FORMS AND REPORTS

Assignment 2A: Creating Tables in Access

In this part of the assignment, you will create your tables in Access. Type in your records. Use the following data. All customers live in Newark, DE 19713. Add your name and street address to the list.

Name	Address
Beth's Bratwurst	101 W. Park
Chris Prescott	700 Oak
Natalie's Knick-knacks	35 Amsterdam
Mark Knightly	23 Crofton
Samuel's Smoothies	180 Elm
Sally Brennan	15 E. 5th
Patti's Pizza	450 Maple
Tom Bell	5 Rt 52
Your Name	**Your Street Address**

Fig. 10-1

- The items to be rented are as follows: Grill, 3 × 5 Table, Folding Chair, 5 × 9 Table, 20 × 14 Tent, and Gazebo.
- Make up the rental data. Each customer should rent any item at least once, and a few customers should rent several items. Assume each customer only rents on one given day, and make all the orders in the same month. Make the appropriate customers business customers.
- Appropriately limit the size of the text fields; for example, a Zip Code field does not need to be the default setting of 50 characters in length.
- Print all tables.

Assignment 2B: Creating Forms, Queries, and Reports

Form

Create a form for taking telephone orders. Base the form on your transaction table.

List Report

Generate a mailing list of business customers. First, create a query to find those specific records, and then bring that query into a report that lists the names and addresses. Your list will resemble the one that follows.

Mailing List

Customer Name	Address
Beth's Bratwurst	101 W. Park, Newark, DE 19713
Natalie's Knick-knacks	35 Amsterdam, Newark, DE 19713
Patti's Pizza	450 Maple, Newark, DE 19713
Samuel's Smoothies	180 Elm, Newark, DE 19713

Fig. 10-2

Report 1

Calculate how many days each item of equipment has been rented this month. Display equipment rentals from the most number of days rented down to least number of days rented.

- You will need to generate a query before creating the report. The query will simply sum the number of days for each item. Make sure that you give the summed field an appropriate heading, such as Frequency of Rental or Number of Times Rented. Also, sort that field in descending order so that the most frequently rented item will be first, and the least frequently rented item will be last. Bring the query into a report.
- Don't group or sum the report. The format of your report will resemble the portion of the report that follows.

Frequency Report

Item Name	Number of Times Rented
Grill	3
3 x 5 Table	2
Gazebo	1
Folding chair	1
5 x 9 Table	1
20 x 14 Tent	1

Fig. 10-3

Report 2

This report involves creating an itemized bill for a customer. Again, a query needs to be generated before the report can be processed.

- The itemized bill should include the customer's name and address, each item rented, and its total cost. (Hint: Make a calculated field in the query to calculate the dollar amount of each item rented; this will involve time arithmetic.) The report should also show the grand total owed for the rental. Assume that all customers pay by check when they receive their bill. Bring the query into the Report Wizard and group on Customer Name and Address. Click the Summary Options button, and sum on Cost (or whatever you called that calculated field). Preview the new report.

- Make sure all appropriate fields are in currency format. If they are not, go to the Design View of the report, right-click on the Sum object, and change the properties to currency.

- You will notice that the address is on a line below the customer's name. Change that in the Design View, so that both name and address are on the same line. (See Creating Reports in the Access tutorial.)

- Delete any italicized lines or duplicate sum objects in the Design View. (See Creating Reports in the Access tutorial.)

- The format of your report will resemble the portion of the report that follows.

Customer's Bill

Customer Name	Address	Item Name	Cost
Beth's Bratwurst	101 W. Park, Newark, DE 19713		
		5 x 9 Table	$10.00
		Grill	$20.00
Total Bill			$30.00
Chris Prescott	700 Oak, Newark, DE 19713		
		Gazebo	$36.00
		20 x 14 Tent	$36.00
Total Bill			$72.00
Mark Knightly	23 Crofton, Newark, DE 19713		
		Grill	$5.00
Total Bill			$5.00

Fig. 10-4

➤ DELIVERABLES

1. Word-processed design of tables
2. Tables created in Access
3. Form: Print out only 1 record
4. List Report
5. Report 1
6. Report 2
7. Diskette
8. Any other required tutorial printouts or tutorial diskette

Staple all pages together. Put your name and class number at the top of each page. Make sure your diskette is labeled.

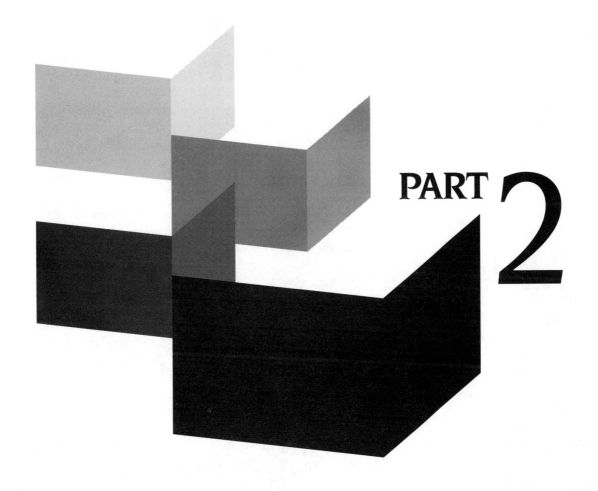

PART 2

Decision Support Cases Using Excel

C
TUTORIAL

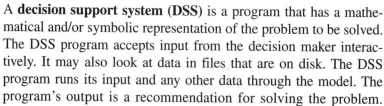

Building a Decision Support System in Excel

A **decision support system (DSS)** is a program that has a mathematical and/or symbolic representation of the problem to be solved. The DSS program accepts input from the decision maker interactively. It may also look at data in files that are on disk. The DSS program runs its input and any other data through the model. The program's output is a recommendation for solving the problem.

A DSS could be written in any programming language that lets the programmer represent the problem. For example, a DSS could be built in a third-generation language, such as Visual Basic, or in a database package, such as Access. A DSS could also be written in a spreadsheet package, such as Excel.

Many kinds of problems can be modeled in Excel. The Excel spreadsheet package has standard built-in arithmetic functions, as well as many statistical and financial functions. So, for example, any accounting, operations, or finance problem could, in theory, be modeled in Excel.

This tutorial has three sections:

1. **Spreadsheet and DSS Basics** In this section, you'll learn how to create a DSS program in Excel. Your program will be in the form of a cash-flow model. This gives you practice in spreadsheet design and in building a DSS program.

2. **Scenario Manager** In this section, you'll learn how to use an Excel tool called the Scenario Manager. One problem with playing "what if" with any DSS package is this: Where do you, physically, record the results from running each set of data? Typically, a user just writes the inputs and related results on a piece of paper. Then—ridiculously enough—the user might have to input the data *back into* a spreadsheet for further analysis! The Scenario Manager solves that problem. It can be set up to capture inputs and results as "scenarios," which are then nicely summarized on a separate sheet in the Excel workbook.

3. **Review of Excel Basics** This section reviews the information you'll need to do the spreadsheet cases that follow this tutorial.

Assume that it is late in 1999, and you are trying to build a model of what a company's net income (profit) and cash flow will be in the next two years (2000 and 2001). That is the "problem," to forecast net income and cash flow. Assume that knowing these forecasts would help to answer some question or make some decision. After researching the problem, you decide that the estimates should be based on 1999 results, estimates of the underlying economy, and the cost of the products that the company sells.

The model will use an accounting income statement and cash-flow framework. The user can input values for two possible states of the economy in years 2000–2001: "O" for an optimistic outlook, "P" for a pessimistic outlook. The state of the economy is expected to affect the number of units the company can sell, as well as the selling price. The better the economy, the more units that can be sold and the higher the price. The user can also input values for two possible cost-of-goods-sold price directions: "U" for up, "D" for down. The "U" means that the cost of an item sold would be higher than in 1999, "D" less.

Presumably, the company will do better with the good economy and lower input costs. But how much better? The relationships are too complex to assess in one's head, but the software model can handle the relationships easily. The user plays "what if" with the input variables and notes the effect on net income and year-end cash levels. "What if" the economy is good, and costs go up: What will net income and cash flow be in that case? What will happen if the economy is down, and costs go down? What would be net income and cash flow in that case? With your Excel software model available, the answers are easily quantified.

Organization of the DSS Model

Your spreadsheets should have these sections:

- CONSTANTS
- INPUTS
- SUMMARY OF KEY RESULTS
- CALCULATIONS of values that will be used in the Income Statement/Cash Flow
- INCOME STATEMENT AND CASH FLOW STATEMENT.

Here, as an extended illustration, a DSS model is built for the forecasting problem described above.

CONSTANTS This section records values that are used in spreadsheet calculations. In a sense, the constants are inputs, except that they do not change. In this tutorial, constants are TAX RATE and the NUMBER OF BUSINESS DAYS.

INPUTS The inputs are the ECONOMIC OUTLOOK and PURCHASING PRICE OUTLOOK (input costs). Inputs could conceivably be entered for *each year* covered by the model (here 2000 and 2001). This would let you enter "O" for year 2000's economy in one cell, and "P" for year 2001's in another cell, or one input for the two-year period could be entered in one cell. For simplicity, this tutorial uses the *latter* approach.

SUMMARY OF KEY RESULTS This section will capture years 2000 and 2001 NET INCOME (profit) and YEAR-END CASH levels, which are (assume) the two relevant outputs of this model. The summary merely repeats, in one easy-to-see place, results that are shown in otherwise widely spaced places in the spreadsheet. This just makes the answers easy to see while inputting data. (It also makes it easier to *graph* results later).

CALCULATIONS This area is used to compute the following:

1. The NUMBER OF UNITS SOLD IN A DAY (a function of a certain *1999* value and of the ECONOMIC OUTLOOK input)

2. The SELLING PRICE PER UNIT (similarly derived)

3. The COST OF GOODS SOLD PER UNIT (a function of a *1999* value and of the PURCHASING PRICE OUTLOOK)

4. The NUMBER OF UNITS SOLD IN A YEAR (the NUMBER OF UNITS SOLD IN A DAY times the NUMBER OF BUSINESS DAYS)

These formulas could be embedded in the INCOME STATEMENT AND CASH FLOW STATEMENT. But doing that would cause the expressions there to be complex and difficult to understand. Putting the intermediate calculations into a separate section breaks the work up into modules. This is good form because it simplifies your programming.

INCOME STATEMENT AND CASH FLOW STATEMENT This is the "body" of the spreadsheet. It shows the following:

1. BEGINNING OF THE YEAR CASH ON HAND, which equals cash at the end of the *prior* year

2. SALES (revenue), which equals the units sold in the year times the unit selling price

3. COST OF GOODS SOLD, which is units sold in the year times the cost of goods sold per unit

4. PRE-TAX PROFIT MARGIN, which equals sales (revenue) less total costs

5. TAX EXPENSE, which is zero if there are losses, otherwise the pre-tax margin times the constant tax rate

6. NET INCOME, which equals pre-tax margin less tax expense

7. END OF THE YEAR CASH ON HAND, which is BEGINNING OF YEAR CASH ON HAND plus NET INCOME (In the real world, cash-flow estimates must account for changes in receivables and payables. Assume that Sales are collected immediately—there are no receivables or bad debts. Assume that suppliers are paid off right away—there are no payables.)

Construction of the Spreadsheet Model

Build your spreadsheet model in three steps:

1. Make a "skeleton" of the spreadsheet.

2. Fill in the "easy" cell formulas.

3. Enter the "hard" spreadsheet formulas.

Make a Skeleton

Your first step is to set up a skeleton worksheet. This should have the headings, text string labels, and the constants, but no formulas.

To set up the skeleton, you must get a grip on the problem, *conceptually*. The best way to do that is to work *backwards* from what the "body" of the spreadsheet will look like. Here, the body is the INCOME STATEMENT AND CASH FLOW STATEMENT. Set that up, in your mind or on paper, then do the following:

- Decide what amounts should be in the CALCULATIONS area. In this tutorial's model, SALES (revenue) will be NUMBER OF UNITS SOLD PER DAY times SELLING

PRICE PER UNIT, in the income statement. The intermediate amounts (NUMBER OF UNITS SOLD and SELLING PRICE PER UNIT) are calculated in the CALCULATIONS area.

- Set up the SUMMARY OF KEY RESULTS by deciding what important *outputs* are needed to solve the problem. The INPUTS area should be reserved for amounts that can change—the controlling variables—which are the ECONOMIC OUTLOOK and the PURCHASING PRICE OUTLOOK.

- Use the CONSTANTS area for values that you will need to use, but that are not in doubt, i.e., you will not have to input them or calculate them. Here, the TAX RATE is a good example.

⌑ AT THE KEYBOARD

Type in the skeleton below.

Note: (1) "NA" means that a cell will not be used in any formula in the worksheet. The 1999 values are needed only for certain calculations, so for the most part, the 1999 column's cells just show "NA." (Recall that the forecast is for 2000 and 2001.) (2) You can "break" a text string in a cell, by typing Alt and Enter at the same time at the breakpoint. (This makes the cell "taller.")

	A	B	C	D
1	TUTORIAL EXERCISE			
2		1999	2000	2001
3	CONSTANTS			
4	TAX RATE EXPECTED	NA	0.33	0.35
5	NUMBER OF BUSINESS DAYS	NA	300	300
6				
7	INPUTS			
8	ECONOMIC OUTLOOK (O = OPTIMISTIC; P = PESSIMISTIC)	NA		
9	PURCHASING PRICE OUTLOOK (U = UP; D = DOWN)	NA		
10				
11	SUMMARY OF KEY RESULTS			
12	NET INCOME FOR YEAR	NA		
13	YEAR-END CASH ON HAND	NA		
14				
15	CALCULATIONS			
16	NUMBER OF UNITS SOLD/DAY	1000		
17	SELLING PRICE/UNIT	7		
18	COST OF GOODS SOLD/UNIT	3		
19	NUMBER OF UNITS SOLD/YEAR	NA		

Fig. C-1

	A	B	C	D
20				
21	**INCOME STATEMENT AND** **CASH FLOW STATEMENT**			
22	BEGINNING OF YEAR CASH ON HAND	NA		
23				
24	SALES	NA		
25	COST OF GOODS SOLD	NA		
26	PRE-TAX PROFIT MARGIN	NA		
27	TAX EXPENSE	NA		
28	NET INCOME	NA		
29				
30	END OF YEAR CASH ON HAND (BEGINNING OF YR CASH, PLUS NET INCOME FOR YEAR)	10000		
31				

Fig. C-2

Fill in the "Easy" Formulas

The next step is to fill in the "easy" formulas. The cells affected (and what you should enter) are discussed next.

The summary of results is just an "echo" of results shown in other places. The idea is C28 holds the NET INCOME. You want to echo that amount to C12. So, the formula that should be typed into C12 is: =C28. Translation: "Copy what is in C28 into C12." It's that simple. (Note: with the cursor in C12, the contents of that cell—in this case the formula =C28—shows in the editing window, which is above the lettered column indicators.)

C12	▼	**=**	=C28	
	A	B	C	D
11	**SUMMARY OF KEY RESULTS**			
12	NET INCOME FOR YEAR	NA	0	
13	YEAR-END CASH ON HAND	NA		
14				

Fig. C-3

At this point, C28 is empty (and thus has a zero value), but that does not prevent you from copying. Copy cell C12's formula to the right, to cell D12. The copy operation does not actually "copy." Copying puts =D28 into D12, which is what you want. (Year 2001's NET INCOME is in D28.)

To copy:

1. *Select (click in) the cell that you want to copy.*

2. *Choose Edit—Copy.*

3. *Select the cell (or cell range) to be copied to by clicking (and then dragging if the range has more than one cell).*

4. *Press the Enter key.*

END OF YEAR CASH ON HAND for year 2000 cash is in cell C30. Echo the cash results in cell C30 to cell C13 (put =C30 in cell C13).

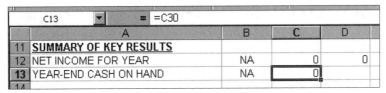

	C13	▼	=	=C30		
	A			B	C	D
11	**SUMMARY OF KEY RESULTS**					
12	NET INCOME FOR YEAR			NA	0	0
13	YEAR-END CASH ON HAND			NA	0	

Fig. C-4

Copy the formula from C13 to D13. At this point, the CALCULATIONS formulas will not be entered because they are not all "easy" formulas. Move on to the easier income statement formulas, as if the calculations were already done. Again, the empty calculations cells do not stop you.

BEGINNING OF YEAR CASH ON HAND is the cash on hand at the end of the *prior* year. In C22 (for the year 2000), type in =B30. (See the "skeleton" you just entered. B30 has the 1999 END OF YEAR CASH ON HAND.) Copy the formula to the right.

	C22	▼	=	=B30		
	A			B	C	D
21	**INCOME STATEMENT AND CASH FLOW STATEMENT**					
22	BEGINNING OF YEAR CASH ON HAND			NA	10000	
23						
24	SALES			NA		
25	COST OF GOODS SOLD			NA		
26	PRE-TAX PROFIT MARGIN			NA		
27	TAX EXPENSE			NA		
28	NET INCOME			NA		
29						
30	END OF YEAR CASH ON HAND (BEGINNING OF YR CASH, PLUS NET INCOME FOR YEAR)			10000		

Fig. C-5

SALES (revenue) is just NUMBER OF UNITS SOLD PER YEAR times SELLING PRICE PER UNIT. In C24 enter =INT(C17*C19).

	C24	▼	=	=INT(C17*C19)		
	A			B	C	D
15	**CALCULATIONS**					
16	NUMBER OF UNITS SOLD/DAY			1000		
17	SELLING PRICE/UNIT			7		
18	COST OF GOODS SOLD/UNIT			3		
19	NUMBER OF UNITS SOLD/YEAR			NA		
20						
21	**INCOME STATEMENT AND CASH FLOW STATEMENT**					
22	BEGINNING OF YEAR CASH ON HAND			NA	10000	0
23						
24	SALES			NA	0	
25	COST OF GOODS SOLD			NA		

Fig. C-6

C17*C19 multiplies units sold for the year times selling price. The INT function lops off any decimal portion from the result. (C17 and C19 are empty now, which is why SALES shows as zero after the formula is entered.) Copy the formula to the right (to D24).

COST OF GOODS SOLD is handled similarly. In C25, type =INT(C18*C19). This equals NUMBER OF UNITS SOLD IN THE YEAR times COST OF GOODS SOLD PER UNIT. Copy to the right.

In cell C26, the formula for PRE-TAX PROFIT MARGIN is =C24–C25. Enter the formula. Copy to the right.

Income taxes are only paid on positive pre-tax profits in the U.S. In cell C27, the TAX EXPENSE is zero if the PRE-TAX PROFIT MARGIN is zero or less, otherwise TAX EXPENSE equals the TAX RATE times the PRE-TAX PROFIT MARGIN. The TAX RATE is a constant (in C4). An =IF() statement is needed to express this logic:

IF(PRE-TAX PROFIT MARGIN is <= 0, put zero tax in C27,

else in C27 put a number equal to multiplying the

TAX RATE times the PRE-TAX PROFIT MARGIN)

C26 stands for the concept PRE-TAX PROFIT MARGIN, and C4 stands for the concept TAX RATE. So, in Excel, substitute those cell addresses in the pseudo-code:

=IF(C26 <= 0, 0, INT(C4 * C26))

(The INT function, again, just gets rid of the pennies.) Copy the tax expense formula to the right.

In cell C28, NET INCOME is just PRE-TAX MARGIN less TAX EXPENSE: =C26–C27. Enter; copy to the right.

The END OF YEAR CASH is BEGINNING OF YEAR CASH plus NET INCOME. In cell C30, enter =C22+C28. The resulting value is shown. Then copy to the right.

	C30	▼	=	=C22+C28	
	A		B	C	D
21	INCOME STATEMENT AND CASH FLOW STATEMENT				
22	BEGINNING OF YEAR CASH ON HAND		NA	10000	10000
23					
24	SALES		NA	0	0
25	COST OF GOODS SOLD		NA	0	0
26	PRE-TAX PROFIT MARGIN		NA	0	0
27	TAX EXPENSE		NA	0	0
28	NET INCOME		NA	0	0
29					
30	END OF YEAR CASH ON HAND (BEGINNING OF YR CASH, PLUS NET INCOME FOR YEAR)		10000	10000	

Fig. C-7

Put in the "Hard" Formulas

The next step is to finish the spreadsheet by filling in the "harder" formulas.

⌨ **AT THE KEYBOARD**

First, in C8 enter "O" (no quotes) for OPTIMISTIC, and in C9 enter "U" (no quotes) for UP. There is nothing magic about these particular values—they just give the worksheet formulas some input to process. Recall that the inputs will cover both years 2000 and 2001. Enter NA in D8 and D9, just to remind yourself that these cells will not be used for input:

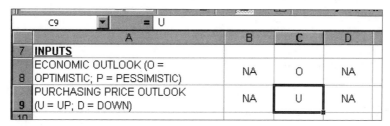

	A	B	C	D
7	**INPUTS**			
8	ECONOMIC OUTLOOK (O = OPTIMISTIC; P = PESSIMISTIC)	NA	O	NA
9	PURCHASING PRICE OUTLOOK (U = UP; D = DOWN)	NA	U	NA
10				

Fig. C-8

The entries in D8 and D9 are shown centered in the cells. If you want that formatting, see instructions at the end of this tutorial.

Recall that CALCULATIONS cell addresses are already referred to in income statement formulas. The next step is to enter formulas for the calculations.

The easiest CALCULATIONS formula is the NUMBER OF UNITS SOLD FOR THE YEAR, which is the calculated NUMBER OF UNITS SOLD PER DAY (in C16) times the NUMBER OF BUSINESS DAYS (in C5). In C19, enter =C5*C16.

C19 = =C5*C16

	A	B	C	D
3	**CONSTANTS**			
4	TAX RATE EXPECTED	NA	0.33	0.35
5	NUMBER OF BUSINESS DAYS	NA	300	300
6				
7	**INPUTS**			
8	ECONOMIC OUTLOOK (O = OPTIMISTIC; P = PESSIMISTIC)	NA	O	NA
9	PURCHASING PRICE OUTLOOK (U = UP; D = DOWN)	NA	U	NA
10				
11	**SUMMARY OF KEY RESULTS**			
12	NET INCOME FOR YEAR	NA	0	0
13	YEAR-END CASH ON HAND	NA	10000	10000
14				
15	**CALCULATIONS**			
16	NUMBER OF UNITS SOLD/DAY	1000		
17	SELLING PRICE/UNIT	7		
18	COST OF GOODS SOLD/UNIT	3		
19	NUMBER OF UNITS SOLD/YEAR	NA	0	
20				

Fig. C-9

Copy the formula to cell 19 for year 2001.

Assume that if the ECONOMIC OUTLOOK is OPTIMISTIC, the year 2000's NUMBER OF UNITS SOLD PER DAY will be 6% more than 1999's, and year 2001's will be 6% more than *2000*'s. Assume that if the ECONOMIC OUTLOOK is PESSIMISTIC, year 2000's

NUMBER OF UNITS SOLD PER DAY will be 1% less than 1999's, and 2001's will be 1% less than 2000's. An =IF() statement is needed in C16 to express this idea:

IF(economy variable = OPTIMISTIC,

   then UNITS SOLD PER DAY will go UP 6%,

      else UNITS SOLD PER DAY will go DOWN 1%)

Substituting cell addresses:

=IF(C8 = "O", INT(1.06 * B16), INT(.99 * B16))

Note: multiplying by 1.06 results in a 6% rise. Multiplying by .99 results in a 1% decrease. The INT function just gets rid of decimal parts of a unit.

Enter that formula into cell C16. Absolute addressing is needed (C8) because the address is in a formula that gets copied, *and* you do not want this cell reference to change when you copy the formula to the right. Absolute addressing maintains the C8 reference when the formula is copied. Use C8 for input for the economy variable—do not use D8 for 2001.

	C16		=	=IF(C8="O",INT(1.06*B16),INT(0.99*B16))

	A	B	C	D
3	**CONSTANTS**			
4	TAX RATE EXPECTED	NA	0.33	0.35
5	NUMBER OF BUSINESS DAYS	NA	300	300
6				
7	**INPUTS**			
8	ECONOMIC OUTLOOK (O = OPTIMISTIC; P = PESSIMISTIC)	NA	O	NA
9	PURCHASING PRICE OUTLOOK (U = UP; D = DOWN)	NA	U	NA
10				
11	**SUMMARY OF KEY RESULTS**			
12	NET INCOME FOR YEAR	NA	0	0
13	YEAR-END CASH ON HAND	NA	10000	10000
14				
15	**CALCULATIONS**			
16	NUMBER OF UNITS SOLD/DAY	1000	1060	
17	SELLING PRICE/UNIT	7		

Fig. C-10

Copy cell C16 into D16.

The SELLING PRICE PER UNIT is also a function of the ECONOMIC OUTLOOK. The two-part rule is (assume):

- If the ECONOMIC OUTLOOK is OPTIMISTIC, year 2000's SELLING PRICE will be 1.07 times year 1999's; year 2001's will be 1.07 times 2000's.

- On the other hand, if the ECONOMIC OUTLOOK is PESSIMISTIC, the SELLING PRICE in year 2000 and 2001 will equal year 1999's SELLING PRICE (i.e., the price will not change).

Test your understanding of the selling price calculation by figuring out what the formula should be for cell C17. Enter it and copy it to the right. You will need to use absolute addressing. (Can you see why?) Do *not* use the INT function—you do not want to lose the pennies in the price.

The COST OF GOODS SOLD PER UNIT is a function of the raw materials PURCHASING PRICE OUTLOOK. The two-part rule is (assume):

- If the PURCHASING PRICE OUTLOOK is UP ("U"), year 2000's COST OF GOODS SOLD PER UNIT will be 1.25 times year 1999's, and year 2001's will be 1.25 times 2000's.

- On the other hand, if the PURCHASING PRICE OUTLOOK is DOWN ("D"), the multiplier in each year will be 1.01.

Again, to test your understanding, figure out what the formula should be in cell C18. Enter it and copy it to the right. You will need to use absolute addressing. Do *not* use the INT function—you do not want to lose the pennies in the cost.

Your SELLING PRICE and COST OF GOODS sold formulas, given O and U inputs, should yield the calculated values shown here:

	A	B	C	D
15	**CALCULATIONS**			
16	NUMBER OF UNITS SOLD/DAY	1000	1060	1123
17	SELLING PRICE/UNIT	7	7.49	8.0143
18	COST OF GOODS SOLD/UNIT	3	3.75	4.6875
19	NUMBER OF UNITS SOLD/YEAR	NA	318000	336900
20				

Fig. C-11

That completes the body of your spreadsheet! The values in the calculations area ripple through the income statement because the income statement formulas reference the calculations. The final income and cash flow numbers should look like this:

	A	B	C	D
21	**INCOME STATEMENT AND CASH FLOW STATEMENT**			
22	BEGINNING OF YEAR CASH ON HAND	NA	10000	806845
23				
24	SALES	NA	2381820	2700017
25	COST OF GOODS SOLD	NA	1192500	1579218
26	PRE-TAX PROFIT MARGIN	NA	1189320	1120799
27	TAX EXPENSE	NA	392475	392279
28	NET INCOME	NA	796845	728520
29				
30	END OF YEAR CASH ON HAND (BEGINNING OF YR CASH, PLUS NET INCOME FOR YEAR)	10000	806845	1535365
31				

Fig. C-12

➤ SCENARIO MANAGER

You are now ready to use the Scenario Manager to capture inputs and results as you play "what if" with the spreadsheet.

Note that there are four possible combinations of input values: O-U (Optimistic-Up), O-D (Optimistic-Down), P-U (Pessimistic-Up), and P-D (Pessimistic-Down). Financial results for each combination will be different. Each combination can be referred to as a "scenario." Excel's Scenario Manager records each combination of inputs as a separate scenario and then shows a summary of all scenarios in a separate worksheet. These summary worksheet values can be used as a raw table of numbers, which can be printed or copied into a Word document. The table of data could be the basis for a chart (i.e., an Excel graph), which could also be printed or put into a memo.

You have four possible Economy-Purchasing Price scenarios: Optimistic-Up, Optimistic-Down, Pessimistic-Up, and Pessimistic-Down. The four input-value sets produce different financial results. When you use the Scenario Manager, you define the four scenarios, then have Excel (1) sequentially run the input values "behind the scenes," and (2) then put the results for each input scenario in a summary sheet.

When you define a scenario, you give the scenario a name and tell Excel what the input cells and input values are. You do this for each scenario. Then you create the summary sheet. When you create the summary sheet, you tell Excel where the *output* cells are. That lets Excel capture the outputs.

☐ AT THE KEYBOARD

To start, select Tools—Scenarios:

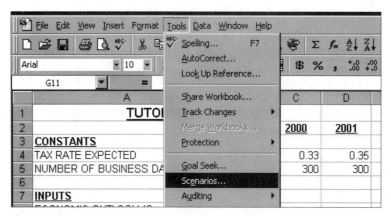

Fig. C-13

This leads you to a Scenario Manager window. Initially there are no scenarios defined, and Excel tells you that.

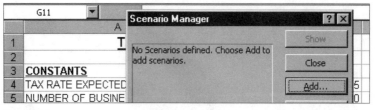

Fig. C-14

With this window you are able to add scenarios, delete them, or change (edit) them. You are also able to create the summary sheet, toward the end of the process. (Note: When working with this window and its successors, do **not** hit the Enter key to navigate. Use mouse clicks to move from one step to the next.)

Click the Add button. In the resulting Add Scenario window, give the first scenario a name: OPT-UP. Then type the input cells in the Changing Cells window. Here these are C8:C9, which are your INPUT cells. Note: Excel may add dollar signs to the cell address—do not be concerned about this.

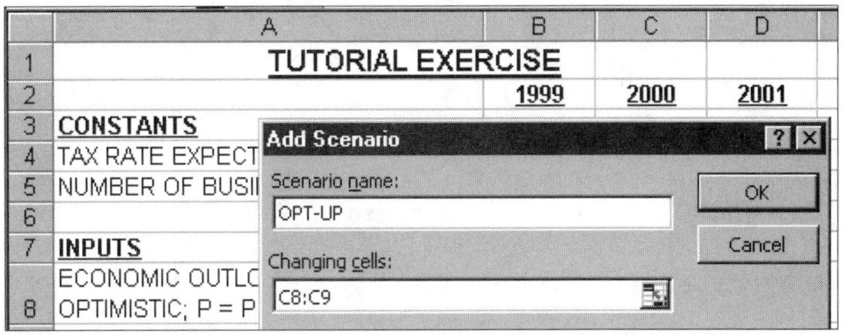

Fig. C-15

Now click OK. This moves you to the Scenario Values window. Here you indicate what the INPUT *values* would be for the scenario. (Note: The values in the cells *currently in* the spreadsheet will be displayed. They might—or might not—be correct for the scenario you are defining.) For the OPT-UP scenario, O and U would need to be entered. Enter those values if need be, then click OK to move on.

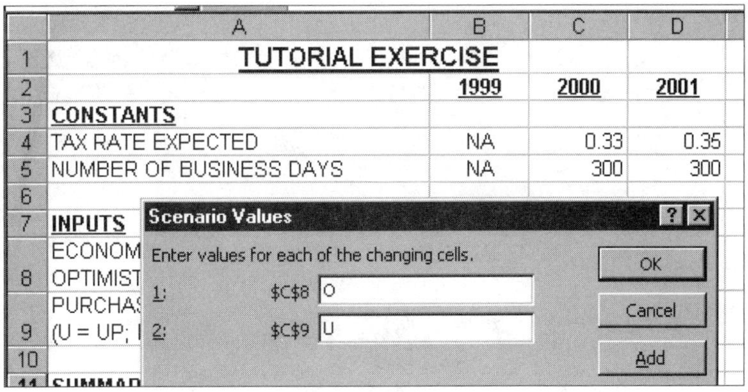

Fig. C-16

This takes you back to the Scenario Manager window. You are now able to enter the other three scenarios, following the same steps. Do that now! Enter the OPT-DOWN, PESS-UP, and PESS-DOWN scenarios. Then, you should see the names and the changing cells for the four scenarios have been entered:

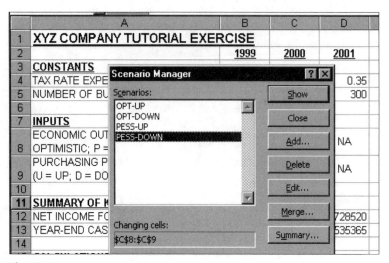

Fig. C-17

You are now able to create the summary sheet, which shows the results of running the four scenarios. Click the Summary button. You'll get the Scenario Summary window. You must tell Excel what the output cell addresses are—these will be the same for all four scenarios. (The output *values* change in those output cells as input values are changed, but the addresses of the output cells do not change.)

Assume that you are primarily interested in the results that have accrued at the end of the two-year period. These are your two-year 2001 SUMMARY OF KEY RESULTS cells for NET INCOME and YEAR-END CASH (D12 and D13). Type these addresses into the window's input area.

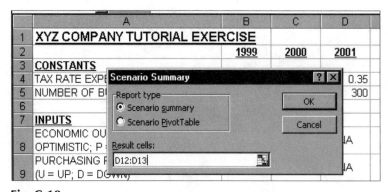

Fig. C-18

Then click OK. Excel runs each set of inputs and collects results as it goes. (You do not see this happening on the screen.) Then, Excel makes a *new* sheet, titled Scenario Summary (denoted by the sheet's lower tab) and takes you there:

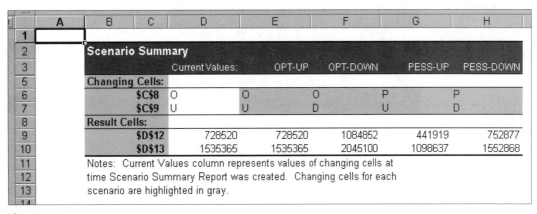

Fig. C-19

One annoying thing here is that the Current Values in the spreadsheet itself are given an output column. This duplicates one of the four defined scenarios. You should delete that extra column by (1) clicking on its column designator (here column D), and (2) clicking on Edit—Delete. (Do *not* select Edit—Delete *Sheet*!)

Another annoying thing is that Column A goes unused. You can click and delete it in the same way to move everything over to the left. This should make the columns of data easier to see on the screen, without scrolling. You can also edit cell values to make the results more clear. Enter words for the cell addresses. Use Alt—Enter to break long headings. Center values using the Format—Cells menu option. (See Review of Excel Basics in this tutorial.)

When you're done, your summary sheet should look something like this:

	A	B	C	D	E	F
1	Scenario Summary		OPTIMISTIC	OPTIMISTIC	PESSIMISTIC	PESSIMISTIC
2			UP	DOWN	UP	DOWN
4	Changing Cells:					
5	ECONOMY		O	O	P	P
6	PURCHASE PRICES		U	D	U	D
7	Result Cells:					
8	NET INCOME		728520	1084852	441919	752877
9	YEAR END CASH		1535365	2045100	1098637	1552868
10	Notes: Current Values column represents values of changing cells at					
11	time Scenario Summary Report was created. Changing cells for each					
12	scenario are highlighted in gray.					
13						

Fig. C-20

The way you read this is in columns. Column C shows the OPTIMISTIC-UP case. NET INCOME in that scenario is $728,520, and YEAR-END CASH is $1,535,365. Columns D, E, and F show the other scenario results.

Here is an important postscript to this exercise: DSS spreadsheets are used to guide decision making. This means that the spreadsheet's results must be interpreted in some way. Let's practice, in a simple way, with the results above. With the data here, what combination of year 2001 NET INCOME and CASH would be best? Clearly, O-D is the best result, right? Highest income, highest cash. What is the worst combination? P-U, right? Lowest income and lowest cash.

Results are not always this easy to interpret, but the method is the same. You have a complex situation that you cannot understand without software assistance. Build a model of the situation in the spreadsheet. Enter the inputs, collect the results. Interpret the results to guide decision making.

Summary Sheets

When you do the spreadsheet case studies, you'll need to manipulate Summary Sheets and their data.

1. Rerunning the Scenario Manager

    To rerun the Scenario Manager, merely click the Summary button and then the OK button. This makes another summary sheet. It does not overwrite a prior one.

2. Deleting an Unwanted Scenario Manager Summary Sheet

    With the sheet on the screen, select Edit—Delete Sheet. You will be asked if you really mean it. If so, click to remove it, or else cancel out.

3. Charting a Summary Sheet Data

    The summary sheet results are conveniently charted, using the Chart Wizard. The stumbling blocks are at the beginning, before the Wizard is invoked: How do you select the X and Y axis values? You must select the *Y axis* values first, then the X axis values. To select the Y axis values, merely highlight the block of data, in the normal click-and-drag way. To select the X axis values, first hold down the Ctrl key and then select the values by clicking and dragging. You will then see that both data ranges are highlighted. (Normally, selecting a data range *de*-selects a previously selected range. Holding the Ctrl key down tells Excel not to do that.) For Example: in the tutorial's summary sheet, C8 .. F9 would have been the Y range and C1 .. F2 would have been the X range. A nice double-bar chart could have been made for the 2001 cash and income values. Using the Chart Wizard, you could have then made this chart:

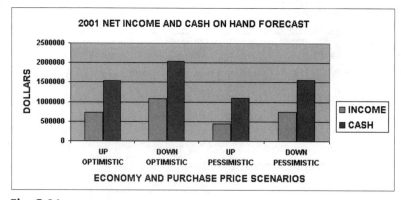

Fig. C-21

4. Copying Summary Sheet Data to the Clipboard

You may want to put the summary sheet data into the Clipboard to use later in a Word document. To do that, first highlight the data range. The best way to do that is to click on the cell at the lower right of the range (in the tutorial example above, cell F12), then click and drag to the upper-left cell (A1, previously). Then use Edit—Copy to put the graphic into the clipboard. Then: File—Save, File—Close, File—Exit Excel. (You may be asked whether you want to leave a graphic in the clipboard—you do want to.) Open up your Word document. Put your cursor where you want the upper-left part of the graphic to be. Edit—Paste.

❧ REVIEW OF EXCEL BASICS

If you're having difficulties, this review may help you do the spreadsheet cases in this book.

1. Formatting Cells

You may have noticed that some data in the tutorial spreadsheet was centered in the cells. The way to do that is to use the Format menu option. Highlight the cell range to format. Then: Format, Cells, Alignment, choose Center for both Horizontal and Vertical, then OK.

It is also possible to put a border around cells. This might be desirable highlighting for input section cells. Again, use Format: Format, Cells, Border, Outline, choose the outline Style you want, then OK.

2. Showing Excel Cell Formulas

Press the Ctrl key and the "back quote" key (`) at the same time. (The back quote is the quote that orients from Seattle to Miami—on most keyboards it is next to the exclamation point key and shares the key with the tilda diacritic mark.) To restore, press Ctrl and back quote again.

3. Understanding a Circular Reference

A formula has a circular reference if the *formula refers to the cell that the formula is in*. The formula cannot be evaluated because the value of the cell is not yet known, but the value in the cell cannot be known until the formula is evaluated. This is a circular reference. Excel will point out circular references, if any exist, when you Open a spreadsheet, and Excel will point them out as you insert them during development. Excel actually puts a circular marker in the cell or cells that have the offending formula. You *must* fix a circular reference. Your spreadsheet is not going anywhere if you have one.

4. Using the "And" Function and the "Or" Function in =IF Statements

An =IF() statement has this syntax:

=IF(test condition, result if test is True, result if test is False)

The test conditions in the tutorial's =IF statements tested only one cell's value. A test condition could test more than one cell's values.

Assume, for the sake of illustration, that year 2000's selling price per unit depended on the economy and the purchase price outlook. If the economic outlook is optimistic *and* the purchase price outlook is down, then the selling price will be 1.10 times the prior year's price. Assume that in all other cases, the selling price will be 1.03 times the prior year's price. The first test requires two things to be true *at the same time*: C8 = "O" *AND* C9 = "D." So, the AND() function would be needed. The code in cell C17 would be this:

=IF(AND(C8 = "O", C9 = "D"), 1.10 * B17, 1.03 * B17)

On the other hand, the test might be this: If the economic outlook is optimistic *or* the purchase price outlook is down, then the selling price will be 1.10 times the prior year's price. Assume that in all other cases, the selling price will be 1.03 times the prior year's price. The first test requires *only one of* two things to be true: C8 = "O" *OR* C9 = "D". So, the OR() function would be needed. The code in cell C17 would be:

=IF(OR(C8 = "O", C9 = "D"), 1.10 * B17, 1.03 * B17)

5. Using IF() Statements Inside IF() Statements

An =IF() statement has this syntax:

=IF(test condition, result if test is True, result if test is False)

In the examples shown so far, only two courses of action were possible, so only one test has been needed in the =IF() statement. Situations can be more complex, and this means that the "result if False" clause needs to show further testing.

Assume, for the sake of illustration, that year 2000 selling price per unit depended on the economy and the purchase price outlook. Logic: (1) If the economic outlook is optimistic *and* the purchase price outlook is down, then the selling price will be 1.10 times the prior year's price. (2) If the economic outlook is optimistic *and* the purchase price outlook is up, then the selling price will be 1.07 times the prior year's price. (3) In all other cases, the selling price will be 1.03 times the prior year's price. The code in cell C17 would be:

=IF(AND(C8 = "O", C9 = "D"), 1.10 * B17,

IF(AND(C8 = "O", C9 = "U"), 1.07 * B17, 1.03 * B17))

(The line is broken here, because the page is not wide enough, but in Excel the formula would not be typed into two lines) Note the second right parenthesis at the end. Note also that the embedded "IF" is not preceded by an equal sign.

6. Borrowings and Repayment of Debt in the Cases that Follow

To do some of the cases in this section, you must assume two things about a company's borrowings and repayments of debt. First, assume that the company wants to have a certain minimum cash level at the end of a year (and thus to start the next year). For borrowings, assume that a bank will provide a loan to reach the minimum cash level if year-end cash falls short of that level.

Here are some numerical examples to test your understanding. Assume "NCP" stands for "net cash position" and equals beginning-of-year cash plus net income for the year. NCP is the cash available at year end, before any borrowings or repayments. Compute the amount to borrow in the three examples. (The answers will be shown later in this section.)

Examples of Borrowing

Example	NCP	Minimum Cash Required	Amount to Borrow
1	50,000	10,000	?
2	8,000	10,000	?
3	−20,000	10,000	?

Fig. C-22

Second, assume that a company would use its excess cash at year end to pay off as much debt as possible, without going below the minimum-cash threshold.

In the following examples, compute excess cash (above the minimum), and then compute the amount to repay. (The answers will be shown later in this section.)

Examples of Repayment

Example	NCP	Minimum Cash Required	Beginning of Year Debt	Repay
1	12,000	10,000	4,000	?
2	12,000	10,000	10,000	?
3	20,000	10,000	10,000	?
4	20,000	10,000	0	?
5	60,000	10,000	40,000	?
6	−20,000	10,000	10,000	?

Fig. C–23

Your spreadsheet will need two bank financing sections beneath the income statement and cash-flow statement. The first section will calculate any needed borrowings or repayments at year end to compute year-end cash. The second section will calculate the amount of debt owed at the end of the year, after borrowings or repayments.

Continuing this tutorial's spreadsheet example, the first new section would look like this:

	A	B	C	D
30	NET CASH POSITION (NCP) BEFORE BORROWINGS AND REPAYMENTS OF DEBT (BEG CASH + NET INCOME)	NA	806845	1535365
31	ADD: BORROWINGS	NA		
32	LESS: REPAYMENTS	NA		
33	EQUALS: CASH AT THE END OF YEAR	10000		

Fig. C-24

The heading in cell A30 was previously END OF YEAR CASH ON HAND. But BORROWINGS increase cash and REPAYMENTS of debt decrease cash. So CASH AT THE END OF THE YEAR is now computed two rows down (in C33 for year 2000, for example). The value in row 30 must be a subtotal for the BEGINNING OF YEAR CASH plus the year's NET INCOME. That subtotal is called the NET CASH POSITION before BORROWINGS and REPAYMENTS (NCP). (Note: Previously, the formula in cell C22 for BEGINNING OF YEAR CASH was =B30. Now that formula would be =B33.)

The second new section looks like this:

	A	B	C	D
35	**DEBT OWED**			
36	OWED AT BEGINNING OF YEAR	NA		
37	ADD: BORROWINGS	NA		
38	LESS: REPAYMENTS	NA		
39	EQUALS: DEBT OWED AT END OF YEAR	15000		
40				

Fig. C–25

This section just computes DEBT OWED AT THE END OF THE YEAR. Previously the assumption was that $15,000 was owed at the end of 1999. Debt owed at the end of a year would be the DEBT OWED AT THE BEGINNING OF THE YEAR, plus any new BORROWINGS (which increase debt owed), less any REPAYMENTS of debt (which reduce it). So the formula in cell C39 would be this:

=C36 + C37 - C38.

Assume that the amounts for BORROWINGS and REPAYMENTS are calculated in the first new section. Thus, the formula in cell C37 would be this: =C31. The formula in cell C38 would be this: =C32. (The formula in cell C36 for BEGINNING OF YEAR DEBT will also be an echo formula. *Can you see what it would be*? It's an exercise for you to complete.)

Now that you have seen how the borrowings and repayments data is shown, the logic of the borrowings and repayments formulas can be discussed.

Calculation of Borrowings

The logic of this in English is:

> If(cash on hand before financing transactions is greater than the
>
> minimum cash required, then borrowings are not needed,
>
> otherwise borrow enough to get to the minimum)

Or (a little more precisely):

> If(NCP is greater than the minimum cash required,
>
> then borrowings = 0, otherwise,
>
> borrow enough to get to the minimum)

Suppose that the desired minimum cash at year-end is $10,000, and that value is a constant in cell C6. Our formula (getting closer to Excel) would be this:

IF(NCP > MIN, 0, otherwise borrow enough to get to the minimum)

You have cell addresses that stand for NCP and Minimum Cash. Substitute those cell addresses for "NCP" and "Minimum Cash". The harder logic is the "otherwise" clause. At this point, you should look ahead to the borrowings answers at the end of this section. In example two, $2,000 had to be borrowed. *Which cell was subtracted from which other cell to calculate the amount to borrow?* Substitute cell addresses in the Excel formula below for the year 2000 borrowings formula in cell C31:

$$=IF(\qquad > \qquad , 0 , \qquad - \qquad)$$

Calculation of REPAYMENTS

The logic of this in English is:

> IF(beginning of year debt = 0, repay zero because there is nothing owed, but
>> IF(NCP is less than the min, repay zero, because you must borrow, but
>>> IF(extra cash equals or exceeds the debt, repay the whole debt,
>>>> ELSE (to stay above the min, repay only the extra cash)))

Look at the following formula. In cell C32, substitute cell addresses for concepts to complete the formula for year 2000 repayments. (Clauses are on different lines because of page width limitations.)

$$=IF(\qquad = 0, 0,$$
$$IF(\qquad < \qquad , 0,$$
$$IF((\qquad - \qquad) > \qquad , \qquad ,$$
$$(\qquad - \qquad))))$$

Answers, Examples of Borrowing

Example	NCP	Minimum Cash Required	Borrow	Comments
1	50,000	10,000	Zero	NCP > Min.
2	8,000	10,000	2,000	Need 2,000 to get to Min. 10,000 – 8,000.
3	–20,000	10,000	30,000	Need 30,000 to get to Min. 10000 - (-20,000).

Fig. C–26

Answers, Examples of Repayment

Example	NCP	Minimum Cash Required	Beginning of Year Debt	Repay	Ending Cash
1	12,000	10,000	4,000	2,000	10,000
2	12,000	10,000	10,000	2,000	10,000
3	20,000	10,000	10,000	10,000	10,000
4	20,000	10,000	0	0	20,000
5	60,000	10,000	40,000	40,000	20,000
6	–20,000	10,000	10,000	NA	NA

Fig. C–27

In Examples 1 and 2, only $2,000 is available for debt repayment (12,000 – 10,000) to avoid going below the minimum cash.

In Example 3, cash available for repayments is $10,000 (20000 - 10000) so all beginning debt can be repaid, leaving the minimum cash.

In Example 4, there is no debt owed, so no debt need be repaid.

In Example 5, cash available for repayments is $50,000 (60,000 – 10,000) so all beginning debt can be repaid, leaving more than the minimum cash.

In Example 6, no cash is available for repayments. The company must borrow.

7. Saving Files After Using Microsoft Excel

Save you work at the end of a session in this three-step procedure: (1) Save the file. Presumably you want to save to your diskette, so do not forget the A: in the file name. (2) Use File — Close to tell Windows to close the file. If saving to your diskette, make sure it is in Drive A: when you close. If you violate this rule, you may lose your work. (3) Exit from Windows by selecting File — Exit. In theory, you may exit from Windows after you have saved a file (short-cutting the File — Close step), but that is not a recommended shortcut.

Preliminary Case
The Meat and Potatoes
Restaurant Local Decision

DECISION SUPPORT USING EXCEL

➤ PREVIEW

You and your former college roommate are planning to open a new restaurant called Meat and Potatoes. You need to choose a city for its location. In this case, you will use Excel to make a cash-flow forecast, which will help you make your decision.

➤ PREPARATION

- Review spreadsheet concepts discussed in class and/or in your text.
- Complete any exercises your instructor assigns.
- Complete any part of Tutorial C your instructor assigns, or refer to the tutorial as necessary.
- Review file-saving procedures for Windows programs. These are discussed in Tutorial C.

➤ BACKGROUND

You want to open your restaurant in a city that anticipates population growth. You have identified three possible cities, code-named "A," "B," and "C." Each city had a population of about 120,000 people in 1999; however, each city has a different growth rate.

Cooks and waiters will be hired locally. Because each city has different labor-pool characteristics, labor and salary costs are expected to increase at different rates in each city.

Assume you have established the restaurant at the end of 1999. Your restaurant will begin actual operations in the year 2000. To choose a location, you must forecast net income and cash flow for 2000–2002. Because most restaurants take time to become popular, you believe 2002 will be the key year for decision making. For that year, you want to know projected net income, cash on hand at year end, and debt owed at year end—given values for one key variable: the city in which the restaurant is located!

➤ ASSIGNMENT: CREATING A SPREADSHEET FOR DECISION SUPPORT

In this two-part assignment, you will produce a spreadsheet that models the business decision and then write a memorandum that provides your results.

In *Assignment A*, you will create the spreadsheet model of the decision. The model is an income statement and cash flow forecast for your restaurant for 2000 to 2002. Your spreadsheet should have sections for Constants, Inputs, Summary of Key Results, Calculations, Income Statement and Cash Flow, and Debt Owed. You are shown how each section should be set up before you enter cell formulas.

In *Assignment B*, you will use the model to develop information so that you can decide where to locate the restaurant. You will then document the decision in a memorandum.

Assignment A: Creating the Spreadsheet

A discussion of each spreadsheet section follows. The discussion is about (1) how each section should be set up, and (2) the logic of the formulas in the section's cells. *When you type in the spreadsheet skeleton, follow the order given in this section.*

Constants You should have these constants:

A	B	C	D	E
THE RESTAURANT LOCATION PROBLEM				
CONSTANTS	**1999**	**2000**	**2001**	**2002**
TAX RATE	NA	0.3	0.31	0.32
FIXED COSTS IN YEAR	NA	12000	13000	14000
INTEREST RATE FOR YEAR	NA	0.1	0.1	0.1
MIN CASH NEEDED AT YEAR END	NA	15000	15000	15000
AVG SELLING PRICE OF A MEAL	NA	13	14	15
AVG MEAL INGREDIENTS COST	NA	4	5	6
NUMBER OF WORKERS (COOKS, WAITERS)	NA	4	4	4

Fig. 11-1

- Income tax rates are expected to increase somewhat each year.
- The restaurant's fixed costs will be $12,000 in year 2000 in all three cities, but costs are expected to increase for years 2001 and 2002.

- A 10% interest rate is expected in all forecast years. This rate is applied to debt owed at the *beginning* of the year to compute interest expense for the year.
- The target minimum amount of cash to have on hand at the end of each year (and thus to start the next year) is $15,000. Your roommate's uncle is willing to lend enough money to reach the minimum if net income in a year is insufficient. (In fact, money is already owed to him for financing the start-up—for working capital, the purchase of equipment, and so on. At the end of 1999, $15,000 will be on hand, and you expect to owe the uncle $50,000.)
- The *average* selling price of a meal in all cities is expected to be $13 in 2000, increasing in following years.
- The average meal ingredient cost in all cities is expected to be $4 in 2000, increasing in the following years.
- You expect to have a total of 4 cooks and waiters employed in each year.

Inputs You should have this input:

A	B	C	D	E
INPUTS	1999	2000	2001	2002
LOCATION (A = CITY A; B = CITY B;C = CITY C)	NA		NA	NA

Fig. 11-2

The key input variable is the location. Entering the letter "A" in the input cell means that city A will be chosen. Entering "B" means that city B will be chosen, and entering "C" means that city C will be chosen. The value that is input applies to each year in the three-year forecast period. (Enter nothing in cells that contain "NA.")

Summary of Results You should show these results:

A	B	C	D	E
SUMMARY OF KEY RESULTS	1999	2000	2001	2002
CASH ON HAND AT YEAR END	NA			
DEBT OWED AT YEAR END	NA			
NET INCOME FOR YEAR	NA			

Fig. 11-3

For each year, your spreadsheet should show (1) cash on hand, (2) debt owed to the uncle, and (3) net income for the year. These amounts are computed in the spreadsheet body and echoed to this section.

Calculations You should calculate the following intermediate results, based on the expected yearly inflation rate and on the expected population growth. The calculated amounts are then used in the Net Income and Cash Flow forecast. The formulas in the calculations cells may need to use the input value. Use absolute addressing when called for. Calculated amounts should have no decimals (no pennies).

A	B	C	D	E
CALCULATIONS	1999	2000	2001	2002
AVG YEARLY SALARY OF WORKERS	30000			
POPULATION IN THE AREA	120000			
NUMBER OF MEALS SERVED IN THE YEAR	NA			

Fig. 11-4

- An employee's average annual salary in each city is based on that city's expected inflation rate. *Explanatory example*: Assume that in 1999, a worker will earn $30,000 in each city, and that the average annual salary will increase in each city at its rate of inflation. If inflation were expected to be 5% (.05), then the 2000 average salary would be (30,000 + (.05 * 30,000)) = $31,500; the average salary in 2001 would be (31,500 + (.05 * 31,500)) = $33,075, and so on.

  This table shows the expected inflation rate in each city for years 2000–2002:

Yearly Inflation Rate Expected in Each City in Each Year

City	Inflation Expected in 2000, 2001, and 2002
A	.01
B	.04
C	.06

Fig. 11-5

- The number of meals sold is a function of the number of people living in a city. *Explanatory example*: Assume that at the end of 1999, the population in each city will be 120,000. However, a different population growth rate is expected in each city, for 2000, 2001, and 2002. If yearly population growth is expected to be 5% (.05) in a city, then the population in 2000 would be (120,000 + (.05 * 120,000)) = 126,000. The population in 2001 would be (126,000 + (.05 * 126,000)) = 132,300, and so on for 2002.

  This table shows population growth expected in each city for years 2000–2002:

Population Growth Rate Expected in a City in Each Year

City	Growth Rate Expected in Years 2000, 2001, and 2002
A	.02
B	.03
C	.04

Fig. 11-6

- The number of restaurant meals served in a year is expected to be 13% (.13) of a city's population. *Explanatory example*: If 100,000 people were living in the city, the number of meals served in the year would be 13,000. The 13% factor will apply in all cities in all three forecast years.

Income Statement and Cash Flow The net income and cash flow forecast starts with the cash on hand at the beginning of the year. This is followed by the income statement, and concludes with the calculation of cash on hand and debt position at the end of the year. Your results in this section should have no pennies. Some of the line items are discussed next.

A	B	C	D	E
INCOME STATEMENT AND CASH FLOW STATEMENT	1999	2000	2001	2002
CASH AT BEGINNING OF YEAR	NA			
REVENUE FROM SELLING MEALS	NA			
MEAL INGREDIENT COSTS	NA			
LABOR COSTS (COOKS, WAITERS)	NA			
FIXED COSTS	NA			
TOTAL OF ALL COSTS	NA			
PRE-INTEREST EXPENSE MARGIN	NA			
INTEREST EXPENSE	NA			
PRE-TAX MARGIN	NA			
TAX EXPENSE	NA			
NET INCOME	NA			

Fig. 11-7

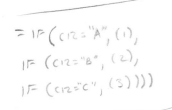

- Note that cash at the beginning of a year is the cash at the end of the *prior* year.
- Total costs are from the cost of ingredients, salaries of workers, and the fixed costs.
- Interest expense is based on the year's interest rate and the amount of debt owed to the uncle at the *start* of the year.
- Income tax expense is zero if pre-tax profit margin is zero or less. Otherwise, apply the rate for the year to the pre-tax profit margin.

Line items for the year-end cash calculation are discussed next.

A	B	C	D	E
NET CASH POSITION (NCP) BEFORE BORROWINGS AND REPAYMENTS OF DEBT (BEG CASH + NET INCOME)	NA			
ADD: BORROWINGS	NA			
LESS: REPAYMENTS (NONE TILL 2005)	NA			
EQUALS: CASH AT END OF YEAR	15000			

Fig. 11-8

- You will have $15,000 cash at the end of 1999.
- The Net Cash Position (NCP) at the end of a year equals the cash at the beginning of a year, plus the year's net income. (Assume there are no receivables or payables).
- Your roommate's uncle will lend enough money at the end of a year to get to your minimum cash target. If the NCP is less than the minimum cash at the end of a year, you must borrow.
- Repayments of debt principal owed to the uncle do not start until 2005. Thus, debt principal repayments in the next three years are zero. So, your "formula" for repayments is just the number 0 (i.e., use no =IF formula for repayments).

Debt Owed The spreadsheet body ends with a calculation of debt owed at year end.

A	B	C	D	E
DEBT OWED	**1999**	**2000**	**2001**	**2002**
OWED AT BEGINNING OF YEAR	NA			
ADD: BORROWINGS	NA			
LESS: REPAYMENTS (NONE TILL 2005)	NA			
EQUALS: DEBT OWED AT END OF YEAR	50000			

Fig. 11-9

- The sum of $50,000 is owed to the uncle at the end of 1999.
- Cash owed at the beginning of a year equals cash owed at the end of the prior year.
- Amounts borrowed and repaid have been calculated and can be echoed to this section.
- The amount owed at the end of a year equals what was owed at the start of the year, plus any borrowings for the year, less the repayments (which are zero).

Assignment B: Using the Spreadsheet for Decision Support

You will now complete the case by (1) using the spreadsheet to gather the data you need to make the location decision and (2) documenting your recommendation in a memorandum.

Use the Spreadsheet to Gather Data

You have built the spreadsheet to model the restaurant location decision. Now run "what if" scenarios with the input value (A, B, C). The way you do this depends on whether or not your instructor has told you to use the Scenario Manager.

- If your instructor told you *not* to use the Scenario Manager, you must now manually enter the input values. Note the results for each on a separate sheet of paper. (They will show in the Summary of Key Results section as you work.)
- If your instructor told you to use the Scenario Manager, perform the procedures set forth in Tutorial C. Record the three scenarios possible (A, B, C). The changing cell is the restaurant location input cell. Output cells are for year 2002 (only) net income, cash, and debt.
- If you are using the Scenario Manager, copy the results from the Summary page into the Clipboard before ending your work with the spreadsheet. (Tutorial C explains this procedure.) The graphic will then be available when you write your memorandum.
- In either case, when you are done gathering data, print the entire workbook. Then save the .xls file, close the file (with the diskette in drive A:), and finally exit from Excel.

Document Your Recommendation in a Memorandum

Write a short memo to the uncle, summarizing the results.

- Your memorandum should have a proper heading (DATE/ TO/ FROM/ SUBJECT). You may wish to use a Word memo template (File — New, click Memos, choose Contemporary Memo).

- In the first paragraph, state your preferred location, based on the best combination of 2002 net income, debt, and cash. Provide no background—assume the uncle expects your memo.
- Support your recommendation graphically in one of two ways: (1) If you're using the Scenario Manager, include a copy of the Summary Sheet results. (2) Otherwise, summarize results in a table. (In MS Word, select the Table menu option. Enter the number of rows and columns. Select Autoformat. Choose the format—Grid 1 is a good choice; that is what is shown here.) Your table should look like this:

Projected 2002 Financial Results

City	Cash at Year End	Debt at Year End	Net Income in Year
A			
B			
C			

Fig. 11-10

- Run the spell checker. Print the memorandum. Then save the file, close it (with the diskette in drive A:), and exit from the word processor.

☛ DELIVERABLES

1. Spreadsheet printouts
2. Memorandum
3. Diskette, which should have your memo file and your Excel file.

Staple the printouts together, with the memo on top. Handwrite your instructor a note, stating the name of the model's .xls file.

12
CASE

The JED Manufacturing Co. Outsourcing Decision

DECISION SUPPORT USING EXCEL

➤ PREVIEW

JED Manufacturing Company has been profitable and its financial condition is good; however, management is considering outsourcing some administrative tasks. In this case, you will use Excel to make a net income and cash-flow forecast, which will help JED management consider the merits of different outsourcing alternatives. You will document your recommendations in a memorandum.

➤ PREPARATION

- Review spreadsheet concepts discussed in class and/or in your text.
- Complete any exercises your instructor assigns.
- Complete any part of Tutorial C your instructor assigns.
- Review file-saving procedures for Windows programs. These are discussed in Tutorial C.

⤷ BACKGROUND

In-The-Black Consulting Company has offered to take over various accounting and clerical jobs for JED Manufacturing Company. If the consulting company were hired, JED would cut the number of its employees from 30 to 15, which would reduce JED's salary and employee benefits expenses. JED Manufacturing would pay In-The-Black Consulting a fee for their services. If the outsourcing fee is less than the laid-off workers' salaries and benefits, JED's profit will increase.

In-The-Black Consulting can be paid in one of two ways: Under the "flat fee" plan, JED would pay a fixed dollar amount per year to In-The-Black. Under the "percent of sales" plan, JED would pay In-The-Black a certain percentage of JED's revenue (sales) each year. Of course, if JED does not outsource, the outsourcing fee is zero.

Every year JED makes a net income and cash-flow forecast for the coming four years. Assume 1999 is now coming to an end. Management needs a forecast for the years 2000–2003. The forecast must be based on what has happened in 1999, on how good the economy may be in the four-year period, and on the possible outsourcing options. You must make a DSS in Excel that lets management answer this question: "Given possible economic and outsourcing scenarios, what will be our net income in each of those years, and what will cash on hand and bank debt be at the end of each of those years?"

In your DSS, the inputs are for (1) two states of the economy in the four-year period: Optimistic or Pessimistic, and (2) the outsourcing method used: None, Flat Fee, or Percentage of Sales. Your DSS must account for the effects of the input values on variables such as number of employees, number of units sold, selling price per unit, cost of each unit sold, interest rate paid on bank debt, and salary and benefits costs. Your model lets JED's owners play "what-if" with the inputs, see the results, then decide what to do.

⤷ ASSIGNMENT: CREATING A SPREADSHEET FOR DECISION SUPPORT

In this two-part assignment, you will produce a spreadsheet that models a business decision and then a memorandum that explains your recommendation for action.

In *Assignment A*, you will create the spreadsheet model of the outsourcing decision. The model is an income statement and cash-flow forecast for the years 2000 to 2003. Your spreadsheet should have sections for Constants, Inputs, Summary of Key Results, Calculations, Income Statement and Cash Flow, and Debt Owed. You are shown how each section should be set up before you enter cell formulas.

In *Assignment B*, you will use the model to develop information so you can recommend an outsourcing strategy. You will then document your recommendation in a memorandum.

Assignment A: Creating the Spreadsheet

A discussion of each spreadsheet section follows. The discussion is about (1) how each section should be set up, and (2) the logic of the formulas in the section's cells. *When you type in the spreadsheet skeleton, follow the order given in this section.*

Constants You should have these constants:

A	B	C	D	E	F
OUTSOURCING DECISION					
	1999	**2000**	**2001**	**2002**	**2003**
CONSTANTS					
EMPLOYEE BASE SALARY	NA	40000	41000	42000	43000
NUMBER OF BUSINESS DAYS	NA	250	250	250	250
OUTSOURCE PRICE -- % OF SALES	NA	0.28	0.28	0.28	0.28
OUTSOURCE PRICE -- FLAT FEE	NA	800000	840000	882000	926100
TAX RATE EXPECTED	NA	0.3	0.31	0.32	0.33
MIN CASH RQRD AT START OF YEAR	NA	10000	10000	10000	10000
BENEFITS COST -- % OF SALARY	NA	0.5	0.52	0.53	0.54

Fig. 12-1

- The employee base salary is the average salary paid. This increases each year.
- Each year has 250 business days.
- In-The-Black's "flat fee" is $800,000 in 2000 and goes up each year. The flat fees for 2000–2003 are shown. The alternate "percentage of sales" fee is 28% of revenue (sales) each year.
- The tax rate on pre-tax profits is expected to go up each year.
- JED's policy is to have at least $10,000 in cash on hand at the end of each year. JED's banker is willing to lend whatever is needed at the end of a year in order to begin the next year with $10,000.
- The average cost of employee benefits will be 50% of base salary in 2000. The percentage goes up each year after that.

Inputs You should have these inputs:

A	B	C	D	E	F
INPUTS	**1999**	**2000**	**2001**	**2002**	**2003**
ECONOMIC OUTLOOK (O = OPTIMISTIC; P = PESSIMISTIC)	NA			NA	NA	NA
OUTSOURCE METHOD (N = NONE; F = FLAT FEE; P = PERCENT OF SALES)	NA			NA	NA	NA

Fig. 12-2

- The user enters **O** for an optimistic four-year outlook or **P** for a pessimistic one. Assume the value applies to all four years.
- The user enters **N** for "no outsourcing," **F** for outsourcing paid for by the "flat fee" method, and **P** for outsourcing paid for by the "percentage of sales" method.
- In-The-Black requires that a method apply to all four years. Thus, JED could not use percentage of sales for the first two years and flat fee for the last two years.

Summary of Key Results You should show these results:

A	B	C	D	E	F
SUMMARY OF KEY RESULTS	**1999**	**2000**	**2001**	**2002**	**2003**
NET INCOME FOR YEAR	NA				
END OF YEAR CASH ON HAND	NA				
OWED TO BANK AT END OF YEAR	NA				

Fig. 12-3

For 2000 to 2003, show net income for the year, cash on hand at year end, and debt owed at year end. These amounts are computed in the spreadsheet body and echoed to this section.

Calculations You should calculate these intermediate results, which are then used in the Income Statement and Cash Flow Statement. Calculations are based on the values of the inputs, and possibly based on 1999 values.

A	B	C	D	E	F
CALCULATIONS	**1999**	**2000**	**2001**	**2002**	**2003**
OUTSOURCING COST	NA				
NUMBER OF UNITS SOLD/DAY	1500				
NUMBER OF EMPLOYEES	30				
SELLING PRICE PER UNIT	7.9				
COST OF GOODS SOLD PER UNIT	3				
INTEREST RATE FOR YEAR	NA				
COST OF SALARIES	NA				
NUMBER OF UNITS SOLD IN YEAR	NA				

Fig. 12-4

- Outsourcing Cost is based on the outsourcing input. The cost is zero if no outsourcing is chosen. The cost is equal to the year's constant value if "flat fee" is chosen. The cost is equal to total revenue (sales) times the year's percentage if the "percentage of sales" is chosen. In the percentage of sales case, use the INT function in your formula to get rid of pennies.

- If an Optimistic economy exists, number of units sold per day will rise by 10% each year in the four-year period. For example, 2000's units would be 110% of 1999's units, 2001's would be 110% of 2000's, and so on. Otherwise, units sold per day will rise only 1% each year. Use the INT function to avoid partial units.

- If no outsourcing is used, the number of salaried employees will increase by 1 per year. (For example, in 2000 there will be 31, in 2001 there will be 32, etc.) With either form of outsourcing, JED will have 15 salaried employees in each of the four years.

- If an Optimistic economy exists, selling price per unit will rise by 6% a year each year in the four-year period. Otherwise, selling price will rise only 1% a year each year. Do *not* use the INT function in your formula—retain the pennies in the price.

- If an Optimistic economy exists, cost of goods sold per unit will rise by 2% each year in the four-year period; otherwise, the cost will rise 1% each year. Do *not* use the INT function.

- Interest must be paid on debt owed to the bank. If an Optimistic economy exists, expect an interest rate of 6% (.06); otherwise, expect an interest rate of 5%. This rule applies in all four years.

- Cost of salaries equals the number of JED employees multiplied by the average salary for an employee. The former value has been calculated. The latter value is a constant. Use the INT function in your formula.
- Number of units sold for the year is a function of the units sold per day and the number of business days in the year. The former value has been calculated. The latter value is a constant.

Income Statement and Cash Flow The net income and cash-flow forecast starts with the cash on hand at the beginning of the year. This is followed by the income statement and concludes with the calculation of the cash on hand at year end. Your results in this section should have no pennies. Some of the line items are discussed next.

A	B	C	D	E	F
INCOME STATEMENT AND CASH FLOW STATEMENT	1999	2000	2001	2002	2003
BEGINNING OF YEAR CASH ON HAND	NA				
REVENUE (SALES)	NA				
COSTS AND EXPENSES:	NA				
COST OF GOODS SOLD	NA				
SALARIES AND OUTSOURCING	NA				
COST OF BENEFITS	NA				
TOTAL COSTS AND EXPENSES	NA				
PRE-INTEREST EXPENSE MARGIN	NA				
INTEREST EXPENSE	NA				
PRE-TAX PROFIT MARGIN	NA				
TAX EXPENSE	NA				
NET INCOME	NA				

Fig. 12-5

- Note that the cash at the beginning of a year is the cash at the end of the *prior* year.
- The cost of benefits is a function of salaries and the benefits percentage prevailing in the year.
- Interest expense equals the rate for the year times the amount of debt owed to the bank at the *beginning* of the year.
- Tax expense is zero if pre-tax profit margin is zero or negative; otherwise, apply the rate for the year to the pre-tax profit margin.

Line items for the year-end cash calculation are discussed next.

A	B	C	D	E	F
NET CASH POSITION (NCP) BEFORE BORROWINGS AND REPAYMENTS OF DEBT(BEG CASH + NET INCOME)	NA				
ADD: BORROWINGS FROM BANK	NA				
LESS: REPAYMENTS TO BANK	NA				
EQUALS: END OF YEAR CASH ON HAND	10000				

Fig. 12-6

- The 1999 values are mostly NA, except $10,000 cash at year end, the minimum cash.

- The net cash position (NCP) at the end of a year equals the cash at the beginning of a year, plus the year's net income. (Assume there are no receivables or payables.)

- JED's banker will lend JED enough money at the end of a year to get to the minimum cash. If the NCP is less than the minimum, then JED must borrow enough to reach the minimum.

- If the NCP is more than the minimum cash at the end of a year and there is outstanding debt, then some or all of it should be repaid (but not to take JED below its minimum cash).

- Cash at the end of the year equals the NCP, plus any borrowings, less any repayments.

Debt Owed The spreadsheet body ends with a calculation of debt owed at year end.

A	B	C	D	E	F
	1999	2000	2001	2002	2003
DEBT OWED					
OWED TO BANK AT BEGINNING OF YEAR	NA				
ADD: BORROWINGS FROM BANK	NA				
LESS: REPAYMENTS TO BANK	NA				
EQUALS: OWED TO BANK AT END OF YEAR	0				

Fig. 12-7

- 1999 values are mostly NA, except that zero debt was owed at year end.

- Cash owed to the bank at the beginning of a year equals cash owed to the bank at the end of the prior year.

- Amounts borrowed and repaid have been calculated and can be echoed to this section.

- The amount owed at the end of a year equals the amount owed at the beginning of a year, plus any borrowings, and less any repayments.

Assignment B: Use the Spreadsheet for Decision Support

You will now complete the case by (1) using the spreadsheet to gather the data you need to make the outsourcing decision and (2) documenting recommendations in a memorandum.

Use the Spreadsheet to Gather Data

You have built the spreadsheet to model the outsourcing decision. Now run "what if" scenarios with the possible Economy-Outsourcing input values (O-N, O-F, O-P, P-N, P-F, P-P). The way you do this depends on whether your instructor has told you to use the Scenario Manager.

- If your instructor has told you not to use the Scenario Manager, you must now manually enter the input value combinations. Note the results for each on a sheet of paper. (They will show in the Summary of Key Results section as you work.)

- If your instructor told you to use the Scenario Manager, perform the procedures set forth in Tutorial C. Record the six scenarios possible (O-N, O-F, O-P, P-N, P-F, P-P). The changing cells are the two cells used to input the Economy and the Outsourcing values. Output cells are 2003 values *only*—2003 net income, cash at year end 2003, and debt at year end 2003.

- If you're using the Scenario Manager, copy the results from the Summary page into the Clipboard before ending your work. (Tutorial C refers to this procedure.) The graphic will then be available when you write your memorandum.

- In either case, when you are done gathering data, print the entire workbook. Then save the .xls file, close it (with the diskette in drive A:), and finally exit from Excel.

Document Your Recommendation in a Memorandum

Write a brief memo to JED's Chief Information Officer (CIO). The CIO needs to know the answers to these questions: (1) Given an Optimistic economy, which outsourcing scenario gives the best net income, year-end cash, and year-end debt in 2003? (2) Given a Pessimistic economy, which outsourcing scenario gives the best net income, year-end cash, and year-end debt in 2003?

- Your memorandum should have a proper heading (DATE/ TO/ FROM/ SUBJECT). You may wish to use a Word memo template (File — New, click Memos, choose Contemporary Memo).

- In the first paragraph, recommend what JED should do both in an Optimistic economy and a Pessimistic economy. Do this by answering the CIO's questions. Provide no background—the CIO understands the problem and expects your analysis.

- Support your statements graphically in one of two ways: (1) If you used the Scenario Manager to gather data, include a copy of the Summary Sheet results. Copy this from the Clipboard. (2) Otherwise, make two summary tables, one for each scenario, after the first paragraph. (To make a table In MS Word, select the Table menu option. Enter the number of rows and columns. Select Autoformat. Choose the format— Grid1 is a good choice; that is what is shown here). Your tables should look like this:

Projected 2003 Financial Results—Optimistic Economic Scenario

	Cash at Year End	Debt at Year End	Cash at Year End
No Outsourcing			
Flat Fee			
Percent of Sales			

Fig. 12-8

Projected 2003 Financial Results—Pessimistic Economic Scenario

	Cash at Year End	Debt at Year End	Cash at Year End
No Outsourcing			
Flat Fee			
Percent of Sales			

Fig. 12-9

ᐅ DELIVERABLES

1. Memorandum
2. Spreadsheet printouts
3. Diskette, which should have your memo file and your Excel file.

Staple the printouts together, with the memo on top. Handwrite your instructor a note, stating the name of the model's .xls file.

The TUV Bond Fund Investment Policy Decision

DECISION SUPPORT USING EXCEL

➤ PREVIEW

TUV Investment Company manages a family of mutual funds. TUV recently started a new fund called the Bond Fund. The Bond Fund's management needs to know whether they should choose high-risk or low-risk investments—and how their choice might be affected by a changing economy. They've asked for your help. In this case, you'll use Excel to give decision support to TUV management for that decision.

➤ PREPARATION

- Review spreadsheet concepts discussed in class and/or in your text.
- Complete any exercises your instructor assigns.
- Complete any part of Tutorial C your instructor assigns.
- Review file-saving procedures for Windows programs. These are discussed in Tutorial C.

To help you understand their operation, Fund managers have told you about their history, their current operation, and their goals.

History

In late 1999, Fund managers started the Fund by borrowing money from their bank and selling shares in the Fund. The managers invested in safe securities, and 1999 net income was $6,000,000. The Fund had invested $100,000,000, so the return on the beginning investment was 6%. The initial $100,000,000 was financed by $10,000,000 owed to the bank and $90,000,000 from Fund shareholders. At the end of 1999, the Fund investment level was $106,000,000 (the original investment plus the 6 million net income, which was reinvested in the fund by year end).

Current Operation

The new Bond Fund invests only in securities that pay interest; common stocks will not be purchased by the fund.

Bond Fund managers pay Fund expenses (including their own salaries) by charging the fund an administration fee. Fund managers charge the Fund 1% of total dollars invested, which is a typical charge in the mutual fund industry. That charge is an expense to the Fund. Other Fund expenses include taxes and losses when bond issuers default, because of insolvency or bankruptcy.

Bond Fund managers *gain* money to invest in bonds in three ways:

- The Fund reinvests its net income in new securities.

- Investors send in money for shares of the Bond Fund. This is called the "inflow factor."

- Bond Fund managers borrow money if total dollars invested at the end of a year fall below $100,000,000.

The Bond Fund's invested dollars are *reduced* in two ways:

- Bond Fund investors cash out their shares. Fund managers must liquidate some Fund investments to pay these investors. This is called the "liquidation factor."

- A bond issuer defaults, announcing it is not going to repay its debt. This means that the now-worthless investment must be written off as an expense in the Fund income statement.

The Future

The Bond Fund managers must determine which kind of investment policy to adopt for the next four years. They might adopt a "high risk" policy or a lower-risk "safe" policy.

High risk and high reward go hand-in-hand. Companies in high-risk industries must offer high interest rates on bonds they issue to attract investors (such as TUV), who know the chance of default is greater with high-risk companies. By contrast, companies in low-risk industries can offer lower rates on their debt. The lowest risk is on U.S. Government securities, because the U.S. Government can't default on its bonds. The next higher level of risk is on bonds issued by blue-chip corporations, followed by the bonds of solid companies and stable states and municipalities.

Another factor affecting interest rates is the general state of the economy. In a good economy, companies compete for capital, so rates offered to investors go up. In a recession economy, the reverse happens: rates go down. In a good economy defaults are less likely. In a recession economy, companies (and governments) have trouble making ends meet, and defaults increase.

Your Decision Analysis

Whatever course of action TUV's Bond Fund management chooses, they must maintain it for the next four years because the Fund's advertising will be keyed to their investment policy. You must make a DSS in Excel that lets management answer this question: "Given an estimate of the economy and given the two possible investment policies, what will Fund net income and year-end cash be for 2000, 2001, 2002, and 2003?"

In your DSS, the inputs are for (1) three states of the economy in the four-year period: Good, Neutral, and Recession, and (2) two possible investment strategies, High Risk and Safe Risk. Your DSS must account for the effects of the input values on these variables: average investment interest income, cash inflow rates, default rates, and the interest rate paid to the Fund's banker on any debt. Your DSS lets management play what-if with the inputs, see the results, then decide which investment policy to use.

❧ ASSIGNMENT: CREATING A SPREADSHEET FOR DECISION SUPPORT

In this two-part assignment, you will produce a spreadsheet that models the business decision and then write a memorandum that provides your results.

In *Assignment A*, you will create the spreadsheet model of the decision. The model is an income statement and cash-invested forecast for the years 2000 to 2003. Your spreadsheet should have sections for Constants, Inputs, Summary of Key Results, Calculations, Income Statement and Cash Flow Statement, and Debt Owed. You are shown how each section should be set up before you enter cell formulas.

In *Assignment B*, you will use the model to develop your spreadsheet. The spreadsheet should have a summary of the six scenarios possible in this decision (3 economy values * 2 investment policy values). You will then document your findings in a memorandum.

Assignment A: Creating the Spreadsheet

A discussion of each spreadsheet section follows. The discussion is about (1) how each section should be set up, and (2) the logic of the formulas in the sections' cells. *When you type in the spreadsheet skeleton, follow the order given in this section.*

Constants You should have these constants:

A	B	C	D	E	F
CONSTANTS	1999	2000	2001	2002	2003
FUND ADMIN EXPENSE PERCENTAGE	NA	0.01	0.01	0.01	0.01
TAX RATE EXPECTED	NA	0.3	0.31	0.32	0.33
MIN FUND INVESTMENT DOLLARS AT BEGINNING OF YEAR	NA	100000000	101000000	102010000	103030100

Fig. 13-1

- Administrative expenses will be 1% of dollars invested at the beginning of year.

- The tax rate on pre-tax profit is expected to increase each year.
- The desired minimum invested dollars at the end of each year are shown. The Bond Fund's bankers are willing to loan money so the Fund can reach its end-of-year cash-invested target. Any borrowings would be immediately invested.

Inputs   You should have these inputs:

A	B	C	D	E	F
INPUTS	**1999**	**2000**	**2001**	**2002**	**2003**
EXPECTED ECONOMY (G=GOOD; N = NEUTRAL; R = RECESSION)	NA		NA	NA	NA
FUND RISK LEVEL (H = HIGH; S = SAFE)	NA		NA	NA	NA

Fig. 13-2

- The user enters a **G** for a "good" four-year economic outlook, an **N** for a "neutral" outlook, or an **R** for a "recession" outlook. The value entered applies to all four years (thus the "NA" in most cells).
- The user enters an **H** for a "High Risk" investment policy or an **S** for a "Safe" policy. The entry applies to all years.

Summary of Key Results   You should show these results:

A	B	C	D	E	F
SUMMARY OF KEY RESULTS	**1999**	**2000**	**2001**	**2002**	**2003**
FUND INVESTMENT LEVEL AT YEAR END	NA				
NET INCOME FOR YEAR	NA				
RETURN ON THIS YEAR'S INVESTMENT	0.06				
OWED TO BANK AT END OF YEAR	10000000				

Fig. 13-3

Some pertinent 1999 results are shown. "Echo" results for 2000–2003 from cells in the spreadsheet body to this section. "Return on This Year's Investment" (ROI) represents net income divided by dollars invested. (Note: format the ROI cells for three decimals: Format, Cells, Number; select 3 decimal places.)

Calculations   You should calculate these intermediate results, which then get used in the net income and cash-invested forecast formulas that follow:

A	B	C	D	E	F
CALCULATIONS	**1999**	**2000**	**2001**	**2002**	**2003**
APPRECIATION FACTOR	NA				
DEFAULT (LOSSES) FACTOR	NA				
CASH INFLOW FACTOR	NA				
LIQUIDATION FACTOR	NA				
INTEREST RATE FOR YEAR	NA				
RETURN ON THIS YEAR'S INVESTMENT	NA				

Fig. 13-4

Your formulas will calculate 2000–2003 values, based on the values of the inputs. Rules for each calculation are discussed next.

- *Appreciation Factor* This is the average investment interest rate in a year. The investment portfolio "appreciates" (earns income) at that average rate. The better the economy and the higher the risk taken, the higher the appreciation factor. The following table shows the appreciation factor in the six possible situations.

Appreciation Factor in Each of the Four Years

	Good Economy	Neutral Economy	Recession Economy
High Risk Policy	14%	12%	10%
Safe Policy	10%	9%	9%

Fig. 13-5

Explanatory example: Assume $100,000,000 is invested. With a Good Economy and a High Risk Policy, the average interest rate on money invested would be 14%, and appreciation revenue would be $14,000,000 in the income statement.

- *Default (Losses) Factor* The following table shows the percentage of investment dollars that will be defaulted in the six possible situations.

Default Factor in Each of the Four Years

	Good Economy	Neutral Economy	Recession Economy
High Risk Policy	1%	3%	5%
Safe Policy	1%	1%	2%

Fig. 13-6

Explanatory example: Assume $100,000,000 is invested. With a Recession Economy and a High Risk Policy, the average loss rate would be 5%. Bond default expense in the income statement would be $5,000,000.

- *Cash Inflow Factor* Management thinks the willingness of investors to provide new investment funds in a year is a function of the economy and also of the Bond Fund's prior year ROI (potential investors watch that performance measure). The better the economy and the better the prior year's ROI, the higher the inflow. (Using *prior* year ROI simplifies this calculation.) The following table shows the factor in the six possible situations.

Cash Inflow Factor in Each of the Four Years

	Good Economy	Neutral Economy	Recession Economy
Prior Yr. ROI > .05	10%	8%	8%
Prior Yr. ROI <= .05	8%	3%	3%

Fig. 13-7

Explanatory example: Assume $100,000,000 is invested. With a Good economy and a prior year ROI of .06, the inflow rate would be 10%, and new investment funds would be $10,000,000.

- *Liquidation Factor* Management thinks the tendency of investors to liquidate their investments is a function of the economy. The following table shows the factor in the three possible situations.

Investment Liquidation Factor in Each of the Four Years

Good Economy	Neutral Economy	Recession Economy
5%	7%	8%

Fig. 13-8

Explanatory example: Assume $100,000,000 is invested. In a Good Economy, investors would be expected to cash in $5,000,000 of the fund.

- *Interest Rate for Year* Management expects this to be only a function of the economy. The following table shows the rate in the three possible economies.

Interest Rate on Bank Debt in Each of the Four Years

Good Economy	Neutral Economy	Recession Economy
6%	7%	8%

Fig. 13-9

- *Return on This Year's Investment* This is the year's net income divided by the total dollars invested at the *beginning* of the year.

Income Statement and Cash Flow Invested The net income and cash flow statement starts with the income statement. This is followed by a calculation of dollars invested at year end. Your results in this section should have no pennies. Some of the line items are the subject of explanatory examples in the Calculations section. Other line items are discussed next.

INCOME STATEMENT AND CASH FLOW STATEMENT	1999	2000	2001	2002	2003
APPRECIATION REVENUE	NA				
COSTS OF INVESTMENTS:	NA				
FUND ADMIN EXPENSES	NA				
BOND DEFAULTS (LOSSES)	NA				
TOTAL COSTS OF INVESTMENTS	NA				
PRE-INTEREST EXPENSE MARGIN	NA				
INTEREST EXPENSE	NA				
PRE-TAX PROFIT MARGIN	NA				
TAX EXPENSE	NA				
NET INCOME FOR YEAR	NA				

Fig. 13-10

- Fund administration expenses are a function of beginning-of-year dollars invested and the administration expense constant.

- Interest expense is a function of the year's interest rate and the amount of debt owed at the *beginning* of the year.

- Tax expense is zero if pre-tax profit is zero or negative. Otherwise, apply the rate for the year to the pre-tax profit margin.

The next part of your spreadsheet should calculate the year-end cash invested. The Calculations section has explanatory examples of investment inflows and liquidations. Other line items are discussed next.

	1999	2000	2001	2002	2003
FUND INVESTMENT LEVEL AT BEGINNING OF YEAR	NA				
ADD: FUND NET INCOME FOR YEAR	NA				
ADD: INVESTMENT INFLOW	NA				
LESS: LIQUIDATIONS	NA				
FUND INVESTMENT LEVEL BEFORE FINANCINGS					
ADD: BORROWINGS FROM BANK	NA				
LESS: REPAYMENTS TO BANK	NA				
FUND INVESTMENT LEVEL AT YEAR END	106000000				

Fig. 13-11

- The amount invested in the fund at the beginning of a year is the amount invested at the end of the *prior* year. Cash invested at the end of 1999 was $106,000,000.

- Fund net income in a year can be echoed down from the income statement.

- At the end of a year, the Fund's bankers will lend enough money to get the Fund back to the minimum investment level. If the Fund's investment level before financing is less than the minimum investment required at year end, the Bond Fund must borrow.

- However, if the fund investment level is more than the minimum *and* there is outstanding bank debt, some or all of it should be repaid (but not to take the Fund below its minimum required investment).

Debt Owed at Year End The next part of your spreadsheet should show a calculation of year-end debt owed to banks.

A	B	C	D	E	F
DEBT OWED	**1999**	**2000**	**2001**	**2002**	**2003**
OWED TO BANK AT BEGINNING OF YEAR	NA				
ADD: BORROWINGS IN YEAR	NA				
LESS: DEBT REPAYMENTS/YR	NA				
EQUALS: OWED TO BANK AT END OF YEAR	10000000				

Fig. 13-12

- Debt owed to the bank at the beginning of a year equals debt owed to the bank at the end of the prior year. The fund owed $10,000,000 at the end of 1999.

- Amounts borrowed and repaid were calculated and can be echoed to this section.

Assignment B: Use the Spreadsheet for Decision Support

You will now complete the case by (1) using the spreadsheet to gather the data you need to make the investment-policy decision and (2) documenting recommendations in a memorandum.

Use the Spreadsheet to Gather Data

You have built the spreadsheet to model the decision. Now run "what if" scenarios with the possible Economy-Policy input values (G-H, G-S, N-H, N-S, R-H, R-S). The way you do this depends on whether your instructor has told you to use the Scenario Manager.

- If your instructor told you *not* to use the Scenario Manager, you must now manually enter the input value combinations. Note the results for each on a sheet of paper. (They will show in the Summary of Key Results section as you work.)

- If your instructor told you to use the Scenario Manager, perform the procedures set forth in Tutorial C. Record the six possible scenarios. The changing cells are the two Input cells (Economy and Investment Policy). The output cell is the 2003 ROI ratio cell, *only*.

- If you're using the Scenario Manager, copy the results from the Summary page into the Clipboard before ending your work. (Tutorial C refers to this procedure.) The graphic will then be available when you write your memorandum.

- In either case, when you are done gathering data, print the entire workbook. Then save the .xls file, close it (with the diskette in drive A:), and exit from Excel.

Document Your Recommendation in a Memorandum

Write a brief memo to the Bond Fund's managers. Assume they would consider an investment policy only if its 2003 ROI was greater than 5%. Thus, the managers need the answers to these questions: (1) Given each state of the economy (Good , Neutral, Recession), which investment policy (or policies) produce an ROI greater than 5%? (2) Are there economic scenarios in which the 5% minimum ROI cannot be earned? If the managers know the answers to these questions, they can decide which investment policy to pursue.

- Your memorandum should have a proper heading (DATE/ TO/ FROM/ SUBJECT). You may wish to use a Word memo template (File — New, click Memos, choose Contemporary Memo).

- In the first paragraph, tell Fund managers which scenarios generate the minimum return (or more) and which scenarios do not yield the minimum. Provide no background—management understands the problem and expects your analysis.
- Support your statements graphically in one of two ways: (1) If you used the Scenario Manager to gather data, include a copy of the Summary Sheet results. Copy this from the Clipboard. (2) Otherwise, summarize ROI data in a table after the first paragraph. (To make a table In MS Word, select the Table menu option. Enter the number of rows and columns. Select Autoformat. Choose the format—Grid 1 is a good choice; that is what is shown here). Your table should look like this:

TUV Bond Fund Return on Investment (2003)

	Good Economy	Neutral Economy	Recession Economy
High Risk Policy			
Safe Policy			

Fig. 13-13

⇒ DELIVERABLES

1. Memorandum
2. Spreadsheet printouts
3. Diskette, which should have your memo file and your Excel file.

Staple the printouts together, with the memo on top. Handwrite your instructor a note, stating the name of the model's .xls file.

The Cup O' Joe Coffee House Decision

DECISION SUPPORT USING EXCEL

➤ PREVIEW

You'd like to open a coffee shop on Home Town's Main Street. The street is about a mile long and is heavily traveled each day, in part by college students who attend the local college. In this case, you will use Excel to make a net income and cash-flow forecast, which will help you to decide whether the coffee house is likely to succeed.

➤ PREPARATION

- Review spreadsheet concepts discussed in class and/or in your text.
- Complete any exercises your instructor assigns.
- Complete any part of Tutorial C your instructor assigns.
- Review file-saving procedures for Windows programs. These are discussed in Tutorial C.

➤ BACKGROUND

Home Town currently has no coffee shop where people can go for good coffee and a snack. This is surprising, considering the popularity of such places, and you're considering filling the void with a place called the Cup O' Joe Coffee House.

You want to serve coffee and a small menu of food items, such as cake, pie, cookies, and sandwiches. A local bakery could deliver the menu items daily. You'd order the coffee beans each week and grind them daily to make the coffee.

You think you would not be alone for long. At least one other coffee house, or coffee shop, would open once you've proved there's a market. The question is this: How *much* competition will arise? You think Main Street would be able to support no more than three coffee houses like yours. Actually, you are not sure more than *one* could be supported.

Your success will depend on (1) how many coffee houses open to compete with yours, and (2) how much advertising you do. You think you should use year 2002 to make an accurate forecast of how the business would fare. You need to build a DSS program to predict net income, cash on hand, and money owed to the bank at the end of years 2000–2002.

In your DSS, the inputs would be for (1) the number of competing coffee houses in the three-year period, and (2) the advertising intensity chosen: low, medium, or high. Your DSS must account for the effects of the input values on variables like market share, selling prices, and other variables. Your model will let you play what-if with the inputs, see the results, and then decide what to do.

➤ ASSIGNMENT: CREATING A SPREADSHEET FOR DECISION SUPPORT

In this two-part assignment, you will produce a spreadsheet that models the decision, and then write a memorandum to your banker, explaining your recommendations.

In *Assignment A*, you will create the spreadsheet model of the decision. The model is an income statement and cash-flow forecast for the years 2000–2002. Your spreadsheet should have sections for Constants, Inputs, Summary of Key Results, Calculations, Income Statement and Cash Flow Statement, and Debt Owed. You are shown how each section should be set up before you enter your cell formulas.

In *Assignment B*, you will use the model to develop information that will let you decide what to do. You will document your findings in a memorandum to your banker (who may have to lend you money so you can start your business).

Assignment A: Creating the Spreadsheet

A discussion of each spreadsheet section follows. The discussion is about (1) how each section should be set up, and (2) the logic of the formulas in the section's cells. *When you type in the spreadsheet skeleton, follow the order given in this section.*

Constants Your spreadsheet should have these constants:

A	B	C	D	E
CONSTANTS	**1999**	**2000**	**2001**	**2002**
TAX RATE EXPECTED	NA	0.31	0.32	0.33
INTEREST RATE FOR YEAR	NA	0.1	0.1	0.1
NUMBER OF EMPLOYEES	NA	2	2	2
BASE HOURLY WAGE	NA	6	6.5	7
NUMBER OF PEOPLE IN TOWN	NA	13000	13500	14000
BASE COFFEE SELLING PRICE	NA	2	2.1	2.2
MIN CASH RQRD AT START OF YR	NA	10000	10000	10000
CITY BUSINESS LICENSE/YR	NA	1000	1100	1200
NUMBER OF BUSINESS DAYS	NA	300	300	300
RENT EXPENSE -- FIXED PORTION/YR	NA	12000	14400	16800
MARKET SHARE FACTOR	NA	0.07	0.073	0.077
NUMBER OF HOURS OPEN/DAY	NA	10	10	10

Fig. 14-1

- The tax rate is applied to pre-tax profits. It is expected to increase each year.
- The interest rate applies to any bank debt you take on to finance the coffee house.
- You think you would always need two hourly employees at work, not counting yourself.
- The base hourly wage rate is needed to attract and retain good people. Each year this rate is expected to increase.
- About 13,000 people live in Home Town in 2000. This number increases each year because college enrollment is expected to increase.
- The base selling price for a cup of coffee is $2. This is the average floor price for all the kinds of coffee you will sell. (Actual selling prices are more than this base, as you will see.)
- You want to have at least $10,000 in cash at the beginning of each year. Your banker will lend you whatever you need at the end of a year in order to begin the next year with $10,000.
- Your coffee house will have a few small tables on the sidewalk. The city charges a license fee for that privilege, which will be $1,000 in 2000. The fee will increase each year.
- The coffee house will be open 300 days a year, 10 hours per day.
- Your building rent will be a fixed fee, plus a percentage of sales. The fixed fee per year is shown. Your prospective landlord tells you this fee will go up each year.
- The market share factor is the percentage of people in town who are likely to buy from a coffee house in a day. You think this percentage will rise in your town as coffee houses become established.
- The total number of cups of coffee sold in a day is the "market share factor" times the total number of people in Home Town.

Inputs   You should have these inputs for 2000, 2001, and 2002:

INPUTS	1999	2000	2001	2002	
NUMBER OF COFFEE SHOPS IN TOWN (INCLUDE YOURS) = N	NA				
ADVERTISING LEVEL (1 = HI; 2 = MED; 3 = LOW) = A	NA				

Fig. 14-2

- The number of coffee houses in Home Town in a year is expected to range from 1 (assume yours is 1) to 3 (you and 2 competitors). You need not enter the same digit for all 3 years: You could show 1 in 2000, 2 in 2001, and 3 in 2002.

- You can advertise heavily (enter a 1), lightly (enter a 3), or somewhere in between (2). Even if yours is the only coffee house, you'll have to advertise somewhat, so zero is not a possible input. You need not enter the same digits for all 3 years.

Summary of Results   You should show these results:

SUMMARY OF KEY RESULTS	1999	2000	2001	2002	
NET INCOME FOR YEAR	NA				
CASH AT END OF YEAR	NA				
BANK DEBT AT END OF YEAR	NA				

Fig. 14-3

For 2000 to 2002, show net income for the year, cash on hand at the end of the year, and debt owed to your bank at the end of the year. These amounts are computed in the spreadsheet body and echoed to this section.

Calculations   You should calculate these intermediate results, which are then used in the Net Income Statement and Cash Flow Statement. Calculations may use input values, constants, and possibly other calculated values.

CALCULATIONS	1999	2000	2001	2002	
TOTAL MARKET IN TOWN (CUPS/DAY)	NA				
NUMBER OF CUPS SOLD/DAY	NA				
AVG SELLING PRICE/CUP	NA				
# OF CAKES (ETC)/DAY	NA				
AVG SELLING PRICE/CAKE	NA				
COST OF SALES PER CUP	NA				
COST OF SALES PER CAKE	NA				
COST OF SALARIES/DAY	NA				

Fig. 14-4

- The cups of coffee that could be sold per day in the town is a function of the total population and the market share factor. (Use the -INT function to lop off decimal cups of coffee.)

- You expect that the number of cups sold per day at your coffee house will be the number of cups expected in the total market divided by the number of coffee houses, which is an input. Use the =INT() function to lop off decimal cups of coffee.

- You need to calculate an average selling price that applies to all cups of coffee sold. The equation, in English is:

Avg price   =   ((base coffee selling price) +
                        ((number of coffee houses + 1)/(advertising level + 1)) –
                        (number of coffee houses * $.50))

Explanatory example: If yours was the only coffee house and you had "low" advertising, then the average 2000 selling price for a cup of coffee sold would be:

$$(2) + ((1 + 1)/(3 + 1)) – (1 * \$.50) = (2) + (.5) – (.5) = 2$$

- Most people who buy a cup of coffee will get a roll or a piece of cake or a sandwich, but not all coffee buyers will do so. You think that the number of cakes, sandwiches, and so forth sold in a day will be 80% of the number of cups of coffee sold in a day. (Use the INT function to remove decimal values.)

- Your research shows that what is spent over and above the cup of coffee is a function of how much was spent *on* the cup of coffee. You think that the average selling price of a supplemental item will be twice the average selling price of a cup of coffee.

- You think that the average cost of sales per cup of coffee will be 110% of the "base coffee selling price" (a constant). (This cost per cup does not include rent, employee salaries, the town business license, or interest and taxes, which are charged separately.)

- The average unit cost for a supplemental food item is expected to be 75% of the selling price of these items.

- The cost of salaries for a day is a function of the number of employees, the hourly wage rate, and the expected number of hours per day.

Income Statement and Cash Flow Statement The net income and cash-flow forecast starts with the cash on hand at the beginning of the year. This is followed by the income statement and concludes with the calculation of cash on hand at year end. Use the =INT() function to avoid showing pennies in this section. Some of the line items are discussed next.

A	B	C	D	E
INCOME STATEMENT AND CASH FLOW STATEMENT	**1999**	**2000**	**2001**	**2002**
BEGINNING OF YEAR CASH ON HAND	NA			
REVENUE (SALES):	NA			
COFFEE	NA			
CAKES, ETC.	NA			
TOTAL REVENUE (SALES)	NA			
COSTS AND EXPENSES:	NA			
COST OF SALES -- COFFEE	NA			
COST OF SALES -- CAKES, ETC.	NA			
COST OF SALARIES	NA			
RENT EXPENSE	NA			
ADVERTISING EXPENSE	NA			
BUSINESS LICENSE EXPENSE	NA			
TOTAL COSTS AND EXPENSES	NA			
PRE-INTEREST EXPENSE MARGIN	NA			
INTEREST EXPENSE	NA			
PRE-TAX PROFIT MARGIN	NA			
TAX EXPENSE	NA			
NET INCOME	NA			

Fig. 14-5

- Cash on hand at the beginning of a year is the cash at the end of the *prior* year.

- Rent expense is equal to the fixed portion (a constant) plus 5% of total revenues.

- Your advertising agency fees are in proportion to the your level of advertising: $10,000 a year for low level; $20,000 a year for medium level; and $30,000 a year for high level.

- Interest expense is the rate for the year times the amount of debt owed to the bank at the *beginning* of the year.

- Tax expense is zero if pre-tax income is zero or negative. Otherwise, apply the rate for the year times the pre-tax profit margin.

Line items for the year-end cash calculation are discussed next.

A	B	C	D	E
NET CASH POSITION (NCP) BEFORE BORROWINGS AND REPAYMENTS OF DEBT (BEG CASH PLUS NET INCOME)	NA			
ADD: BORROWINGS FROM BANK	NA			
LESS: REPAYMENTS TO BANK	NA			
EQUALS: END OF YEAR CASH ON HAND	10000			

Fig. 14-6

- Values for 1999 are mostly NA, except that cash at year end was $10,000, the minimum cash.

- The Net Cash Position (NCP) at the end of a year equals the cash at the beginning of the year, plus the year's net income. (Assume there are no receivables or payables.)

- If need be, your banker will lend enough money at the end of a year to get you back to the minimum cash. If the NCP is less than the minimum, you must borrow enough to get to the minimum.

- If the NCP is more than the minimum cash *and* there is outstanding debt from prior years, then some or all of the debt should be repaid (but not to take your company below the minimum cash level).
- Cash at the end of the year equals the NCP, plus any borrowings, less any repayments.

Debt Owed The spreadsheet body ends with a calculation of debt owed at year end.

A	B	C	D	E
DEBT OWED	**1999**	**2000**	**2001**	**2002**
OWED TO BANK AT BEGINNING OF YEAR	NA			
ADD: BORROWED FROM BANK	NA			
LESS: REPAYMENTS TO BANK	NA			
EQUALS: OWED TO BANK AT END OF YEAR	0			

Fig. 14-7

- Values for 1999 are NA, except that no debt was owed at the end of 1999.
- Cash owed to the bank at the beginning of a year equals cash owed to the bank at the end of the prior year.
- Amounts borrowed and repaid have been calculated and can be echoed to this section.
- The amount owed at the end of a year equals the amount owed at the beginning of a year, plus any borrowings, less any repayments.

Assignment B: Use the Spreadsheet for Decision Support

You will now complete the case by (1) using the spreadsheet to gather the data you need to determine your strategy, and (2) documenting recommendations in a memorandum.

Use the Spreadsheet to Gather Data

Assume that you and your banker believe you will probably have Main Street to yourself in 2000, that there will be 1 competing coffee house in 2001, and 2 competing houses in 2002. Thus, the Number of Coffee Houses pattern you want to use is this: 1 in 2000, 2 in 2001, and 3 in 2002. You will run "what if" scenarios with various Advertising Level input values. Six advertising scenarios should be considered:

- Heavy ad campaign in all three years (1-1-1 input pattern)
- Medium ad campaign in all three years (2-2-2 pattern)
- Low ad campaign in all three years (3-3-3)
- Graduated low-medium-high campaign (3-2-1)
- Graduated low-to-medium campaign (3-2-2)
- Graduated low-to-high campaign (3-1-1)

The way you gather data depends on whether your instructor has told you to use the Scenario Manager:

- If your instructor told you not to use the Scenario Manager, you must now manually enter the Number of Coffee Houses and Advertising Level input values. Note the results for each combination on a sheet of paper. (Results will show in the Summary of Key Results.)

- If your instructor told you to use the Scenario manager, perform the procedures set forth in Tutorial C. Assume the 1-2-3 Number of Coffee Houses pattern. Record the six possible scenarios (advertising patterns 1-1-1, 2-2-2, and so on). The changing cells are those for advertising levels in 2000–2002. Output cells are for 2002 net income, cash, and debt.
- If you are using the Scenario Manager, copy the results from the Summary page into the Clipboard before ending your work. (Tutorial C explains this procedure.)
- In either data-gathering case, when you are done, print the entire workbook. Then save the .xls file, close it (with the diskette in drive A:), and, finally, exit from Excel.

Document Your Recommendation in a Memorandum

Write a brief memorandum to your banker to support your request for financing. The banker wants to know, given the competition assumption, which advertising strategy would yield the best results.

- Your memorandum should have a proper heading (DATE/ TO/ FROM/ SUBJECT). You may wish to use a Word memo template (File — New, click Memos, choose Contemporary Memo).
- In the first paragraph, state the competition assumption and then recommend which advertising strategy you want to follow.
- Support your statements graphically in one of two ways: (1) If you used the Scenario Manager to gather data, include a copy of the Summary Sheet results after the first paragraph. Copy this from the Clipboard. (2) Otherwise, make a summary table after the first paragraph. (To make a summary table in MS Word, select the Table menu option. Enter the number of rows and columns. Select Autoformat. Choose the format—Grid 1 is a good choice; that is what is shown here). Your table should look like this:

Year 2002 Financial Results, Given Different Ad Campaigns in 2000–2002

	Year's Net Income	Cash at Year End	Debt at Year End
Heavy (1-1-1)			
Medium (2-2-2)			
Low (3-3-3)			
Low, Medium, High (3-2-1)			
Low to Medium (3-2-2)			
Low to High (3-1-1)			

Fig. 14-8

☛ DELIVERABLES

1. Memorandum
2. Spreadsheet printouts
3. Diskette, which should have your memo file and your Excel file.

Staple the papers together, with the memorandum on top. Handwrite your instructor a note stating the name of the model's .xls file.

15
CASE

The Bob and Babs Warehouse Location Decision

DECISION SUPPORT USING EXCEL

⇥ PREVIEW

New Age Dolls makes Bob and Babs dolls at two locations and leases warehouses at both locations. The warehouse leases expire at the end of 1999. Management has decided to build their own warehouses rather than continue leasing them. In this case, you will use Excel to make a net income and cash-flow forecast, which will help New Age management decide where to build the new warehouses. You will document your recommendations in a memorandum.

⇥ PREPARATION

- Review spreadsheet concepts discussed in class and/or in your text.
- Complete any exercises your instructor assigns.
- Complete any part of Tutorial C your instructor assigns.
- Review file-saving procedures for Windows programs. These are discussed in Tutorial C.

New Age Dolls makes the very successful line of Bob and Babs dolls. After only a few years on the market, the dolls rapidly gained popularity with girls of all ages.

New Age Dolls make dolls at its St. Louis and Boston production sites and has been leasing warehouses in those locations. Warehouses are used for storage and for distribution to retail stores. But management is not happy with the terms of the current leases, which are much too expensive. The leases will be allowed to expire at the end of 1999. Management has decided to build its own warehouses. You have been called in to help analyze choices for new warehouse sites.

New Age management has three possible locations in mind: Portland, Oregon; Phoenix, Arizona; and Atlanta, Georgia. New Age would construct warehouses at only two of these sites. They need help deciding which of the two would be financially the best (or, to put it another way, which one of the three would be financially the worst).

In the next three years (2000, 2001, and 2002), New Age management expects to sell all the dolls they produce in Boston and St. Louis. Production of the two dolls will be divided evenly between the two locations. Here are the expected production (and sales) levels in the next three years:

Number of Dolls to Be Made at Each Site

	2000	2001	2002
Bob—St. Louis	500,000	750,000	1,000,000
Babs—St. Louis	750,000	850,000	1,000,000
Bob—Boston	500,000	750,000	1,000,000
Babs—Boston	750,000	850,000	1,000,000

Fig. 15-1

To reduce distribution and storage risks (from strikes, natural disasters, etc.), management plans to send half of each plant's production to each of the two selected warehouse sites. For example, if Atlanta and Phoenix are selected, then (1) half of Boston's Bob doll production will be sent to Atlanta and half to Phoenix; (2) half of Boston's Babs doll production will be sent to Atlanta and half to Phoenix. St. Louis' doll production would be similarly split between the Atlanta and Phoenix warehouses.

Shipping costs from each plant to each of the three sites differ. Also, storage costs *at* each of the three warehouse sites will differ. Management has analyzed how much it will cost to ship and store a doll for each of the factory/ warehouse combinations. Here is the data:

Cost to Ship and Store a Single Doll

(from) Factory	(to) Warehouse	2000	2001	2002
St Louis	Portland	4.50	4.95	5.45
St Louis	Atlanta	5.50	6.05	6.66
St Louis	Phoenix	3.50	3.85	4.24
Boston	Portland	6.00	6.60	7.26
Boston	Atlanta	4.50	4.95	5.45
Boston	Phoenix	5.50	6.05	6.66

Fig. 15-2

In 1999, a Bob doll sells for $11.25, and the slightly more popular Babs doll sells for $12.25. If the economy remains steady, the selling prices of Bob and Babs dolls are not expected to change in 2000–2002. But if the economy inflates, or "heats up," selling prices would rise; selling prices of each doll would rise 4% from one year to the next.

In 1999, it costs $5.00 to make and market a St. Louis-made doll. In 1999, it costs $5.50 to make and market a Boston-made doll. Production and marketing costs are expected to go up in the next three years. Management sees no chance of an economic downturn in the next few years. The economy could be flat or heat up. In the latter case, prices would rise quickly. Here are the expected year-to-year rates of increase in costs, depending on the production site and on the state of the economy.

Expected Year-to-year Increase in Production and Marketing Costs

	Economy is Flat	Economy Heats Up
Doll made in St Louis	1% per year	15% per year
Doll made in Boston	2% per year	5% per year

Fig. 15-3

The St. Louis labor market is "tighter" than Boston's, so management thinks wage rates and other costs would go up more in St. Louis if the economy heats up.

In your DSS, the inputs are for (1) the expected state of the national economy in the three years: a flat (steady) or hot economy, and (2) for the warehouse location *not* chosen: Portland, Atlanta, or Phoenix. Your model lets you play what-if with the inputs, see the results, and then decide what to do.

➤ ASSIGNMENT: CREATING A SPREADSHEET FOR DECISION SUPPORT

In this two-part assignment, you will produce a spreadsheet that models a business decision and then write a memorandum that explains your recommendation for action.

In *Assignment A*, you will create the spreadsheet model of the warehouse location decision. The model is an income statement and cash-flow forecast for the years 2000 to 2002. Your spreadsheet should have sections for Constants, Inputs, Summary of Key Results, Calculations, Income Statement and Cash Flow Statement, and Debt Owed. You are shown how each section should be set up before you enter cell formulas.

In *Assignment B*, you will use the model to develop information so you can recommend a warehousing strategy. You will then document your recommendation in a memorandum.

Assignment A: Creating the Spreadsheet

A discussion of each spreadsheet section follows. The discussion is about (1) how each section should be set up, and (2) the logic of the formulas in the section's cells. *When you type in the spreadsheet skeleton, follow the order in this section.*

Constants   Your spreadsheet should have these constants:

CONSTANTS	1999	2000	2001	2002
BOB PRODUCTION - STL	NA	500000	750000	1000000
BABS PRODUCTION - STL	NA	750000	850000	1000000
BOB PRODUCTION - BSN	NA	500000	750000	1000000
BABS PRODUCTION - BSN	NA	750000	850000	1000000
PER UNIT SHIPPING AND WAREHOUSING COSTS (FROM-TO)				
STL --> PTLD	NA	4.5	4.95	5.45
STL --> ATL	NA	5.5	6.05	6.66
STL --> PHX	NA	3.5	3.85	4.24
BSN --> PTLD	NA	6	6.6	7.26
BSN --> ATL	NA	4.5	4.95	5.45
BSN --> PHX	NA	5.5	6.05	6.66
TAX RATE EXPECTED	NA	0.29	0.3	0.31
MIN CASH RQRD AT START OF YR	NA	10000	10000	10000
FIXED ADMINISTRATIVE COSTS	NA	1200000	1200000	1200000

Fig. 15-4

- Unit production is expected to increase each year.
- Unit shipping and warehousing costs are expected to increase each year.
- The tax rate on pre-tax profit margin is expected to increase each year.
- New Age wants to have at least $10,000 in cash at the beginning of each year. The company's banker will lend whatever is needed at the end of a year to begin the next year with $10,000.
- Fixed administrative costs will be $1,200,000 each year.

Inputs   Your spreadsheet should have these inputs:

INPUTS	1999	2000	2001	2002
EXPECTED STATE OF ECONOMY: F = FLAT, H = HOT	NA			
WAREHOUSE LOCATION *NOT* USED: PT = PORTLAND; AT = ATLANTA; PX = PHOENIX	NA		NA	NA

Fig. 15-5

- The user enters an **F** for a flat (steady) economic outlook in a year and an **H** for a hot one. Use a string of three values to show the economic outlook for all three years. For example, **FHH** indicates the economy will be flat in 2000 but will heat up in the next two years.

- The user makes one entry for the location *not* used. For example, entering **PT** means the Portland warehouse will *not* be used for warehousing. (Atlanta and Phoenix will be used.)

Summary of Results   Your spreadsheet should show these results:

SUMMARY OF KEY RESULTS	1999	2000	2001	2002
NET INCOME FOR YEAR	NA			
END OF YEAR CASH ON HAND	NA			
OWED TO BANK AT END OF YEAR	NA			

Fig. 15-6

For 2000 to 2002, show net income for the year, cash on hand at year end, and debt owed at year end. These values are computed in the spreadsheet body and echoed to this section.

Calculations   Your spreadsheet should calculate these intermediate results, which are then used in the Income Statement and Cash Flow Statement. Calculations are based on the values of the inputs and, in some cases, on 1999 values.

CALCULATIONS	1999	2000	2001	2002
INTEREST RATE FOR YEAR	NA			
NUMBER OF DOLLS SHIPPED				
FROM STL TO PTLD	NA			
FROM STL TO ATL	NA			
FROM STL TO PHX	NA			
FROM BSN TO PTLD	NA			
FROM BSN TO ATL	NA			
FROM BSN TO PHX	NA			
SHIPPING & WAREHOUSING COSTS				
FROM STL TO PTLD	NA			
FROM STL TO ATL	NA			
FROM STL TO PHX	NA			
FROM BSN TO PTLD	NA			
FROM BSN TO ATL	NA			
FROM BSN TO PHX	NA			

Fig. 15-7

UNIT SELLING PRICE - BOB	11.25			
UNIT SELLING PRICE - BABS	12.25			
DOLLARS OF SALES (REVENUES) - BOB	NA			
DOLLARS OF SALES (REVENUES) - BABS	NA			
UNIT PRODUCTION & MARKETING COSTS:				
ST LOUIS (BOTH DOLLS)	5			
BSN (BOTH DOLLS)	5.5			
TOTAL PRODUCTION & MARKETING COSTS:				
ST LOUIS (BOTH DOLLS)	NA			
BOSTON (BOTH DOLLS)	NA			

Fig. 15-8

- Interest must be paid on debt owed to the bank. The rate will be 8% if the economy is flat in a year, but 10% if the economy is heating up in a year.
- You must know how many dolls get shipped from point A to point B, so you can compute shipping and storage costs. If a warehouse site is *not* selected, then no dolls are shipped there; otherwise, a factory's doll production is divided evenly between the two selected sites.
- Shipping and warehousing costs for dolls shipped from point A to point B are a function of the number of units shipped and the per unit cost for the city-to-city combination. The former amount is a Calculation; the latter amount is a Constant. Use the INT() function to get rid of pennies.
- The selling price of a doll is a function of the Economy. If there is a selling price change, 2000's prices are based on 1999's, 2001's are based on 2000's, and so on. Do not use the INT() function (keep the pennies in the unit price).
- Revenue (Sales) is a function of the number of units sold times the unit selling price. The former amount is a Constant, and the latter is a Calculation. Use the INT() function to get rid of pennies.
- Unit production and marketing costs are a function of the production location and the state of the economy, and 1999 values. Do not use the INT() function (keep the pennies).
- Total production and marketing costs are a function of the units produced and unit costs for a location. The former amount is a Constant; the latter is a Calculation. Use the INT() function, to get rid of pennies.

Income Statement and Cash Flow The net income and cash-flow forecast starts with the cash on hand at the beginning of the year. This is followed by the income statement and concludes with the calculation of cash on hand at year end. Your results in this section should have no pennies. Some of the line items are discussed next.

G19	=			
A	B	C	D	E
INCOME STATEMENT AND CASH FLOW STATEMENT	**1999**	**2000**	**2001**	**2002**
BEGINNING OF YEAR CASH ON HAND	NA			
REVENUE (SALES)	NA			
COSTS AND EXPENSES:				
PRODUCTION AND MARKETING COSTS	NA			
SHIPPING AND WAREHOUSE COSTS	NA			
FIXED ADMIN COSTS	NA			
TOTAL COSTS	NA			
PRE-INTEREST EXPENSE MARGIN	NA			
INTEREST EXPENSE	NA			
PRE-TAX PROFIT MARGIN	NA			
TAX EXPENSE	NA			
NET INCOME	NA			

Fig. 15-9

- Note that the cash at the beginning of a year is the cash at the end of the *prior* year.
- Doll Revenue (Sales), Production and Marketing Costs, and Shipping and Warehouse Costs have already been calculated.
- The fixed administrative cost is a Constant, which you should echo here.

- Interest expense equals the rate for the year times the amount of debt owed to the bank at the *start* of the year.
- Tax expense is zero if the pre-tax profit margin is zero or negative; otherwise, apply the rate for the year times pre-tax income.

Line items for the year-end cash calculation are discussed next.

G19	▼	=			
A		B	C	D	E
NET CASH POSITION (NCP) BEFORE BORROWINGS AND REPAYMENTS OF DEBT (BEG CASH PLUS NET INCOME)		NA			
ADD: BORROWINGS FROM BANK		NA			
LESS: REPAYMENTS TO BANK		NA			
EQUALS: END OF YEAR CASH ON HAND		10000			

Fig. 15-10

- Cash at the end of 1999 was $10,000, the minimum cash required.
- The Net Cash Position (NCP) at the end of the year equals the cash at the beginning of the year plus the year's net income. (Assume there are no receivables or payables.)
- New Age's banker will lend enough money at the end of a year to attain the minimum cash level. If the NCP is less than the minimum, then New Age must borrow to reach the minimum.
- If the NCP is more than the minimum cash at the end of a year, and there is outstanding debt, then some or all of the debt should be repaid (but not to take the company below its minimum cash).
- Cash at the end of the year equals the NCP, plus any borrowings, less any repayments.

Debt Owed   The spreadsheet body ends with a calculation of debt owed at year end.

G19	▼	=			
A	B	C	D	E	
DEBT OWED	1999	2000	2001	2002	
OWED TO BANK AT BEGINNING OF YEAR	NA				
ADD: BORROWINGS FROM BANK	NA				
LESS: REPAYMENTS TO BANK	NA				
EQUALS: OWED TO BANK AT END OF YEAR	3000000				

Fig. 15-11

- Note that $3,000,000 of debt was owed at the end of 1999.
- Cash owed to the bank at the *beginning* of a year equals cash owed to the bank at the end of the *prior* year.
- Amounts borrowed and repaid were calculated and can be echoed to this section.
- The amount owed at the end of a year equals the amount owed at the beginning of a year, plus any borrowings, less any repayments.

Case 15

Assignment B: Use the Spreadsheet for Decision Support

You will now complete the case by (1) using the spreadsheet to gather the data you need to make the warehouse location decision, and (2) documenting recommendations in a memorandum.

Use the Spreadsheet to Gather Data

You have built the spreadsheet to model the outsourcing decision. Now run "what ifs" for the six scenarios that New Age management is interested in. These are: (1) a Flat (steady) economy with the three possible warehouse combinations (F-PT, F-AT, F-PX) and (2) a Hot economy with the three possible warehouse combinations (H-PT, H-AT, H-PX). The way you do this depends on whether your instructor has told you to use the Scenario Manager.

- If your instructor told you not to use the Scenario Manager, you must manually enter the input combinations. Note the results for each on a sheet of paper. (They will show in the Summary of Key Results section.)

- If your instructor told you to use the Scenario Manager, perform the procedures set forth in Tutorial C. The input cells for the six scenarios are the three economy inputs and the warehouse input. (Suppose your input cells were C24, D24, E24, and C25. You'd enter these addresses separated by commas: C24, D24, E24, C25). Output cells are the 2002 *(only)* net income, cash, and debt cells in the Summary of Key Results section.

- If you are using the Scenario Manager, copy the results from the Summary sheet into the Clipboard before ending your work.

- In either data-gathering case, when you are done, print the entire workbook. Then save the .xls file, close it (with the diskette in drive A:), and, finally, exit from Excel.

Document Your Recommendation in a Memorandum

Write a brief memorandum to New Age's vice president of finance. Tell her which warehousing combination yields the best financial results given (1) a Flat (steady) economy, and (2) a Hot economy.

- Your memorandum should have a proper heading (DATE/ TO/ FROM/ SUBJECT). You may wish to use a Word memo template (File — New, click Memos, choose Contemporary Memo).

- In the first paragraph, recommend what should be done in a Flat economy and in a Hot economy. You should provide no background—The vice president understands the problem and expects your analysis.

- Support your statements graphically in one of two ways: (1) If you used the Scenario Manager to gather data, include a copy of the Summary Sheet results. Copy this from the Clipboard. (Tutorial C explains this procedure.) (2) Otherwise, make two summary tables, one for each Economy scenario, after the first paragraph. (To make a table in MS Word, select the Table menu option. Enter the number of rows and columns. Select Autoformat. Choose the format—Grid 1 is a good choice; that is what is shown here). Your tables should look like this:

Projected 2002 Financial Results—Flat Economy for Three Years

	Phoenix Out (build— Atlanta, Portland)	Atlanta Out (build— Phoenix, Portland)	Portland Out (build— Atlanta, Phoenix)
2002 net income			
cash at 12/31/2002			
debt at 12/31/2002			

Fig. 15-12

Projected 2002 Financial Results—Hot Economy for Three Years

	Phoenix Out (build— Atlanta, Portland)	Atlanta Out (build— Phoenix, Portland)	Portland Out (build— Atlanta, Phoenix)
2002 net income			
cash at 12/31/2002			
debt at 12/31/2002			

Fig. 15-13

➤ DELIVERABLES

1. Memorandum
2. Spreadsheet printouts
3. Diskette, which should have your memorandum file and your Excel file.

Staple the printouts together, with the memo on top. Handwrite your instructor a note, stating the name of the model's .xls file.

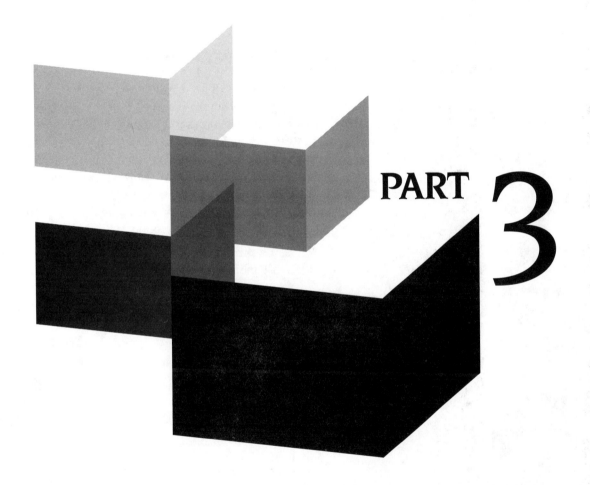

PART 3

Decision Support Cases
Using the Excel Solver

D
TUTORIAL

Building A Decision Support System Using Excel's Solver

Decision Support Systems (DSS) are programs that help people make decisions. (The nature of DSS programs is discussed in Tutorial C.) This tutorial teaches you how to use the "Solver," Excel's built-in utility, for decision support.

For some business problems, people want to know the best, or optimal, solution. Usually this means maximizing a variable (e.g., net income) or minimizing a variable (e.g., total costs). This optimization is subject to **constraints**, which are rules that must be observed when solving the problem. The Solver computes answers to such optimization problems.

This tutorial has four sections:

1. **Using the Excel Solver** In this section, you'll learn how to use the Solver in decision making. As an example, you use the Solver to create a production schedule for a sporting goods company. This schedule is called the "Base Case."

2. **Extending the Example** In this section, you'll test what you've learned about using the Solver as you modify the sporting goods schedule. This is called the "Extension Case."

3. **Using the Solver on a New Problem** In this section, you'll use the Solver on a new problem.

4. **Trouble-shooting the Solver** In this section, you'll learn how to overcome problems you might encounter using the Solver.

➤ USING THE EXCEL SOLVER

Suppose a company must set a production schedule for its various products, each of which has a different profit margin (selling price less variable costs). At first, you might assume the company will maximize production of all profitable products to maximize net income. However, a company typically cannot make and sell an unlimited number of its products because of "constraints."

One constraint affecting production is the "shared resource problem." For example, several products in a manufacturer's line might require the same raw materials that are in limited supply. Similarly, the manufacturer might require the same machines to make several of its products. In addition, there might also be a limited pool of skilled workers available to make the products.

In addition to production constraints, sometimes management's policies impose constraints. For example, management might decide the company must have a broader product line. As a consequence, a certain production quota of several products must be met, regardless of profit margins.

Thus, management must find a production schedule that will, given the constraints, maximize profit. Optimization programs like the Solver look at each combination of products, one after the other, ranking each combination by profitability. Then the program reports the best answer.

To use the Solver, you'll set up a model of the problem, including the factors that can vary, the constraints on how much they can vary, and the goal you are trying to maximize (usually profit) or minimize (usually total costs). The Solver then figures out the best solution.

Setting Up a Spreadsheet Skeleton

Suppose your company makes two sporting goods products—basketballs and footballs. Assume you will sell all the balls you produce. To maximize net income, you want to know how many of each kind of ball to make in the coming year.

Making each kind of ball requires a certain (and different) number of hours, and each ball has a different raw materials cost. Because you have only a limited number of workers and machines, you can devote a maximum of 40,000 hours to production. This is a shared resource. You do not want that resource to be idle, however. Downtime should be no more than 1,000 hours in the year, so machines should be used for at least 39,000 hours.

Marketing executives say you cannot make more than 60,000 basketballs and may not make less than 30,000. Furthermore, you must make at least 20,000 footballs, but not more than 40,000. Marketing says the ratio of basketballs to footballs produced should be between 1.5 and 1.7—i.e., more basketballs than footballs, but within limits.

What would be the best production plan? This problem has been set up in the Solver. The spreadsheet sections are discussed in the pages that follow.

AT THE KEYBOARD

You should enter the skeleton and formulas as they are discussed.

Changing Cells These are the variables the Solver is allowed to change while it looks for the solution. Here is the skeleton and the values that you should enter.

	A	B	C	D	E
1		SPORTING GOODS EXAMPLE			
2	**Changing Cells**				
3	Number of Basketballs	1			
4	Number of Footballs	1			

Fig. D-1

- In the example, the changing cells are for the number of basketballs and footballs to be made and sold. The changing cells are like input cells, except Solver (not you) plays "what-if" with the values, trying to maximize or minimize some value (in this case, maximize net income).

- Note that some number must be put in the changing cells each time before the Solver is run. It's customary to put the number 1 into the changing cells (as shown). Solver will change these values when the program is run.

Constants Your spreadsheet should have a section for values that will not change. Here is the skeleton and the values that you should enter.

	A	B	C	D	E
6	**Constants**				
7	Basketball Selling Price	14			
8	Football Selling Price	11			
9	Tax Rate	0.28			
10	# Hours to make a Basketball	0.5			
11	# Hours to make a Football	0.3			
12	Cost of labor -- 1 machine hour	6			
13	Cost of materials -- 1 Basketball	2			
14	Cost of materials -- 1 Football	1.25			

Fig. D-2

- The selling prices for one basketball and for one football are shown.
- The tax rate is the rate applied to pre-tax income to compute income tax expense.
- The number of machine hours needed to make a basketball and football are shown. A ball-making machine can produce two basketballs in an hour.
- A ball is made by a worker using a ball-making machine. A worker is paid $6 for each hour he or she works at a machine.
- The costs of raw materials for a basketball and football are shown.

Notice that the profit margins (selling price less costs of labor and materials) for the two products are not the same. They have different selling prices and different inputs (raw materials, hours to make)—and the inputs have different costs per unit. Also note that you cannot tell from the data how many hours of the shared resource (machine hours) will be devoted to basketballs and how many to footballs, because you don't know in advance how many basketballs and footballs will be made.

Calculations Calculate intermediate results that (1) will be used in the spreadsheet body, and/or (2) will be used as constraints. Here are the skeleton and formulas that you should enter:

	A	B	C
16	**Calculations**		
17	Ratio of Basketballs to Footballs	=B3/B4	
18	Total Basketball hours used	=B3*B10	
19	Total Football hours used	=B4*B11	
20	Total machine hours used (FB + BB)	=B18+B19	

Fig. D-3

- The ratio of basketballs to footballs (B17) will be needed in a constraint.
- The number of machine hours needed to make all basketballs (B3 * B10) is computed in B18. Cell B10 has the constant for the hours needed to make one basketball. Cell B3 (a changing cell) has the number of basketballs made. (Currently, this cell shows one ball, but that number will change when the Solver works on the problem.)
- The machine hours needed to make all footballs is calculated similarly, in B19.
- Total machine hours needed to make both kinds of balls (B20) will be a constraint; this value is the sum of the hours just calculated for footballs and basketballs.

Notice that constants in the Excel cell formulas in Fig. D–3 are referred to by their cell addresses. Use the cell address of a constant rather than hard-coding a number in an Excel expression: If the number must be changed later, you only have to change it in the Constant cell, not in every cell formula in which you used the value.

Also notice that *you* do not calculate the amounts in the changing cells! (Here, the number of basketballs and footballs to produce.) The *Solver* will compute those numbers. Also notice you can use the changing cell addresses in your formulas. When you do that, you assume the Solver has put the optimal values in each changing cell; your expression makes use of that number.

Excel evaluates the formulas and yields these cell values:

	A	B	C	D	E
16	**Calculations**				
17	Ratio of Basketballs to Footballs	1			
18	Total Basketball hours used	0.5			
19	Total Football hours used	0.3			
20	Total machine hours used (FB + BB)	0.8			
21					

Fig. D-4

Income Statement The target value is calculated in the spreadsheet body. This is the value that the Solver is expected to maximize or minimize. The spreadsheet body can take any form. In this book's Solver cases, the spreadsheet body will be an income statement, which is a form business students understand.

Here are the skeleton and formulas that you should enter:

	A	B	C
22	**Income Statement**		
23	Basketball revenue	=B3*B7	
24	Football revenue	=B4*B8	
25	Total Revenue	=B23+B24	
26	Basketball materials cost	=B3*B13	
27	Football materials cost	=B4*B14	
28	Cost of labor	=B20*B12	
29	Total cost of goods sold	=SUM(B26:B28)	
30	Pre-tax income	=B25-B29	
31	Income tax expense	=IF(B30<=0,0,B30*B9)	
32	Net Income	=B30-B31	

Fig. D-5

Note that income statement cells were formatted for two decimals (Format — Cells — Numbers — Decimals — 2). The INT() function is not used so that correct values show when ones are in the changing cells. For example, footballs material cost is $1.25; only $1.00 would show if INT() were used.

Cell formulas are discussed next.

- Revenues (B23, B24) equal the number of balls times the respective unit selling price. The number of balls is in the changing cells, and the selling prices are constants.

- Materials costs (B26, B27) follow a similar logic: number of units times unit cost.

- The cost of labor is the calculated number of machine hours times the hourly labor rate for machine workers.

- This is the logic of income tax expense: If pre-tax income is less than or equal to zero, the tax is zero, else the tax equals the tax rate times the pre-tax income. An =IF() statement is needed in B31.

Excel evaluates the formulas and yields these cell values:

	A	B	C	D	E
22	**Income Statement**				
23	Basketball revenue	14.00			
24	Football revenue	11.00			
25	Total Revenue	25.00			
26	Basketball materials cost	2.00			
27	Football materials cost	1.25			
28	Cost of labor	4.80			
29	Total cost of goods sold	8.05			
30	Pre-tax income	16.95			
31	Income tax expense	4.75			
32	Net Income	12.20			

Fig. D-6

Constraints These are rules that the Solver must observe when computing the optimal answer. There isn't a section on the face of the spreadsheet for constraints. However, constraints will need to refer to calculated values, or to values in the spreadsheet body. Therefore, you must build those calculations into the spreadsheet design, so they are available to your constraint expressions. You'll use a separate window to enter constraints.

These are English and Excel expressions for the basketball and football production problem constraints:

Solver Constraint Expressions

Expression in English	Excel Expression
TOTAL MACHINE HOURS >= 39000	B20 >= 39000
TOTAL MACHINE HOURS <= 40000	B20 <= 40000
MIN BASKETBALLS = 30000	B3 >= 30000
MAX BASKETBALLS = 60000	B3 <= 60000
MIN FOOTBALLS = 20000	B4 >= 20000
MAX FOOTBALLS = 40000	B4 <= 40000
RATIO BB'S TO FB'S-MIN = 1.5	B17 >= 1.5
RATIO BB'S TO FB'S-MAX = 1.7	B17 <= 1.7
NET INCOME MUST BE POSITIVE	B32 >= 0

Fig. D-7

- Notice that a cell address in a constraint expression can be a changing cell address, a cell address in the calculations section, or a cell address in the spreadsheet body.
- You'll often need to set minimum and maximum boundaries for variables. For example, the number of basketballs ranges between 30,000 and 60,000.

- Often, a boundary value is zero because you want the Solver to find a non-negative result. For example, here you want only answers that yield a positive net income. You tell the Solver the amount in the net income cell must equal or exceed zero, so that the Solver does not find an answer that produces a loss.

- Machine hours must be shared between the two kinds of balls. The constraints for the shared resource are: B20 >= 39000 and B20 <= 40000, where B20 shows the hours used to make the basketballs and footballs together. The shared-resource constraint seems to be the most difficult kind of constraint for students to master when learning the Solver.

Running the Solver: Mechanics

To set up, you must tell the Solver these things:

1. The cell address of the "target" variable that you are trying to maximize (or minimize, as the case may be)

2. The changing cell addresses

3. The expressions for the Constraints

The Solver will put its answers in the changing cells and on a separate sheet.

Beginning to Set Up the Solver

🖳 AT THE KEYBOARD

To start setting up the Solver, select Tools — Solver.

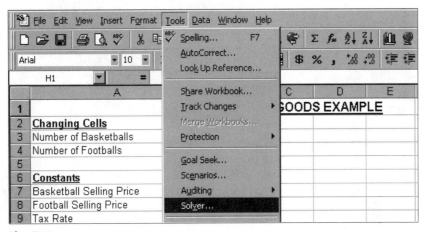

Fig. D-8

The first thing you see is a "Solver Parameters" window. Use this window to specify the target cell, the changing cells, and the constraints.

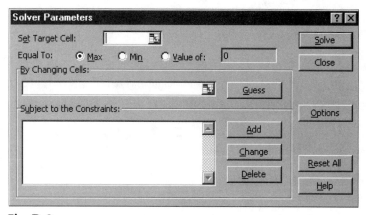

Fig. D-9

Setting the Target Cell

The target cell is net income, B32. To set the target cell, click in that window and enter B32. Max is the default; accept it here. Enter no desired net income value ("Value of").

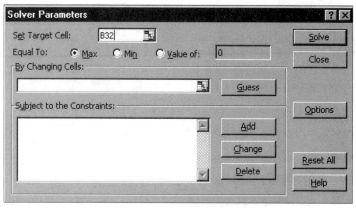

Fig. D-10

DO NOT hit Enter when you finish. You'll navigate within this dialog box by clicking in the next input window. (Note: When you enter the cell address, Solver may put in dollar signs, as if for absolute addressing. Ignore them—do not try to delete them.)

Setting the Changing Cells

The changing cells are the cells for the balls, which are in the range B3:B4. So, click in the changing cell window, and enter B3:B4. (Do not then hit Enter.)

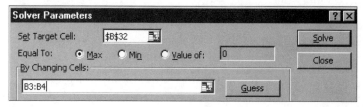

Fig. D-11

Entering Constraints

You are now ready to enter the constraint formulas. The constraints get entered one by one. To start, Click the "Add" button. You'll see the "Add Constraint" window (here, shown with the minimum basketball production constraint entered):

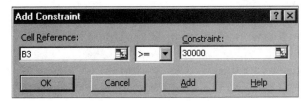

Fig. D-12

- To enter a constraint expression, do four things: (1) type in the variable's cell reference (its address) in the left window; (2) select the operator (<=, =, >=) in the little middle window; (3) enter the right-hand side value, which is either a raw number or the cell address of a value; and (4) click Add to enter the constraint into the program. If you change your mind about the expression and do not want to enter it, click Cancel.

- The minimum basketballs constraint is: B3 >= 30000. Enter that constraint now. (Later Solver may put an equal sign in front of the 30000 and dollar signs in the cell reference.)

- After entering the constraint formula, click the Add button. This puts the constraint into the Solver model. It also leaves you in the Add Constraint window, allowing you to enter other constraints. You should enter those now.

- When you're done entering constraints, click the Cancel button. This takes you back to the Solver Parameter window.

You are not allowed to put an *expression* into the Cell Reference window or into the Constraint window. For example, the constraint for the minimum basketball-to-football ratio is this: B3/B4 >= 1.5. You may not put =B3/B4 into the Cell Reference box. *This is why the ratio is computed in the Calculations section of the spreadsheet* (in cell B17). When adding that constraint, enter B17 in the Cell Reference box.

After entering all the constraints, you'll be back at the Solver Parameters window. You will see the constraints have been entered into the program. The top part of the window's constraints area looks like this:

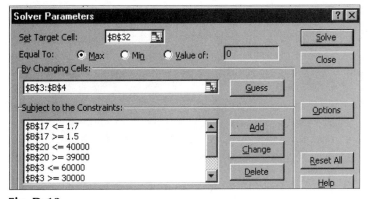

Fig. D-13

Use the scroll arrow, and the rest of the constraints are revealed:

Fig. D-14

Computing the Solver's Answer

To have the Solver actually calculate the answers, click "Solve" in the upper-right-hand corner of the Solver Parameters window. Solver does its work in the background—you do not see the internal calculations. Then the Solver gives you a Solver Results window:

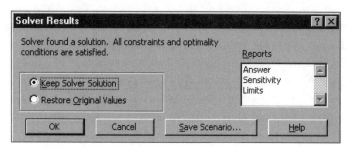

Fig. D-15

In the Solver Results window, the Solver tells you it has found a solution and the "optimality conditions" were met. This is a very important message—you should always check for it. It means an answer was found *and* the constraints were satisfied.

By contrast, your constraints might prohibit the Solver from finding an answer. For example, suppose you had a constraint that said, in effect: "Net income must be at least a billion dollars." That amount cannot be reached with so few basketballs and footballs and these prices. The Solver would report that no answer is feasible.

On the other hand, the Solver may find an answer by ignoring some constraints. Solver would tell you that too. In either case, there is something wrong with your model, and you'll need to rework it.

There are two ways to see your answers. One is to click OK. This lets you see the new changing cell values. A more formal (and better) way is to click Answer in the Reports window and then OK. This puts detailed results into a new sheet in your Excel book. The new sheet is called an "Answer Report." Answer Reports are numbered sequentially as you run the Solver.

To see the Answer Report, click its tab (here, Answer Report 1):

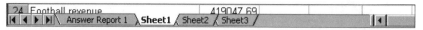

Fig. D-16

That takes you to the Answer Report:

6	Target Cell (Max)					
7	**Cell**	**Name**		**Original Value**	**Final Value**	
8	B32	Net Income SPORTING GOODS EXAMPLE		12.20	588342.87	
9						
10						
11	Adjustable Cells					
12	**Cell**	**Name**		**Original Value**	**Final Value**	
13	B3	Number of Basketballs SPORTING GOODS EXAMPLE		1	57142.85348	
14	B4	Number of Footballs SPORTING GOODS EXAMPLE		1	38095.2442	
15						
16						
17	Constraints					
18	**Cell**	**Name**	**Cell Value**	**Formula**	**Status**	
19	B20	Total machine hours used (FB + BB) SPORTING GOODS EXAMPLE	40000	B20<=40000	Binding	
20	B20	Total machine hours used (FB + BB) SPORTING GOODS EXAMPLE	40000	B20>=39000	Not Binding	
21	B17	Ratio of Basketballs to Footballs SPORTING GOODS EXAMPLE	1.499999663	B17<=1.7	Not Binding	0
22	B17	Ratio of Basketballs to Footballs SPORTING GOODS EXAMPLE	1.499999663	B17>=1.5	Binding	
23	B32	Net Income SPORTING GOODS EXAMPLE	588342.87	B32>=0	Not Binding	
24	B3	Number of Basketballs SPORTING GOODS EXAMPLE	57142.85348	B3>=30000	Not Binding	2
25	B3	Number of Basketballs SPORTING GOODS EXAMPLE	57142.85348	B3<=60000	Not Binding	
26	B4	Number of Footballs SPORTING GOODS EXAMPLE	38095.2442	B4>=20000	Not Binding	
27	B4	Number of Footballs SPORTING GOODS EXAMPLE	38095.2442	B4<=40000	Not Binding	

Fig. D-17

At the start, the changing cells had a 1, and the income was $12.20 ("Original Value"). The optimal solution values ("Final Value") are also shown: $588,343 for net income (the target), and 57,143 basketballs and 38,095 footballs for the changing (adjustable) cells. (This ignores decimal values. The Solver can be asked to find only integer solutions; this technique is discussed at the end of this tutorial.)

The report also shows detail for the constraints: the constraint expression and the value that the variable has in the optimal solution. "Binding" means the final answer caused Solver to bump up against the constraint. For example, the maximum number of machine hours was 40,000, and that is how many Solver used in finding the answer.

"Not Binding" means the reverse. A better word for "binding" might be "constraining." The 60,000 maximum basketball limit did not constrain, for example.

The procedures used to change (edit) or delete a constraint are discussed later in this tutorial.

Print the Solver spreadsheets, save the Excel files, and exit from Excel in the normal way. These procedures are reviewed at the end of this tutorial.

➤ EXTENDING THE EXAMPLE

Next, you'll modify the sporting goods spreadsheet. Management wants to know what net income would be if certain constraints were changed. In other words, management wants to play "what-if" with certain Base Case constraints. The resulting second case is called the "Extension Case."

- Assume that maximum-production constraints will be removed.

- Similarly, the basketball to football production ratio constraints (1.5, 1.7) will be removed.

- There will still be minimum-production constraints at some low level: Assume that at least 30,000 basketballs and 30,000 footballs will be produced.
- The machine-hours shared resource still imposes the same limits as it did previously.
- A more ambitious profit goal is desired: The ratio of net income to total revenue should be greater than or equal to .33. This constraint will replace the constraint calling for profits greater than zero.

⊞ **AT THE KEYBOARD**

Enter a formula computing the ratio of net income to total revenue in cell B21. The formula should have the net income cell in the numerator and total revenue in the denominator. The value of this ratio for the Solver's optimal answer must be at least .33. Click the Add button and enter this constraint:

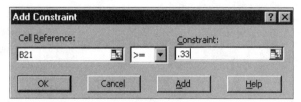

Fig. D-18

Next, in the Solver Parameters window, constraints that are no longer needed are highlighted (select by clicking) and deleted (click the Delete button). Do that for the net income >= 0 constraint and the basketball-football ratio constraints.

The minimum football constraint must be modified, not deleted. Select that constraint, then click Change. That takes you to the Add Constraint window. Edit the constraint so 30,000 is the lower boundary.

When you are finished with the constraints, the Solver Parameter window looks like this:

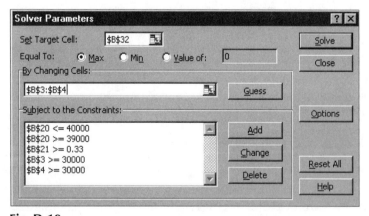

Fig. D-19

The constraints are now only for the minimum production levels, the ratio of net income to revenue, and the machine-hours shared resource.

When the Solver is run, the Answer Report looks like this:

5						
6	Target Cell (Max)					
7	Cell	Name		Original Value	Final Value	
8	B32	Net Income SPORTING GOODS EXAMPLE		12.20	671400.00	
9						
10						
11	Adjustable Cells					
12	Cell	Name		Original Value	Final Value	
13	B3	Number of Basketballs SPORTING GOODS EXAMPLE		1	30000	
14	B4	Number of Footballs SPORTING GOODS EXAMPLE		1	83333.33333	
15						
16						
17	Constraints					
18	Cell	Name	Cell Value	Formula	Status	
19	B21	Ratio of Net Income / Total Revenue SPORTING GOODS EXAMPLE	0.502294264	B21>=0.33	Not Binding	
20	B20	Total machine hours used (FB + BB) SPORTING GOODS EXAMPLE	40000	B20<=40000	Binding	
21	B20	Total machine hours used (FB + BB) SPORTING GOODS EXAMPLE	40000	B20>=39000	Not Binding	
22	B3	Number of Basketballs SPORTING GOODS EXAMPLE	30000	B3>=30000	Binding	
23	B4	Number of Footballs SPORTING GOODS EXAMPLE	83333.33333	B4>=30000	Not Binding	
24						

Fig. D-20

The Extension Case answer differs from the Base Case answer. Which production schedule should management use? The one that has maximum production limits? Or the one that has no such limits?

The question is posed to get you to think about the purpose of using a DSS program. Two scenarios, the Base Case and the Extension Case, were modeled in the Solver. The answers are as shown:

The Solver's Answers to the Two Scenarios

	Base Case	Extension Case
Basketballs	57143	30000
Footballs	38095	83333

Fig. D-21

Are you able to use this output, alone, to decide how many of each kind of ball to produce? No, you cannot. You must also refer to the "Target," which in this case is net income.

The Solver's Answers to the Two Scenarios—With Target Data

	Base Case	Extension Case
Basketballs	57143	30000
Footballs	38095	83333
Net Income	$588,343	$671,400

Fig. D-22

Viewed this way, the Extension Case production schedule looks better, *because it gives you a better target net income.*

⌘ USING THE SOLVER ON A NEW PROBLEM

Here is a short problem that will let you test what you have learned about the Excel Solver.

Assume you run a shirt-manufacturing company. You have two products: (1) polo-style T-shirts, and (2) dress shirts with button-down collars. You must decide how many T-shirts and how many button-down shirts to make. Assume you'll sell every shirt you make.

⊞ AT THE KEYBOARD

Set up a Solver spreadsheet to handle this problem.

Changing Cells The Changing cells should look like this:

	A	B	C	D	E	F	G
1		**SHIRT MANUFACTURING PROBLEM**					
2	**Changing Cells:**						
3	Number of T-Shirts		1				
4	Number of Button Down Shirts		1				

Fig. D-23

Constants The Constants should look like this:

	A	B	C	D	E	F
6	**Constants:**					
7	Tax Rate		0.28			
8	Selling price: T-Shirt		8			
9	Selling price: Button Down		36			
10	Variable cost to make: T-Shirt		2.5			
11	Variable cost to make: Button Down		14			
12	Cotton usage (lbs): T-Shirt		1.5			
13	Cotton usage (lbs): Button Down		2.5			
14	Total cotton available (lbs)		13000000			
15	Buttons per T-Shirt		3			
16	Buttons per Button Down		12			
17	Total buttons available		110000000			

Fig. D-24

The constants cells (and some of your company's operations) are discussed next.

- The tax rate is .28 on pre-tax income, but no taxes are paid on losses.

- You sell a polo-style T-shirt for $8, and a button-down shirt for $36.

- It costs $2.50 to make a T-shirt, and it costs $14 to make a button-down shirt. These variable costs are for machine-operator labor, cloth, buttons, and so forth.

- Each polo T-shirt uses 1.5 pounds of cotton fabric. Each button-down shirt uses 2.5 pounds of cotton fabric. You have only 13 million pounds of cotton on hand to be used to make all the T-shirts and button-down shirts.

- Each polo T-shirt has 3 buttons. Each button-down shirt has a button on each collar tip, 8 buttons down the front, and 1 on each cuff, for a total of 12 buttons. You have 110 million buttons on hand to be used to make all your shirts.

Calculations Your spreadsheet needs these calculations:

	A	B	C	D	E	F
19	**Calculations:**					
20	Ratio of net income to total revenue					
21	Cotton used: T-Shirts					
22	Cotton used: Button Downs					
23	Cotton used: total					
24	Buttons used: T-Shirts					
25	Buttons used: Button Downs					
26	Buttons used: total					
27	Ratio of Button Downs to T-Shirts					

Fig. D-25

Calculations (and related business constraints) are discussed next.

- Your minimum return on sales (net income divided by total revenue) is .20.
- You have a limited amount of cotton and buttons. Use of each resource must be calculated, then used in constraints.
- You think you must make at least 2 million T-shirts and at least 2 million button-down shirts. You want to be known as a balanced shirt maker, so you think the ratio of button-downs to T-shirts should be no greater than 4:1. (Thus, if 9 million button-down shirts and 2 million T-shirts were produced, the ratio would be too high.)

Income Statement Your spreadsheet should have this income statement skeleton:

	A	B	C	D	E	F
29	**Income Statement:**					
30	T-Shirt Revenue					
31	Button-Down Revenue					
32	Total Revenue					
33	Variable costs: T-Shirts					
34	Variable costs: Button Downs					
35	Total Costs					
36	Pre-Tax Revenue					
37	Income Tax Expense					
38	Net Income					

Fig. D-26

The Solver's target is net income, which must be maximized.

You can use this table to write out your constraints before entering them into the Solver.

Solver Constraints

Expression in English	Excel Expression
Net income to revenue	_____ >= _____
Ratio of BDs to Ts	_____ <= _____
Minimum T-shirts	_____ >= _____
Minimum Button Downs	_____ >= _____
Usage of buttons	_____ <= _____
Usage of cotton	_____ <= _____

Fig. D-27

Enter your calculations and income statement formulas. Enter the constraints. Run the Solver to get an answer to the production problem.

➤ TROUBLESHOOTING THE SOLVER

Use this section to overcome problems with the Solver and as a review of some of Windows file-handling procedures.

Rerunning a Solver Model

Assume you have changed your spreadsheet in some way and want to rerun the Solver to get a new set of answers. (For example, you may have changed a constraint or a formula in your spreadsheet.) Before you click "Solve" again to rerun the Solver, you should put the number 1 in the Changing Cells. The Solver can sometimes give odd answers if its point of departure is a set of *prior* answers.

Creating Over-constrained Models

It is possible to set up a model that has no logical solution. For example, in the second version of the sporting goods problem, suppose you specified a need for at least 1 million basketballs. When "Solve" is clicked, the Solver tries to compute an answer, but then admits defeat by telling you that no feasible solution is possible:

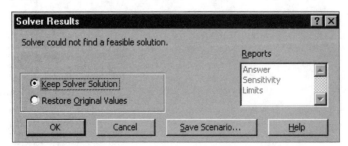

Fig. D-28

In the Reports window, the choices ("Answer", etc.) would be in gray—indicating they are not available as options. Such a model is called an "over-constrained" model.

Setting a Constraint to a Single Amount

It's possible you'll want an amount to be a specific number, as opposed to a number in a range. For example, if the number of basketballs needed to be exactly 30,000, then the "equals" operator would be selected:

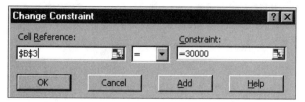

Fig. D-29

Setting a Changing Cell to an Integer

You may want to force changing cell values to be integers. The way to do that is to select the "int" operator (shown here using the Change Constraint window). Assume you wanted the number of basketballs to be an integer.

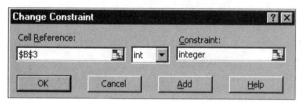

Fig. D-30

In the middle window, select "int" from the drop-down menu. The Solver puts the word "integer" into the Constraint window.

Forcing Solver to find only integer solutions slows the Solver down. The change in speed can be noticeable to the user in some cases. Doing this can also prevent the Solver from seeing a feasible solution—when one can be found if the Solver is allowed to find non-integer answers. For these reasons, it's often best to *not* impose the integer constraint.

Eliminating Decimals from Values

You may want to show Calculations and Income Statement values without decimals. There are two ways to do this, and these are best discussed by examples.

The first way is to use the INT() function in the expression. In the Income Statement in this tutorial's first section, this formula calculated the cost of labor: =B20*B12. The resulting value was 4.80, when 1's were in the changing cells. This formula would have yielded the value 4: =INT(B20*B12), i.e., the pennies would be dropped.

The second way is to use the ROUND() function. The function =ROUND() rounds values up if the decimal value is .50 or greater, or else down. In the Income Statement, this formula would round the cost of labor to a whole number: =ROUND(B20*B12,0). The value in the cell would be 5 (not 4). Just for your information: The "0" in the ROUND() expression means "show zero decimals". If the expression had been =ROUND(B20*B12,2), the value would have been rounded to two decimals.

In the tutorial example, it seems wise to retain decimal values in order to retain accuracy when the number 1 shows in the changing cells.

Deleting Extra Answer Sheets

Suppose you've run different scenarios, each time asking for an Answer Report. As a result, you have a number of Answer Report sheets in your Excel file, but you don't want to keep them all. How do you get rid of an Answer Report sheet?

First, get the unwanted Answer Report sheet on the screen by clicking on the sheet's tab. Then select Edit — Delete Sheet. You will be asked if you really mean it. If you do, click accordingly.

Restarting the Solver with All New Constraints

Suppose you wanted to start over, *with a new set of constraints*. In the Solver Parameter window, click Reset All. You will be asked if you really mean it:

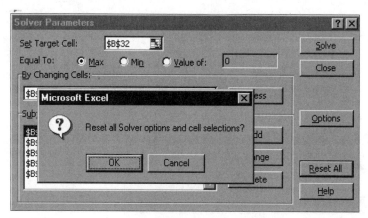

Fig. D-31

If you do, then click OK. This gives you a clean slate (see below) with all constraints deleted. From that point, you can specify a new model.

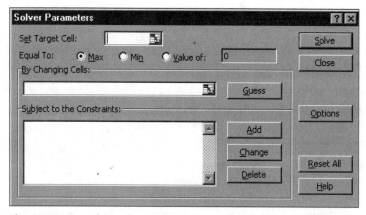

Fig. D-32

Note: If you do this, you really are starting over. If you merely want to add, delete, or edit a constraint, do not use Reset All. Use the Add, Delete, or Change buttons, as the case may be.

Printing Cell Formulas in Excel

To show the Cell Formulas on the screen, press the Ctrl and the left quote (`) keys at the same time: Ctrl-`. (The left quote is usually on the same key as the tilde [~].) This automatically widens cells so the formulas can be read. You can change cell widths by clicking and dragging at the column indicator ("A," "B," etc.) boundaries.

To print the formulas, just use File — Print. Print the sheet as you would normally. To restore the screen to its typical appearance (showing values, not formulas), press Ctrl-` *again*. (It's like a toggle switch.) If you did not change any column widths when in the cell formula view, the widths will be as they were.

Review of Printing, Saving, and Exiting Procedures

Print the Solver spreadsheets in the normal way. Activate the sheet, then select File — Print. You can print an Answer Report sheet in the same way.

To save, use File — Save, or File — Save As. Be sure to select drive A: in the Drive window. When exiting from Excel, always start with File — Close (with the diskette in drive A:), then select File — Exit. If you merely use File — Exit you risk losing your work.

16

Preliminary Case
The Publishing House Decision

DECISION SUPPORT USING THE EXCEL SOLVER

✦ PREVIEW

You run a publishing house that publishes a comic book series and a paperback book series. In this case, you'll use the Excel Solver to decide how many of each to publish to maximize net income in the next year. You will document your recommendation in a memorandum.

✦ PREPARATION

- Review spreadsheet concepts discussed in class and/or in your text.
- Complete any exercises your instructor assigns.
- Complete any part of Tutorial D your instructor assigns.
- Review file-saving procedures for Windows programs. These are discussed in Tutorial D.

⮞ BACKGROUND

Your publishing house produces two products: (1) Computer Man Comix, a comic book series about a brave-hearted programmer, and (2) Keyboard Romance, a line of paperback books about romance between computer programmers.

During the course of a year, you expect to produce 12 new comic book episodes and 6 novel titles. You'll print the same number of comic books for each episode; you'll print the same number of books for each novel title. You must decide how many total comic books and novels to produce in the next year. Because sales have been so good, you assume that you'll sell everything you print.

You sell each issue of the comic book for $1 and each paperback book for $6.75. The variable cost of a comic book is $.33; the variable cost of the paperback book is $2.75. The variable costs are fees for writers and designers and production costs. In addition to variable costs, you will have $2,000,000 of fixed costs (management salary, rent, etc.). Fixed costs are independent of comic book or paperback book production levels.

The romance novels and comic books are printed on the same kind of paper. Each comic book produced requires .15 pounds of paper. Each paperback book requires .50 pounds of paper. Under your current contract with your paper supplier, you expect to have 10 million pounds of paper on hand for next year's comic book and paperback book production. You want to use as much of this resource as possible, so your production should consume at least 9.5 million pounds of paper.

A certain paper broker can provide you with an extra 5 million pounds of paper—if you are willing to pay a higher-than-normal amount for the added resource.

The income tax rate is 28% on pre-tax revenues over zero. No income taxes are paid on losses.

Your minimum return on sales (net income divided by total revenue) is 20%. You feel that you must print at least 1 million issues of the comic book and at least 1 million paperback books. You want to be known as a diversified publisher, so you feel that the ratio of novels to comics published should be no greater than 10:1 but no less than 5:1. Thus, if you produced 11 million novels and 1 million comics, the ratio would be too high; 4 million novels and 1 million comics, and the ratio would be too low.

⮞ ASSIGNMENT 1: CREATING A SPREADSHEET FOR DECISION SUPPORT

In this assignment, you will make two Solver spreadsheets to model the production decision. In the "Base Case," you'll model the production planning decision, without regard to the extra paper that you could buy. In the "Extension Case," you'll include the possibility of having the extra paper to support added production. Each model will be an income statement forecast for the next year.

Your spreadsheets should have sections for Changing Cells, Constants, Calculations, and the Income Statement. You are shown how each section should be set up before you enter cell formulas. Your spreadsheets should also include the decision's constraints, which you'll enter using the Solver.

Then, in Assignment 2, you'll use the models to develop information so you can decide how many comics and novels to publish—and whether you want to buy the extra paper. You'll then document your recommendations in a memorandum.

A discussion of each spreadsheet section follows. The discussion is about (1) how each section should be set up, and (2) the logic of the formulas in the section's cells. When you type in the spreadsheet skeleton, follow the order given in this section.

Changing Cells Your spreadsheet should have these changing cells:

	A	B	C	D	E
	The Publishing House Production Problem				
	Changing Cells				
	Number of comics		1		
	Number of novels		1		

Fig. 16-1

You are asking the Solver model to compute how many comics and paperbacks to make to maximize net income. Start with "1" in each cell. The Solver will change each 1 as it computes the answer.

Constants Your spreadsheet should have these constants:

	A	B	C	D	E
	Constants				
	Selling price of comic		1		
	Selling price of novel		6.75		
	Cost to make a comic		0.33		
	Cost to make a novel		2.75		
	Fixed costs		2000000		
	Paper usage per comic		0.15		
	Paper usage per novel		0.5		
	Available paper		10000000		
	Tax rate expected		0.28		

Fig. 16-2

- The selling prices of a comic and a novel are for the coming year.
- The variable cost to make a comic and novel are for the coming year. These costs include the cost of writers, paper, direct labor, printing, and so on.
- Fixed costs are set for the coming year, no matter how many—or few—comics and novels are produced.
- The pound weight of paper used to make a comic and a novel is shown. The number of pounds of paper available in the coming year is shown.
- The tax rate expected applies to positive pre-tax revenue.

Calculations Your spreadsheet should calculate these intermediate results, which are then used in the Income Statement and/or in the Constraints. Calculated values may be based on the values of the Constants, the Changing Cells, and/or other Calculations.

	A	B	C	D	E
Calculations					
Paper used for comics					
Paper used for novels					
Paper used - total					
Net Income / Revenue ratio					
Novels / Comics ratio					

Fig. 16-3

- Calculate the amount of paper used in making all comics. Do the same for the paper used to make all novels.
- Total paper used is for both comics and novels.
- The net income-to-revenue ratio is the year's net income divided by total revenue.
- The novels-to-comics ratio is the ratio of total novels produced to total comics produced.

Income Statement This statement is for projected net income in the coming year. Some of the line items are discussed next.

	A	B	C	D	E
Income Statement					
Comic revenue					
Novel revenue					
Total revenue					
Fixed Costs					
Cost of making comics					
Cost of making novels					
Total costs					
Pre-tax revenue					
Income tax expense					
Net Income					

Fig. 16-4

- Comic revenue is a function of the number of comics produced and sold and the selling price of a comic. Novel revenue is calculated in the same way.
- The cost of making comics is a function of the number of comics produced and sold and the variable cost of a comic. The cost of making novels is calculated in the same way.
- Income tax expense is zero if pre-tax revenue is zero or negative; otherwise, apply the tax rate times pre-tax income.

Constraints and Running the Solver Determine what the constraints are. Enter the Base Case decision constraints, using the Solver. Run the Solver, and ask for the Answer Report when the Solver tells you a solution has been found that satisfies the constraints.

When you're done, print the entire workbook, including the Solver Report sheet. Save the workbook (File — Save; PubBase.xls would be a good name). Then, in order to prepare for the extension case, use File — *Save As* to make a *new* spreadsheet. (PubExt.xls would be a good file name.)

Assignment 1B: Creating the Spreadsheet—Extension Case

You are able to have 5 million more pounds of paper on hand in the year. This would let you print and sell more comics and novels. You would have to pay the paper supplier 4 million dollars for the added paper, however. You need to know whether the added cost of paper is justified by the added sales.

You would increase the year's fixed costs by the added cost of paper and adjust the pounds-of-paper-available constant. If you had the added paper, you would want to consume at least 14.5 million pounds of paper in your production. Assume the other Base Case constraints remain in force.

Adjust the spreadsheet and the constraints, and then run the Solver. Ask for the Answer Report when the Solver tells you a solution has been found that satisfies the constraints. When you're done, print the entire workbook, including the Solver Report sheet. Save the workbook. Close the file and then exit from Excel.

ASSIGNMENT 2: USING THE SPREADSHEET FOR DECISION SUPPORT

You have built the Base Case and the Extension Case models because you want to know (1) whether you should buy the extra paper, and (2) how many comics and novels to produce in the coming year.

You will now complete the case by (1) using the Answer Reports to gather the data you need to make the production and paper purchasing decisions, and (2) documenting your recommendations in a memorandum.

Assignment 2A: Using the Spreadsheets to Gather Data

You have printed the Answer Report sheets for each paper inventory scenario. Each sheet tells how many comics and novels to print, given the paper available, and the target net income in each case. Note that data for each case by constructing the following table on a separate sheet of paper. In Assignment 2B, you will use your word processor to turn the data into a table.

Summary Table

	10 M lbs. of Paper	15 M lbs. of Paper
Number of Comics		
Number of Novels		
Net Income		

Fig. 16-5

Assignment 2B: Documenting Your Recommendation in a Memorandum

Write a brief memorandum about the results to your manufacturing manager, purchasing manager, and treasurer. (The same memo will go to each person.)

- Your memorandum should have a proper heading (DATE/ TO/ FROM/ SUBJECT). You may wish to use a Word memo template (File — New, click Memos, choose Contemporary Memo).

- Briefly outline the paper-purchasing decision. Then state how much paper to have available, how many comics and novels to produce, and the net income expected.

- Support your recommendations with a summary data table. (To make a table in MS Word, select the Table menu option. Enter the number of rows and columns. Select Autoformat. Choose the format desired—Grid 1 is a good choice.) Your table should show the data you noted in Assignment 2A.

✦ DELIVERABLES

1. Memorandum
2. Base Case and Extension Case spreadsheet printouts
3. Diskette, which should have your memorandum file and your Excel files

Staple printouts together, with the memo on top. Handwrite a note to your instructor, stating the name of the .xls files.

17
CASE

The Branch Library Decision

➤ PREVIEW

Your city's library is about to build a neighborhood branch library. A site has been chosen, but library administrators have yet to stock the library. In this case, you'll use the Excel Solver to help them decide which books, and possibly Internet computers, should be bought. You will document your recommendation in a memorandum.

➤ PREPARATION

- Review spreadsheet concepts discussed in class and/or in your text.
- Complete any exercises your instructor assigns.
- Complete any part of Tutorial D your instructor assigns.
- Review file-saving procedures for Windows programs. These are discussed in Tutorial D.

The city's plan to build a new branch library has elicited a firestorm of controversy. Detractors say the main library is sufficient for everyone's needs and building a branch library is a waste of money. Nevertheless, the town council has voted to build the library. A civic group that supports the plan has promised to donate funds to purchase all reference books and periodicals. You've been asked to help determine what "circulating" books should be purchased. The head librarian says there are three categories of books to buy for the circulating collection: children's books, works of fiction, and works of nonfiction.

The average cost of a book in each category is:

children's: $11.00   *fiction*: $14.00   *nonfiction*: $18.00

Books are shelved "standing up" (vertically). Each book occupies this much horizontal shelf space:

children's: .05 feet   *fiction*: .10 feet   *nonfiction*: .17 feet

(Decimal .05 feet is a little more than a half-inch, .10 feet is about 1.25 inches, and .17 feet is about 2 inches. Use the decimal fractions of a foot in your spreadsheet.)

The new building can accommodate 10,000 feet of bookshelf space. Shelving costs $1 per linear foot.

To silence detractors, town council members insist that the new library be "run like a business" so voters can see its dollar value to the community. This entails using an analogue of the profit-and-loss system. The librarian agrees and suggests that each time a book is checked out, the library will pay itself a "transfer price." No money will actually change hands; the transfer price just represents what the librarian thinks someone would be willing to pay to rent a book for two weeks. For example, someone might be willing to rent a book for $7 rather than paying $30 to buy it.

The town council members say that a projected income statement must be made for the new library. Total transfer price "revenue" should exceed ("pay back") the outlays for new books and shelving within a reasonable period of time—3 years. In fact, the council requires that a net income of 3 million dollars be earned in that time to justify the project. Furthermore, they say that earnings should be "taxed" like any other business and propose a 30% tax rate.

During the 3 years, each book will be checked out an average of this many times:

children's: 45 times   *fiction*: 40 times   *nonfiction*: 20 times

The transfer price to be "earned" with each checkout for each type of book is:

children's: $5.00   *fiction*: $7.00   *nonfiction*: $9.00

Thus, in your system you'll want to maximize the difference between "checkout revenues" and the costs of books and shelving. You can consider that difference the same as a profit-making enterprise's "net income."

The librarian has some other rules:

- No more than 50,000 books can be purchased in total. Libraries usually hold more books than this, but in order to gain city council approval, it was agreed that the branch would not be large enough to "compete" with the main library.

- Enough books must be purchased to occupy at least 4,500 linear feet of shelf space. If more than 4,500 feet is needed, shelving will be purchased as needed, up to the limit of 10,000 feet.

- At least 10,000 fiction books must be purchased, but there cannot be more than 12,000 fiction books.

- The council wants a kid-friendly library, so at least 10,000 children's books must be purchased.

- The number of nonfiction books purchased must be at least twice the number of fiction books purchased.

One of the town council members is the chief information officer (CIO) for a local corporation. She wants Internet access to be available to library patrons—even though the computers would take up some space otherwise used for books. The views of the CIO are discussed in Assignment 1B.

ASSIGNMENT 1: CREATING A SPREADSHEET FOR DECISION SUPPORT

In this two-part assignment, you will make two Solver spreadsheets to model the book-buying decision. In the "Base Case," you will model the book-buying decision without regard to the CIO's view of libraries. In the "Extension Case," you'll factor computers and Internet access into the decision.

Your spreadsheets should have sections for Changing Cells, Constants, Calculations, and the Income Statement. You are shown how each section should be set up before you enter cell formulas. Each Solver model will be an income statement forecast for the three-year period. Your spreadsheets should also include the decision's constraints, which you'll enter using the Solver.

Then, in Assignment 2, you'll use the models to develop information to determine how many of each kind of book to buy and whether computers should be purchased. You'll then document your recommendations in a memorandum.

Assignment 1A: Creating the Spreadsheet—Base Case

A discussion of each spreadsheet section follows. The discussion is about (1) how each section should be set up, and (2) the logic of the formulas in the section's cells. When you type in the spreadsheet skeleton, follow the order given in this section.

Changing Cells Your spreadsheet should have these changing cells:

A	B	C	D	E
The Branch Library Decision				
Changing Cells				
Number of Children's Books	1			
Number of Fiction Books	1			
Number of Nonfiction Books	1			

Fig. 17-1

You are asking the Solver to compute how many of each kind of book to stock. Start with a "1" in each cell. Leave two blank lines after the Changing Cells section for the Extension Case.

Constants Your spreadsheet should have these constants:

A	B	C	D	E
Constants				
Avg width of Children's book	0.05			
Avg width of Fiction book	0.1			
Avg width of Nonfiction book	0.17			
Transfer price, Children's book	5			
Transfer price, Fiction book	7			
Transfer price, Nonfiction book	9			
Avg cost, Children's book	11			
Avg cost, Fiction book	14			
Avg cost, Nonfiction book	18			
Expected # checkouts, Children's book	45			
Expected # checkouts, Fiction book	40			
Expected # checkouts, Nonfiction book	20			
Maximum footage of shelving	10000			
Cost per foot of shelving	1			
Tax rate expected	0.3			

Fig. 17-2

- The average width of each kind of book is shown. Books are shelved vertically.
- The average transfer price for each kind of book is shown. Transfer prices will prevail for the 3-year period.
- The average cost to purchase each kind of book is shown.
- The expected number of times a book will be checked out is shown. Example: The nonfiction book *The All-Thumbs Guide to Home Plumbing* would be checked out an average of 20 times in 3 years.
- The library can hold 10,000 feet of shelf space, but no more.
- Shelving costs $1 per linear foot.
- The tax rate to be applied to pre-tax revenue is 30%.

Leave five blank lines after the Constants section for the Extension Case.

Calculations Your spreadsheet should calculate these intermediate results, which are then used in the Income Statement and/or in the Constraints. Calculated values may be based on the values of the Constants, the Changing Cells, and/or the other Calculations.

A	B	C	D	E
Calculations				
Number of feet of shelving used, Children's				
Number of feet of shelving used, Fiction				
Number of feet of shelving used, Nonfiction				
Total number of feet of shelving used				
# checkouts, Children's books				
# checkouts, Fiction books				
# checkouts, Nonfiction books				
Total number of books bought				
Ratio of Nonfiction to Fiction books				

Fig. 17-3

- Compute the number of linear feet used by each type of book.
- The total number of feet of shelving used is the sum of shelving needed for all books.

- Compute the total checkouts for each type of book.
- Compute the total number of books purchased.
- The ratio of nonfiction to fiction books must be at least 2 to 1.

Leave two blank lines after the Calculations section for the Extension Case.

Income Statement This statement is for projected net income in the three years. Some of the line items are discussed next.

A	B	C	D	E
Income Statement				
Checkout revenue, Children's				
Checkout revenue, Fiction				
Checkout revenue, Nonfiction				
Total checkout revenue				
Cost of shelving				
Cost of Children's books				
Cost of Fiction books				
Cost of Nonfiction books				
Total costs of shelving and books				
Pre-tax revenue				
Income tax expense				
Net Income				

Fig. 17-4

- Checkout revenue for a type of book is a function of the number of checkouts and the transfer price.
- The cost of shelving is a function of the number of feet of shelving needed and the price per linear foot.
- The cost of each type of book is a function of the number of each type stocked and that type's average cost.
- Income tax expense is zero if pre-tax revenue is zero or negative; otherwise, apply the tax rate times pre-tax revenue.

Constraints and Running the Solver Determine what the constraints are. (Of course, part of a book cannot be purchased.) Using the Solver, enter the Base Case decision constraints. Run the Solver. When the Solver tells you a solution has been found that satisfies the constraints, ask for the Answer Report.

When you are done, print the entire workbook, including the Solver Answer Report sheet. Save the workbook (File—Save; LibBase.xls would be a good name). Then, in order to prepare for the Extension Case, use File—Save As to make a new spreadsheet. (LibExt.xls would be a good file name.)

Assignment 1B: Creating the Spreadsheet—Extension Case

The CIO says that the state government has a program that underwrites outfitting libraries for Internet access. Under this program, the cost of computers, printers, paper and other supplies, systems personnel, and Internet access charges are substantially paid for by the state. The average purchase and operating cost of an Internet computer would be only $500 for the 3-year period. The cost of hiring a network administrator to set up and run the computers would be $80,000 (total) for the three years.

The CIO and librarian have agreed there would be at least 20 Internet computers, but no more than 40. Installing computers would mean less space for books. At least 6,000 children's books would be needed. At least 5,000 fiction books would be needed, but no more than 6,000. The ratio of nonfiction to fiction books must still be at least 2 to 1. No more than 30,000 books could be shelved. At least 3,000 feet of shelf space would still be needed, but no more than 6,000.

The CIO and librarian surveyed other libraries that have Internet machines and have learned that each machine would probably be used 10,000 times in the next 3 years to access the Internet. The internal transfer price for each use of an Internet machine will be 25 cents.

You need to know how many books and Internet machines will be needed to maximize net income in the Extension Case. Add constants for the cost of an Internet machine, the expected number of Internet uses per machine, and for the 3-year cost of the network administrator. Add a calculation for the number of total Internet uses in the 3 years. Your income statement should now include Internet access revenue, the cost of the Internet machines, and the cost of the administrator. Adjust the Solver to include a changing cell for the number of Internet machines. (Of course, part of a computer cannot be purchased.) Your target cell address will also change. Add or change constraints as needed for the Extension Case.

Run the Solver. When the Solver tells you a solution has been found that satisfies the constraints, ask for an Answer Report. When you're done, print the entire workbook, including the Solver Answer Report sheet. Save the workbook. Close the file and then exit from Excel.

➥ ASSIGNMENT 2: USING THE SPREADSHEET FOR DECISION SUPPORT

You have built the Base Case and the Extension Case models because you want to know whether to stock the library with books or a mix of books and computers.

Now complete the case by (1) using the Answer Reports to gather data you need to make the decision, and (2) documenting your recommendation in a memorandum.

Assignment 2A: Using the Spreadsheet to Gather Data

You've printed the Answer Report sheets for each scenario. Each sheet tells how many of each kind of book to buy and the target net income in each case. Note that data for each case by constructing the following table on a separate sheet of paper. In Assignment 2B you'll use your word processor to turn this data into a table.

Summary Table

	Base Case	Extension Case
# children's books		
# fiction books		
# nonfiction books		
# Internet machines	None	
Net income		

Fig. 17-5

Assignment 2B: Documenting Your Recommendation in a Memorandum

Write a brief memorandum to the head librarian, stating your results.

- Your memorandum should have a proper heading (DATE/ TO/ FROM/ SUBJECT). You may wish to use a Word memo template (File — New, click Memos, choose Contemporary Memo).

- Briefly outline the library-configuration decision. Then state how many books of each kind to buy and whether the library should be outfitted with Internet machines. If computers are to be purchased, state how many machines should be installed.

- Support your recommendations with a summary table. (To make a table in MS Word, select the Table menu option. Enter the number of rows and columns. Select Autoformat. Choose the format desired—Grid 1 is a good choice; that is what is shown here.) Your table should show the data you noted on paper in Assignment 2A.

➤ DELIVERABLES

1. Memorandum
2. Base Case and Extension Case spreadsheet printouts
3. Diskette, which should have your memorandum file and your Excel files

Staple printouts together, with the memo on top. Handwrite a note to your instructor, stating the names of the .xls files.

The One-Year Investment Portfolio Decision

Decision Support Using the Excel Solver

➤ Preview

An estate attorney must invest 10 million dollars for a year. She's considering 5 specific securities. In this case, you'll use the Excel Solver to help her decide how much to invest in each security. You'll document your recommendation in a memorandum.

➤ Preparation

- Review spreadsheet concepts discussed in class and/or in your text.
- Complete any exercises your instructor assigns.
- Complete any part of Tutorial D your instructor assigns.
- Review file-saving procedures for Windows programs. These are discussed in Tutorial D.

BACKGROUND

An elderly widow in your town has just passed away. People thought she was poor, but a search of her house turned up 10 million dollars in cash, squirreled away in shoe boxes, suitcases, a golf bag, etc. The attorney handling the estate expects it will take about a year to find the widow's heirs. In the meantime, the cash must be invested. At the year's end, taxes on the estate will be paid, and the money will be distributed to the heirs.

The attorney has identified 5 securities: (1) AD&D common stock, (2) King Cola common stock, (3) PolyNet common stock—a red-hot Internet stock, (4) certificates of deposit (CDs) issued by a local bank, and (5) units of a real estate investment trust, DEL REIT, that specializes in Delaware real estate. Here are the purchase prices of the securities:

Security Purchase Price

Security	Cost
1 share AD&D	$50
1 share King Cola	$80
1 share of PolyNet	$130
1 bank CD	$1000
1 unit DEL REIT	$10,000

Fig. 18-1

The attorney tells you that a portfolio generates revenue and incurs expenses. The attorney has profitability and safety goals. She wants to maximize portfolio net income but does not want to take unnecessary risks with the estate capital.

Portfolio Revenue

Portfolio revenue can accrue in three ways: (1) from interest, (2) from dividends, and (3) from gains on the sale of securities. The interest rate and the dividend payout rate are both "rates of return."

The rates of return and expected gains on sales for the five securities are summarized:

Security Rate of Return and Gain on Sale

Security	Expected Annual Rate of Return from Interest and Dividends	Expected Gain from the Sale of a Security
1 share AD&D	7%	10%
1 share King Cola	8%	10%
1 share of PolyNet	0%	40%
1 bank CD	6%	0%
1 unit DEL REIT	15%	20%

Fig. 18-2

Here are four explanatory examples: (1) A bank CD would earn $60 of interest income in the year ($1000 * .06). (2) One share of AD&D would yield $3.50 in dividends ($50 * .07). (3) The gain on selling one share of King Cola at the end of the year would be $8 ($80 * .10). (4) The gain on one CD would be zero—The face value of the CD does not change.

Portfolio Expenses

The attorney explains that administration expenses will arise from keeping track of the portfolio investments during the year. The higher an investment's risk, the more intensively it must be followed, and the higher the administrative expense.

The attorney has quantified the riskiness of each investment and has assigned a risk factor to each. The lower the factor, the lower the risk. For example, a widely traded security is very liquid, which means when the price starts to fall, the security can be sold quickly.

The CD is almost like cash, and it is given a liquidity factor of 1. The AD&D shares are assigned a risk factor of 2. The widely held King Cola shares are assigned a risk factor of 3. The DEL REIT units are assigned a factor of 4. (Land, no matter where it is, is speculative, so the values could go down quickly.) Finally, PolyNet, the risky Internet stock, is assigned a risk factor of 5.

The attorney has assigned an administrative expense rate to each investment, keyed to the risk level. The CD investment is expected to have an administrative cost rate of .001 of the amount invested. For example, if $1,000,000 were invested in CDs, then the cost of keeping track of the CD investment would be .001 * $1,000,000, or $1,000. All rates are applied to the total dollars invested, as in the example.

Security Administrative Expense Rate

Security	Administrative Expense Rate
AD&D	.003
King Cola	.004
PolyNet	.015
CD	.001
DEL REIT	.007

Fig. 18-3

The attorney wants to earn a good return on investment. Net income to total investment revenue must be at least 10%.

Portfolio Safety

The attorney explains that preserving capital is very important when administering an estate. Thus, she has rules designed to spread the risks among the five securities.

- At least $1,000,000 must be invested in each of the 5 securities.
- The entire $10,000,000 can be invested, but at least $9,800,000 must be invested.
- The attorney likes common stocks, but does not want to overinvest in them. She says that the ratio of dollars invested in common stocks (AD&D + PolyNet + King Cola) to total dollars invested must be at least 40% but not more than 67%.

- PolyNet is the common stock most likely to drop dramatically in price. So, the amount invested in AD&D plus King Cola must be at least as much as the amount invested in PolyNet.

- To give the portfolio a safe foundation, 20% of the total funds invested must be in CDs.

The attorney explains that these kinds of rules are just one way to show concern for safety. She has an alternate approach to safety in mind. This approach will be discussed in Assignment 1B.

➥ Assignment 1: Creating a Spreadsheet for Decision Support

In this two-part assignment, you will make two Solver spreadsheets to model the portfolio investment decision. In the "Base Case," you'll model the decision, using the safety rules set forth in the preceding list. In the "Extension Case," you'll incorporate different safety rules into the plan.

Your spreadsheets should have sections for Changing Cells, Constants, Calculations, and the Income Statement. You are shown how each section should be set up before you enter cell formulas. Each Solver model will be an income statement forecast for the year. Your spreadsheets should also include the decision's constraints, which you'll enter using the Solver.

Then, in Assignment 2, you'll use the models to develop information so you can help the attorney decide how much to invest in each of the five securities and to decide which safety rules to follow. You'll then document your recommendation in a memorandum.

Assignment 1A: Creating the Spreadsheet—Base Case

A discussion of each spreadsheet section follows. The discussion is about (1) how each section should be set up, and (2) the logic of the formulas in the section's cells. When you type in the spreadsheet skeleton, follow the order given in this section.

Changing Cells Your spreadsheet should have these changing cells:

A	B	C	D	E
The One-Year Portfolio Decision				
Changing Cells				
Shares of AD&D Common Stock	1			
Number of CD Certificates	1			
Shares of PolyNet Common Stock	1			
Shares of King Cola Common Stock	1			
Shares of Delaware REIT	1			

Fig. 18-4

You are asking the Solver to compute how many units (shares or certificates) of each kind of security to buy to maximize the portfolio's net income. Start with a "1" in each cell.

Constants Your spreadsheet should have these constants:

A	B	C	D	E
Constants				
Tax rate expected	0.3			
Cash available to invest	10000000			
Minimum investment - each security	1000000			
Unit price - AD&D	50			
Rate of return - AD&D	0.07			
Projected gain - AD&D	0.1			
Administrative cost rate - AD&D	0.003			

Fig18-5

- The tax rate to be applied to pre-tax revenue is 30%.
- The attorney has the widow's $10,000,000 to invest for a year.
- At least $1,000,000 must be invested in each security.
- The current stock market price of AD&D is shown.
- The rate of return for AD&D is shown.
- The attorney thinks that the percentage gain in AD&D's market price will be 10% in the year.
- The attorney thinks the cost of following AD&D stock for the year will be .003 times the amount invested in AD&D.

Note: Your constants should also include entries for the unit price, rate of return, projected rate of gain, and administrative cost rate for the other four investment instruments (King Cola, PolyNet, CDs, and DEL REIT).

You should leave five extra spaces after the constants section for the Extension Case.

Calculations Your spreadsheet should calculate these intermediate results, which are then used in the Income Statement and/or in the Constraints. Calculated values may be based on the values of the Constants, the Changing Cells, and/or the other Calculations.

A	B	C	D	E
Calculations				
Amount invested in common stocks				
Total amount invested				
Percentage invested in stocks				
Net income to total revenue ratio				
Total Invested in AD&D and King Cola				
Percentage invested in CDs				
Ratio of (AD&D + King Cola) to PolyNet				
Total invested in AD&D				
Dividends earned on AD&D				
Gain on AD&D				
Administrative cost - AD&D				

Fig. 18-6

- The amount invested in stocks is the total invested in AD&D, PolyNet, and King Cola.
- The percentage invested in stocks is a function of the amount invested in stocks and the total amount invested.

- The ratio of net income to total revenue is a function of net income and total revenue.
- The total invested in AD&D plus King Cola cannot exceed the total invested in PolyNet.
- The percentage invested in CDs is a function of the investment in CDs and the total dollars invested.
- The total invested in AD&D is a function of the number of units (shares) invested in AD&D and the current price of the stock.
- Dividends earned on AD&D are a function of the dividend rate of return and the amount invested in AD&D.
- The gain on AD&D is a function of the amount invested in AD&D and how much the share price is expected to increase in the year.
- The AD&D administrative cost is a function of the AD&D administrative rate and the amount invested in AD&D.

Note: Your calculations should include entries for the amount invested, dividends or interest earned, expected gain, and administrative cost for the other four investments (King Cola, PolyNet, CDs, and DEL REIT).

Leave six extra spaces after the calculations section for the Extension Case.

Income Statement This statement is for projected net income in the coming year. Some of the line items are discussed next.

A	B	C	D	E
Income Statement				
Interest and dividends				
Gains				
Total Revenue				
Administrative costs				
Total Costs				
Pre-tax revenue				
Income tax expense				
Net Income				

Fig.18-7

- Interest and dividends are totaled for all investments. Gains on investments are calculated in the same way.
- Administrative costs are the total for all investments.
- Income tax expense is zero if pre-tax revenue is zero or negative; otherwise, apply the tax rate times pre-tax revenue.

Constraints and Running the Solver Determine what the constraints are. Use the Solver to enter the Base Case decision constraints. Run the Solver. When the Solver tells you a solution has been found that satisfies the constraints, ask for the Answer Report.

When you are done, print the entire workbook, including the Solver Answer Report sheet. Save the workbook (File—Save; PortBase.xls would be a good name). Then, in order to prepare for the Extension Case, use File—Save As to make a new spreadsheet. (PortExt.xls would be a good file name.)

Assignment 1B: Creating the Spreadsheet—Extension Case

The attorney explains that her safety rules (only so much of this and so much of that, etc.) are just one way to provide for investment safety. Another approach she has developed is to quantify a portfolio's "weighted average portfolio risk factor" and then invest in such a way that the index remains within a safety zone.

The attorney has assigned a risk factor to each of the 5 securities. The way to compute a "weighted average portfolio risk factor" for the portfolio is illustrated in the following example. Assume that the sum of $2,000,000 is invested in each security.

Security Weighted Risk Factor

Security	Invested	Risk Factor	Risk Points = Invested * Risk Factor
AD&D	2,000,000	2	4,000,000
King Cola	2,000,000	3	6,000,000
PolyNet	2,000,000	5	10,000,000
CDs	2,000,000	1	2,000,000
DEL REIT	2,000,000	4	8,000,000
		Weighted Total	30,000,000 (A)
		Total Invested	10,000,000 (B)
		Weighted Average Portfolio Risk Factor (A/B)	3.00

Fig. 18-8

The attorney explains that a safe portfolio would be one that has a weighted average risk factor of 2.5 or less. She thinks a factor that low should automatically limit investments in common stocks, which can be risky. This is the only safety rule. All others (CD percentage, relationship of common stocks to total investment, relationship of AD&D and King Cola to PolyNet) would be dropped. At least $1,000,000 would still be required for each security, however.

The attorney would like to know what the net income and invested amounts would be with the new safety rule. The goal is still to maximize net income.

In the Extension Case spreadsheet, add the security risk factors at the end of the constants:

Risk factor - AD&D	2		
Risk factor - CDs	1		
Risk factor - PolyNet	5		
Risk factor - King Cola	3		
Risk factor - DEL REIT	4		

Fig18-9

Then add these calculations at the end of the Calculations section:

Risk points - AD&D				
Risk points - CDs				
Risk points - PolyNet				
Risk points - King Cola				
Risk points - DEL REIT				
Weighted average portfolio risk factor				

Fig18-10

Adjust the Solver's constraints for the Extension Case. Run the Solver. When the Solver tells you a solution has been found that satisfies the constraints, ask for an Answer Report. When you're done, print the entire workbook, including the Solver Answer Report sheet. Save the workbook. Close the file and then exit from Excel.

ASSIGNMENT 2: USING THE SPREADSHEET FOR DECISION SUPPORT

You have built the Base Case and the Extension Case models to compare each scenario's investments and net incomes. You will now complete the case by (1) using the Answer Reports to gather data you need to make the investment level decision, and (2) documenting your recommendation in a memorandum.

Assignment 2A: Using the Spreadsheet to Gather Data

You have printed the Answer Report sheets for each scenario. Each sheet tells how much of each kind of investment to buy and the net income in each scenario. Note that data for each case by constructing the following table on a separate sheet of paper. In Assignment 2B, you'll use your word processor to turn this data into a table.

Summary Table

	Base Case	Extension Case
Number of Shares of AD&D		
Number of $1,000 CDs		
Number of Shares of PolyNet		
Number of Shares of King Cola		
Number of Units of $10,000 DEL REIT		
Weighted Average Liquidity Factor	NA	
Portfolio Net Income		

Fig. 18-11

Assignment 2B: Documenting Your Recommendation in a Memorandum

Write a brief memorandum about the results to the attorney.

- Your memorandum should have a proper heading (DATE/ TO/ FROM/ SUBJECT). You may wish to use a Word memo template (File—New, click Memos, choose Contemporary Memo).

- Briefly outline the investment decision. Then state which portfolio safety approach should be followed: (1) limits on amounts invested for different securities or (2) rely on a weighted average risk factor. Net income is the controlling factor.
- Support your recommendations with a summary table. (To make a table in MS Word, select the Table menu option. Enter the number of rows and columns. Select Autoformat. Choose the format desired—Grid 1 is a good choice; that is what is shown here.) Your table should show the data you noted on paper in Assignment 2A.

➤ DELIVERABLES

1. Memorandum
2. Base Case and Extension Case spreadsheet printouts
3. Diskette, which should have your memorandum file and your Excel files

Staple printouts together, with the memo on top. Handwrite a note to your instructor, stating the names of the .xls files.

19
CASE

The Vet Center Horse Meal Mix Decision

DECISION SUPPORT USING THE EXCEL SOLVER

➤ PREVIEW

The local veterinary center needs a nutritious and cost-effective horse meal. The veterinarian wants to make his own horse meal rather than buy commercial feeds. The meal's main ingredients have been identified, but the veterinarian does not know how much of each ingredient to include in the mix. In this case, you'll use the Excel Solver to help answer that question. You'll document your recommendation in a memorandum.

➤ PREPARATION

- Review spreadsheet concepts discussed in class and/or in your text.
- Complete any exercises your instructor assigns.
- Complete any part of Tutorial D your instructor assigns.
- Review file-saving procedures for Windows programs. These are discussed in Tutorial D.

The local veterinary center's daily boarding rate is $25 per horse. One horse per day can be boarded. The Center's veterinarian is not happy with commercially prepared horse feed and wants to prepare his own horse meal mix. He plans to do this by combining commercial feeds to get a mix that is nutritious, yet economical.

Dry feeds must be purchased by the pound and then mixed to make the meal the horse finally eats. The meal that a horse gets must have minimum units of protein, fiber (sometimes referred to as "carbohydrate"), minerals, and some small amount of fat.

The feeds that the Vet Center will use are called Mighty Horse (MH), Horsey Friend (HF), and Tangy Mush (TM). The number of nutrient units that each feed provides, per pound of feed, is shown in the table below:

Number of Units of Nutrient per Pound of Feed

	MH	HF	TM
Protein	100	200	1
Fiber	400	250	1
Fat	20	15	0

Fig. 19-1

The MH, HF, and TM must be mixed to produce a daily horse meal that will provide at least 1,000 units of protein, 1,500 units of fiber, and between 100 and 150 units of fat. No weight would be lost in the mix. For example, 4 pounds of MH, plus 5 pounds of HF, plus 1 pound of TM would, combined, weigh 10 pounds. (Note: That 10-pound mix would contain a total of 1401 units of protein, 2851 units of fiber, and 155 units of fat.)

You might be wondering why TM would be used at all. Per pound, it provides only 1 unit of protein and fiber, and no fat. But, if you combine only MH and HF, most horses will not eat much of the resulting meal. But if you include some Tangy Mush, a horse will eat enthusiastically! TM seems to act as a condiment acts for humans—it provides a "tang"!

Also, TM has a day's supply of minerals, but MH and HF have some minerals also. (You can assume that any horse meal mix made from MH, HF, and TM will have sufficient minerals.)

A horse should be fed at least 8 pounds of horse meal per day, but no more than 10 pounds.

The minimum amount of MH that could be put into the daily meal mix is 3 pounds. The minimum amount of HF is also 3 pounds. The minimum amount of TM is 1/2 pound. The maximum amount of TM that can be included is 1 pound—you do not want to overdo the condiments!

A pound of MH costs 20 cents. A pound of HF costs 25 cents. A pound of TM costs 1 cent.

Each constituent feed has associated miscellaneous costs for shipping, special storage, special utensils, and so forth. The miscellaneous cost associated with each feed, per pound, is: MH—50 cents, HF—40 cents, TM—$1.

The veterinarian wants a meal mix that is at least minimally nutritious and also provides the greatest daily net income. Moreover, there should be at least a 25% return on sales (net income divided by boarding revenue). The tax rate on positive pre-tax net income is 28%. No taxes are paid on losses.

The Vet Center is next to a working farm. The farmer has offered to let the Center's horses graze in his pasture for free. For millions of years, horses have done pretty well eating from grassland! If the Center fed boarded horses this way, only a small amount of supplemental meal mix would be needed each day. This alternative is discussed more fully in Assignment 1B.

☙ ASSIGNMENT 1: CREATING A SPREADSHEET FOR DECISION SUPPORT

In this assignment, you will make two Solver spreadsheets to model the horse meal mix decision. In the "Base Case," you will model the decision, using MH, HF, and TM. In the "Extension Case," you'll model the possibility of using the pasture and a small supplemental meal. Each Solver model will be an income statement forecast for one day of horse boarding.

Your spreadsheets should have sections for Changing Cells, Constants, Calculations, and the Income Statement. You are shown how each section should be set up before you enter cell formulas. Your spreadsheets should also include the decision's constraints, which you'll enter using the Solver.

Then, in Assignment 2, you'll use the models to develop information so you can decide how to make the horse meal mix and whether to use the pasture. You'll then document your recommendations in a memorandum.

Assignment 1A: Creating the Spreadsheet—Base Case

A discussion of each spreadsheet section follows. The discussion is about (1) how each section should be set up, and (2) the logic of the formulas in the section's cells. When you type in the spreadsheet skeleton, follow the order given in this section.

Changing Cells Your spreadsheet should have these changing cells:

A	B	C	D	E
The Vet Center Horse Meal Mix Decision				
Changing Cells				
Number of pounds of MH	1			
Number of pounds of HF	1			
Number of pounds of TM	1			

Fig. 19-2

You are asking the Solver to compute how many pounds of each feed should be in the daily meal mix. Start with a "1" in each cell. The Solver will change the 1 as it computes its answer.

Constants Your spreadsheet should have these constants:

A	B	C	D	E
Constants				
Tax rate expected	0.28			
Horse boarding fee per day	25			
MH: protein units per lb.	100			
MH: fiber units per lb.	400			
MH: fat units per lb.	20			
MH: cost per lb.	0.2			
MH: misc cost per lb.	0.5			
HF: protein units per lb.	200			
HF: fiber units per lb.	250			
HF: fat units per lb.	15			
HF: cost per lb.	0.25			
HF: misc cost per lb.	0.4			
TM: protein units per lb.	1			
TM: fiber units per lb.	1			
TM: fat units per lb.	0			
TM: cost per lb.	0.01			
TM: misc cost per lb.	1			

Fig. 19-3

- The tax rate to be applied to pre-tax revenue is 28%.
- Horse boarding revenue is $25 per day.
- A pound of MH provides 100 units of protein, 400 units of fiber, and 20 units of fat.
- A pound of MH costs 20 cents to buy; other associated MH costs are 50 cents a pound.
- HF and TM provide units of protein, fiber, and fat, as shown. Purchase costs and miscellaneous costs for HF and TM are shown.

Calculations Your spreadsheet should calculate these intermediate results, which are then used in the Income Statement and/or in the Constraints. Calculated values may be based on the values of the Constants, the Changing Cells, and/or the other Calculations.

A	B	C	D	E
Calculations				
Number of pounds in meal				
Amount of protein in meal				
Amount of fiber in meal				
Amount of fat in meal				
Cost of MH used in meal				
Cost of HF used in meal				
Cost of TM used in meal				
Misc cost of MH in meal				
Misc cost of HF in meal				
Misc cost of TM in meal				
Net income to revenue ratio				

Fig. 19-4

- The number of pounds mixed to make the daily portion of meal is a function of the number of pounds of the feeds in the meal mix. Mixing results in no weight loss.

- The horse meal mix must have certain minimum amounts of protein, fiber, and fat. The amounts should be calculated here.

- Purchase costs and miscellaneous costs of the feeds in the meal mix should be computed here and then used in the income statement.

- The veterinarian has a minimum net income to total revenue ratio goal.

Income Statement This statement is for projected net income for one day of boarding a horse. Some of the line items are discussed next.

	A	B	C	D	E
	Income Statement				
	Boarding revenue -- one day				
	Cost of feed in meal				
	Misc cost of feed in meal				
	Total cost of feed in meal				
	Pre-tax revenue				
	Income tax expense				
	Net income				

Fig. 19-5

- Make an income statement for boarding one horse for one day. A boarded horse gets one serving of meal mix each day. (The horse eats the serving throughout the day, whenever he's hungry.)

- Total cost of the feeds in the meal mix is a function of the costs of each feed in the meal mix.

- Total miscellaneous cost of feeds in the meal mix is a function of the miscellaneous costs of each feed in the meal mix.

- Income tax expense is zero if pre-tax revenue is zero or negative; otherwise, apply the tax rate times pre-tax revenue.

Constraints and Running the Solver Determine what the contraints are. Enter the Base Case decision constraints, using the Solver. Run the Solver. When the Solver tells you a solution has been found that satisfies the constraints, ask for the Answer Report.

When you are done, print the entire workbook, including the Solver Answer Report sheet. Save the workbook (File—Save; VetBase.xls would be a good name). Then, to prepare for the Extension Case, use File—Save As to make a new spreadsheet. (VetExt.xls would be a good file name.)

Assignment 1B: Creating the Spreadsheet—Extension Case

Although the cost of grazing a horse in the farmer's pasture would be zero, another of the Vet Center's costs would rise. Because a boarded horse could become injured in some way as it roams around in the pasture, the veterinarian expects insurance costs to rise $1 per day if horses are fed by grazing.

Even if the horse is allowed to graze, the veterinarian would make a small portion of horse meal mix each day for the boarded horse. This portion would be left in the horse's stall, in case the horse is still hungry after grazing in the pasture. Each day, any uneaten supplemental meal mix from the prior day would be replaced by a fresh portion.

The supplemental meal mix would be made from MH and HF only. The supplemental meal mix would have to provide at least 50 units of protein, at least 75 units of fiber, and 10 to 20 units of fat. At least 1/2 pound of MH and 1/2 pound of HF should be included in the mix. The supplemental meal mix should weigh at least 1 pound but no more than 1.5 pounds.

Although TM would contribute nothing to the supplemental feed, some TM would still be needed. To ensure the horses get enough minerals, exactly a quarter pound of TM would be mixed into the water supply in the horse's stall. Water is refreshed daily.

In the Extension Case, the required return on sales rule would remain the same.

You need to know how many pounds of MH, HF, and TM would be needed in the Extension Case alternative and what the one-day net income would be. You should adjust the Solver model's constraints and income statement. Run the Solver. When the Solver tells you a solution has been found that satisfies the constraints, ask for an Answer Report. When you're done, print the entire workbook, including the Solver Answer Report sheet. Save the workbook. Close the file and then exit from Excel.

➤ ASSIGNMENT 2: USING THE SPREADSHEET FOR DECISION SUPPORT

You have built the Base Case and the Extension Case models because you want to know how the meal mixes should be formulated, whether the pasture should be used, and how much net income would be generated in each case.

You will now complete the case by (1) using the Answer Reports to gather data you need to make the decision, and (2) documenting your recommendation in a memorandum.

Assignment 2A: Using the Spreadsheet to Gather Data

You have printed the Answer Report sheets for each scenario. Each sheet tells how much of each kind of feed to include in the horse meal mix and the net income in each case. Note the data for each case by constructing the following table on a separate sheet of paper. In Assignment 2B, you'll use your word processor to turn this data into a table.

Summary Table

	Base Case	Extension Case
Pounds of MH used		
Pounds of HF used		
Pounds of TM used		
Grazing as a food source?	No	Yes
One-day net income		

Fig. 19-6

Assignment 2B: Documenting Your Recommendation in a Memorandum

Write a brief memorandum to the veterinarian outlining your results.

- Your memorandum should have a proper heading (DATE/ TO/ FROM/ SUBJECT). You may wish to use a Word memo template (File—New, click Memos, choose Contemporary Memo).

- Briefly outline the horse meal mix decision. Then state how the daily horse meal mix should be formulated and whether the pasture should be used. Remember, the veterinarian's goal is to maximize net income.
- Support your recommendations with a summary table. (To make a table in MS Word, select the Table menu option. Enter the number of rows and columns. Select Autoformat. Choose the format desired—Grid 1 is a good choice; that is what is shown here.) Your table should show the data you noted on paper in Assignment 2A.

➡ DELIVERABLES

1. Memorandum
2. Base Case and Extension Case spreadsheet printouts
3. Diskette, which should have your memorandum file and your Excel files

Staple printouts together, with the memo on top. Handwrite a note to your instructor, stating the name of the .xls files.

The Country Inn Expansion Decision

Decision Support Using the Excel Solver

➤ Preview

A country inn will be adding a wing of rooms and a parking lot. The owners wonder how many rooms—and what size of rooms—should be built in the new wing. In this case, you'll use the Excel Solver to help them make that decision. You'll document your recommendation in a memorandum.

➤ Preparation

- Review spreadsheet concepts discussed in class and/or in your text.
- Complete any exercises your instructor assigns.
- Complete any part of Tutorial D your instructor assigns.
- Review file-saving procedures for Windows programs. These are discussed in Tutorial D.

The Country Inn is a family-owned-and-operated business. The family also owns an adjoining 20,000 square-foot parcel of land. They want to build a new wing of rooms and a parking lot on the land. Because the area is increasingly popular with vacationers, the owners are sure that they could rent additional rooms at a reasonable occupancy rate.

Another reason for the expansion is that the Inn's restaurant is so large that many seats go unoccupied, even when the Inn is filled to capacity. Building an addition would increase restaurant patrons.

The owners have decided that the new wing would have only three room sizes: single (for single vacationers), double (for couples), and family (for families with children). The square footage for rooms is: (1) single: 225 square feet, (2) double: 400 square feet, and (3) family: 800 square feet. The owners want to know how many of each room size to build in the new wing.

The size of the parking lot will be dictated by the number of rooms built. Each new unit will have one parking space. A parking space will take up 200 square feet. The cost of grading, paving, and painting the lines of the parking lot is $50 a square foot.

All the new units and the parking lot must fit into the 20,000 square feet available. The owners would like to see all 20,000 feet used, of course, but they understand that may not be possible. They say they expect at least 19,500 square feet would be used.

It so happens that the construction cost per square foot is more for a smaller unit than for a larger one. The construction cost per square foot for each kind of unit is expected to be: (1) single: $250, (2) double: $220, and (3) family: $200. (The cost of the new wing's foundation and outside frame is averaged into these numbers.)

The owners would charge daily rentals as follows: (1) single: $83, (2) double: $115, and (3) family: $175. Prices are *per unit*, not per person.

Of course, all the rooms will not be rented all the time. Based on past rental patterns and on projections of future demand for rooms in the area, the owners expect these occupancy rates: (1) single: 70%, (2) double: 65%, and (3) family: 60%.

The daily cost of upkeep for units is expected to be: (1) single: $20, (2) double: $25, and (3) family: $30, i.e., the bigger the unit, the more it costs to service it. The owners anticipate an upkeep charge only if a unit is rented for the day. Unoccupied rooms require no cleaning, and the heat or AC can be turned off in them.

Added restaurant revenue will be a function of how many people stay in each kind of room, frequency of occupancy, and the amount spent on each person's meals. The owners believe that 1 person will occupy a single. They think that, on average, 2 people will occupy a double unit, and 4 people will occupy a family unit. The owners reason that a single person will favor quick, simple meals and will spend the least amount of money on food. They think that a couple will spend more time dining and will be more likely to have cocktails and dessert. People in single and double units usually eat only once a day at the Inn, management has noted. Families have kids, but kids do not eat expensive meals. But families are more likely to eat more than once a day at the Inn. The daily amounts that visitors are expected to spend in the restaurant are: (1) each person in a single: $10, (2) each person in a double: $25, and (3) each person in a family: $20.

The costs of serving a meal are for ingredients, preparation, and serving. Cost can be expressed as a percentage of the amount spent. These costs vary for each kind of guest. Management has noted that people who stay in singles often have meals that require expensive ingredients and considerable preparation. The average cost of meals for singles is expected to be 75% of the average meal revenue. Couples are more likely to have drinks and desserts, which have high profit margins. The average cost of meals for couples is expected to be only 55% of the average meal revenue. The average cost of meals for those in families will be somewhere in between. Family members often eat meals that require almost no preparation. (How difficult is it to serve cereal to children?) The average cost of meals for families is expected to be 65% of the average meal revenue. Example: If a family spends $200 in the restaurant one day, the restaurant's cost would be $130.

The owners have a 360-day business year.

Expenditures from the addition will be heavy in the beginning, but then the investment pays for itself over time; the new wing and parking lot would be fully depreciated after 10 years. Thus, a 10-year forecasted income statement is needed. Just to keep things simple, the owners assume no inflation in unit rents, upkeep, or meal prices. The owners want to make as much net income from the new rooms as they can.

The owners do not want to build a wing that has more than 30 units, but they feel it should have at least 20 units. There should be at least 5 singles, 5 doubles, and 10 family units. A decimal part of a new unit cannot be built, of course. Net income over the 10 years must be positive.

An alternate expansion idea has been proposed by some members of the family. This involves buying another parcel of land and putting in a large pool. Some in the family think this would increase occupancy rates and positively affect the amount of food sold. This alternative is discussed in Assignment 1B.

➤ ASSIGNMENT 1: CREATING A SPREADSHEET FOR DECISION SUPPORT

In this assignment, you will make two Solver spreadsheets to model the expansion decision. In the "Base Case," you'll model the decision, without regard to the swimming pool option. In the "Extension Case," you'll include the effects of having a swimming pool. Each Solver model will be an income statement forecast for the ten-year period.

Your spreadsheets should have sections for Changing Cells, Constants, Calculations, and the Income Statement. You are shown how each section should be set up before you enter cell formulas. Your spreadsheets should also include the decision's constraints, which you'll enter using the Solver.

Then, in Assignment 2, you'll use the models to develop information so you can decide how many of each kind of unit to build, and whether you should include a swimming pool. You'll then document your recommendations in a memorandum.

Assignment 1A: Creating the Spreadsheet—Base Case

A discussion of each spreadsheet section follows. The discussion is about (1) how each section should be set up, and (2) the logic of the formulas in the section's cells. When you type in the spreadsheet skeleton, follow the order given in this section.

Changing Cells Your spreadsheet should have these changing cells:

	A	B	C	D	E
	The Country Inn Expansion Decision				
	Changing Cells				
	Number of single units	1			
	Number of double units	1			
	Number of family units	1			

Fig. 20-1

You are asking the Solver to compute how many of each kind of unit to include in the new wing. Start with a "1" in each cell. The Solver will change the 1 as it computes its answer.

Constants Your spreadsheet should have these constants:

	A	B	C	D	E
	Constants				
	Tax rate expected	0.3			
	Total footage available	20000			
	Number of business days	3600			
	Parking: square feet per space	200			
	Parking: construction cost per sq foot	50			
	Single: Square feet	225			
	Single: Rental per day	83			
	Single: Occupancy rate	0.7			
	Single: Construction cost per sq foot	250			
	Single: Upkeep cost per day	20			
	Single: Avg number of people	1			
	Single: Restaurant revenue per person	10			
	Single: Restaurant cost percentage	0.75			

Fig. 20-2

- The tax rate to be applied to pre-tax revenue is 30%.
- The site's 20,000 square feet must hold the new wing and its parking lot.
- Each year in the next 10 years will have 360 business days.
- Each parking space will take up 200 square feet of ground.
- The parking lot installation will cost $50 per square foot.
- A single unit will take up 225 square feet in the new wing.
- A single unit will rent for $83 per day in the 10-year period.
- A single unit is expected to be rented 70% of the business days.
- A single unit's construction cost is $250 per square foot.
- It will cost $20 dollars per day to maintain a single unit, each day it's rented.
- A single unit will be occupied by 1 person.
- A single person will, on average, spend $10 a day in the restaurant.
- The average cost of a single person's meal will be 75% of the average price of the meal.

The Constants section should have analogous entries for double units and family units.

Calculations Your spreadsheet should calculate these intermediate results, which are then used in the Income Statement and/or in the Constraints. Calculated values may be based on the values of the Constants, the Changing Cells, and/or the other Calculations.

A	B	C	D	E
Calculations				
Number of units built in new wing				
Square footage used - rooms				
Square footage used - parking lot				
Total square footage used				
Construction cost - parking lot				
Total revenue - single				
Total revenue - double				
Total revenue - family				
Total construction cost - single				
Total construction cost - double				
Total construction cost - family				
Total upkeep cost - single				
Total upkeep cost - double				
Total upkeep cost - family				
Restaurant revenue - single				
Restaurant revenue - double				
Restaurant revenue - family				
Restaurant costs - single				
Restaurant costs - double				
Restaurant costs - family				

Fig. 20-3

- The number of new units is the total of all new single, double, and family units.
- Square footage is taken up by the new wing and the parking lot. The square footage of the new wing equals, assume, just the total of the square footage for the new units.
- The parking lot's construction cost is a function of the lot's square footage and the cost per square foot, a constant.
- Room rentals for the three kinds of units are a function of how many rooms there are, how often they are rented, and the price per day.
- Construction costs for the three kinds of units are a function of how many units are built and how much each unit costs to build.
- Upkeep cost for each kind of room is a function of how many rooms are built, how often they are rented, and the upkeep cost per day.
- Restaurant revenue for the three kinds of units are a function of how many rooms are built, how many people stay in them, and how much each person is likely to spend on food per day.
- Restaurant costs are a function of the restaurant revenue for the kind of unit and its related restaurant cost percentage.

Income Statement This statement is for projected net income in the ten-year period. Some of the line items are discussed next.

A	B	C	D	E
Income Statement				
Room rental revenue				
Restaurant revenue				
Total revenue				
Room construction costs				
Room upkeep costs				
Parking lot construction cost				
Restaurant costs				
Total costs				
Pre-tax revenue				
Income tax expense				
Net Income				

Fig. 20-4

- Room rental revenue and restaurant revenue are for all types of units, combined.
- Room construction and upkeep costs are for all types of units, combined.
- The parking lot construction cost has been calculated and can be echoed to the income statement.
- Restaurant costs are for all types of units, combined.
- Income tax expense is zero if pre-tax revenue is zero or negative; otherwise, apply the tax rate times pre-tax revenue.

Constraints and Running the Solver Determine what the constraints are. Use the Solver and enter the Base Case decision constraints. Run the Solver. When the Solver tells you a solution has been found that satisfies the constraints, ask for the Answer Report.

When you are done, print the entire workbook, including the Solver Answer Report sheet. Save the workbook (File—Save; CIBase.xls would be a good name). Then, in order to prepare for the Extension Case, use File—Save As to make a new spreadsheet. (CIExt.xls would be a good file name).

Assignment 1B: Creating the Spreadsheet—Extension Case

The owners have an option to buy some land next to the 20,000 square-foot site. This other site would be perfect, in size and location, for a large swimming pool.

Some members of the owning family think that a swimming pool would appeal to all kinds of vacationers, but especially to family vacationers. Another Solver model is needed that assumes a swimming pool is available.

The assumptions are these: with a pool, single and double occupancy rates would go to 75%, and family occupancy rates would go to 80%. More food would be sold per person (people lounging by the pool do need their snacks!). The average restaurant revenue per person would go to: (1) single: $15, (2) double: $30, and (3) family: $25. The average markup on snacks and other food eaten at the pool would be higher than that eaten in the restaurant proper. But that advantage would be offset by the added cost of poolside servers. So, the owners expect the restaurant cost factors to remain the same in the extension case: single: 75%; double: 55%; family: 65%.

There would be costs associated with the pool. The combined cost of the land on which the pool would be build, building the pool, and maintaining the pool for 10 years is expected to be $300,000.

A buffer area between the parking lot and the pool would be needed. This would reduce the available space for the new wing from 20,000 square feet to 19,000 square feet (of which at least 18,500 would have to be used).

In the Extension Case, you want to know how many units of each kind should be built and the best resulting net income. Adjust constants and constraints to make the Extension Case spreadsheet. In the income statement, the cost of the pool can be included with the parking lot ("Parking lot and pool construction costs").

Run the Solver. When the Solver tells you a solution has been found that satisfies the constraints, ask for an Answer Report. When you're done, print the entire workbook, including the Solver Answer Report sheet. Save the workbook. Close the file and then exit from Excel.

➤ ASSIGNMENT 2: USING THE SPREADSHEET FOR DECISION SUPPORT

You have built the Base Case and the Extension Case models because the Inn's owners need to know what would be the most profitable way to expand: (1) add a new wing, or (2) add a slightly smaller new wing and a swimming pool.

You will now complete the case by (1) using the Answer Reports to gather data you need to make the decision, and (2) documenting your recommendation in a memorandum.

Assignment 2A: Using the Spreadsheet to Gather Data

You have printed the Answer Report sheets for each scenario. Each sheet tells how many of each kind of unit to build and the net income in each case. Note that data for each case by constructing the following table on a separate sheet of paper. In Assignment 2B, you'll use your word processor to turn this into a table.

Summary Table

	New Wing	New Wing and Pool
Number of Family units		
Number of Single units		
Number of Double units		
Net income		

Fig. 20-5

Assignment 2B: Documenting Your Recommendation in a Memorandum

Write a brief memorandum about the results to the Inn's owners.

- Your memorandum should have a proper heading (DATE/ TO/ FROM/ SUBJECT). You may wish to use a Word memo template (File—New, click Memos, choose Contemporary Memo).

- Briefly outline the expansion decision. Then state how many of each kind of unit should be put into the new wing and whether the pool should be installed.
- Support your recommendations with a summary table. (To make a table in MS Word, select the Table menu option. Enter the number of rows and columns. Select Autoformat. Choose the format desired—Grid 1 is a good choice; that is what is shown here.) Your table should show the data you noted on paper in Assignment 2A.

⇥ DELIVERABLES

1. Memorandum
2. Base Case and Extension Case spreadsheet printouts
3. Diskette, which should have your memorandum file and your Excel files

Staple printouts together, with the memo on top. Handwrite a note to your instructor, stating the name of the .xls files.